Voices of the Civil War

Voices of the Civil War · The Peninsula

By the Editors of Time-Life Books, Alexandria, Virginia

Contents

THE VIRGINIA PENINSULA

This artist's rendering of Virginia's Chesapeake coast shows the numerous rivers that drain the Tidewater region. Federal control of the James and York Rivers provided George McClellan's Army of the Potomac with waterborne lines of communication to support an advance up Virginia's Peninsula to seize the Confederate capital, Richmond.

Hanover Court House

Drewry's Bluff

Richmond

Petersburg

Seven Pines–Fair Oaks

Chickahominy River

Pamunkey River

Norfolk & Petersburg RR

Richmond & York River RR

West Point

Williamsburg

Suffolk

York River

Rappahannock River

James River

Yorktown

Hampton Roads

Hampton

Norfolk

Fort Monroe

Chesapeake Bay

W
S — N
E

Fredericksburg

Alexandria

Washington, D.C.

VIRGINIA

MARYLAND

Potomac River

The Young Napoleon to the Rescue

Mobs of disorganized Federal troops were still stumbling back into Washington after the disastrous defeat at the Battle of First Manassas when President Lincoln fired off an urgent telegram to Major General George B. McClellan at his field headquarters in northwestern Virginia. "Circumstances make your presence here necessary," the wire read. "Come hither without delay."

McClellan came in a hurry, riding horseback 60 miles to the nearest railroad station, then taking a Baltimore & Ohio train to the capital. Arriving in the late hours of July 26, 1861, five days after the Manassas fiasco, he went to the White House the next morning—to be given the astonishing news that he, a relatively inexperienced 34-year-old, had been placed in command of the entire Union army in and around Washington.

The young general's immediate task, of

course, was somehow to take hold of the defeated, demoralized, and disorderly remnants of the Federal army skulking about the city and whip them into shape to protect the nation's capital from the Confederate army camped only 25 miles away. Close on the heels of this emergency was a job far more daunting: to forge a new, larger and better Union army, attack the Rebels, conquer Richmond, and end the civil conflict that had so recently riven the nation.

McClellan, showing formidable organizational skills, would indeed create a large, magnificent army. He would also—after maddening delays—take it on an ambitious roundabout campaign up the Virginia Peninsula and almost to Richmond's gates. But there he would run head-on into a Confederate army led by one of the victors of Manassas, General Joseph E. Johnston. The result was a campaign of grand maneuver and exhausting siege warfare that culminated in a two-day battle at the hamlet of Seven Pines, about 10 miles east of the Rebel capital. The campaign set the stage for the emergence of another of the conflict's outsize figures, General Robert E. Lee, and for a series of battles of heretofore unimagined ferocity, the Seven Days.

Lincoln turned to McClellan because in the

Well-ordered columns of the 96th Pennsylvania Infantry drill in their northern Virginia camp during the early spring of 1862. Their discipline, honed under Major General George B. McClellan's hand, would be tested on Virginia's Peninsula.

weeks before the Manassas defeat the young general had produced virtually the only Federal victories of the war thus far. The battles had been small, true, but at Philippi, Rich Mountain, and then Cheat Mountain, McClellan's troops had smashed the opposing Confederate forces and secured the entire hilly region of western Virginia for the Union. For his deeds McClellan had been hailed by the Northern press as a military genius, a hero on horseback, a "Young Napoleon" who would save the Union.

The sobriquet was not entirely fair to Mc-Clellan. The original Napoleon had been, at the start anyway, a rather crude and scruffy provincial from Corsica. McClellan, by contrast, seemed always the epitome of polish—well spoken, exuding an aura of success. The son of a well-to-do Philadelphia surgeon, he had entered West Point at the age of 15 and immediately dazzled his less brilliant classmates—including a rawboned fellow plebe named Thomas Jonathan Jackson—with his easy mastery of all academic subjects.

Graduating second in his class in 1846, Mc-Clellan went on to distinguish himself in the Mexican War of 1847-1848, then gained further luster as the youngest member of a team of favored officers sent to Europe to study the British, French, and other foreign military establishments. Upon his return, McClellan helped develop a new saddle for the cavalry and introduced a new bayonet drill.

In 1857 McClellan, then a captain, resigned his commission to become chief civil engineer of the Illinois Central Railroad. Excelling there as well, he was soon promoted to vice president of the road and, after marrying the beautiful Ellen Marcy, moved on to become president of the Ohio & Mississippi Railroad's Eastern Division, with offices in Cincinnati.

When the war came, McClellan quickly rejoined the army and, given command of the Department of the Ohio, set up training camps for the thousands of midwestern volunteers who had flocked to the colors. He then led a small army of them east across the Ohio River to gain the victories that made him so quickly and immoderately famous.

Hailed as a hero, McClellan perfectly looked the part. Although he would be nicknamed Little Mac by his troops, he was of nearly average height for his time—about five feet eight inches—and powerfully built, with broad shoulders and a muscular torso. His handsome face featured a strong nose, direct gray eyes, and a neat sandy mustache. His uniforms were impeccable, and he was an expert horseman, riding a magnificent dark bay named Daniel Webster. He seemed, in short, the very model of a major general, radiating youth and dash and what one observer called "an indescribable air of success."

McClellan plunged into his new tasks with energy and boundless self-confidence. Sending 1,000 tough Regular Army soldiers to roust unruly and ill-disciplined troops from Washington's saloons and gambling houses, he swiftly restored order and got the army back on duty. He also cracked down hard on several regiments that threatened mutiny unless allowed to go home on leave.

But he did more than merely apply discipline. He quickly raised morale by improving rations, establishing hospitals, and laying out orderly camps in accordance with army regulations and the principles of good sanitation. Within weeks the troops, proud again to be part of the army, raised lusty cheers whenever McClellan rode by on inspection tours. "I have restored order very completely already," he wrote in one of his daily letters to his wife. "I shall carry this thing *en grande* and crush the rebels in one campaign."

By September McClellan had, in effect, created a brand-new army. Gone were most of the three-month militiamen who had tasted defeat at Bull Run. In their place were fresh recruits who, answering President Lincoln's July 1861 call for 500,000 volunteers, had signed up for three years. Into Washington the new men poured at a rate of about 10,000 a week.

While the green soldiers were set to drilling six to eight hours a day, McClellan acted to sharpen the officer corps as well, setting up strict examination boards that weeded out numbers of unsuitable men. To replace the deadwood, McClellan jumped dozens of well-qualified junior officers from company command to the leadership of regiments or even brigades.

McClellan worked as hard as the troops, sometimes riding on tours of inspection 12 hours a day. These were often splashy events, the general trotting jauntily on his superb horse while behind stretched an impressive retinue that included members of his staff and, for extra panache, a pair of exiled royals McClellan had made honorary captains—the comte de Paris, pretender to the French throne, and his brother the duc de Chartres.

For more pageantry, which he loved, McClellan through the fall of 1861 staged a series of increasingly large full-dress reviews, the troops showing off their new skill in marching and maneuvering while bands played, banners snapped in the breeze—and Little Mac rode along the line, responding to the wild enthusiasm of the men with a snappy salute in which he gave his French-style kepi a little twirl. Confident now that they could whip the Rebels anytime, anyplace, the troops were equally sure that Little Mac was, as a Massachusetts private wrote home, "just the man to lead us on to victory." While drilling, the men sang a new song: "For McClellan's our leader; he is gallant and strong. / For God and our country we are marching along."

But if the troops adored Little Mac, some of his glitter was beginning to fade in the eyes of people outside the service. By midautumn he had transformed the Army of the Potomac into the largest, best-trained, and best-equipped force ever seen in America, but he had thus far

done nothing with it, and grumbling was beginning to be heard in Congress, the press, and elsewhere over his lack of action. The roads in Virginia were firm, the weather excellent. Yet McClellan adamantly refused to attack the Confederates or even deign to say when he might make an offensive move.

For all his confidence, dash, and ability to galvanize his soldiers, McClellan possessed a broad streak of innate caution bordering on timorousness—a trait that would show up again and again during the Peninsula campaign. His hesitancy had several sources: Before accepting command of forces in western Virginia, he had never led anything larger than a company. A number of his corps commanders were many years his senior in the Regular Army. Sensible of the vast responsibility he bore—in his mind the very future of the nation was in his hands—he became overly conscious of the consequences of making a mistake. And he was the victim of faulty intelligence, ladled out in cautionary doses by his secret service chief, Allan Pinkerton.

A Scottish immigrant, Pinkerton had founded one of the nation's first private-detective agencies in Chicago before the war and had done work for McClellan at the Illinois Central Railroad. Following the general to Washington, Pinkerton quickly proved adept at catching Confederate spies. But he and his agents seemed to think that to earn their keep they needed to peg their estimates of enemy

strength as high as possible—a tendency that would play into McClellan's own anxieties and plague the coming campaign. In his first report, Pinkerton estimated the Confederate army in and around Manassas at 100,000 men. Later he would raise the total to "not less than 150,000."

It was a grotesque inflation. In fact, the Rebel army camped around the old Bull Run battlefield totaled at most 42,000 men. Shortly after the Manassas battle the two Confederate commanders, Generals Joseph Johnston and P. G. T. Beauregard, had considered taking the offensive and even—as all of Washington feared—attacking the capital. But unable to get reinforcements, they had quickly given up the idea. Then Beauregard, after an unseemly tiff with Confederate president Jefferson Davis, was transferred west—to fight at the Battle of Shiloh. Since then Johnston had been content to hold Manassas while trying desperately, like McClellan, to forge a better-organized fighting force.

The Federals had seen signs of Confederate weakness in August after a New Jersey colonel, angry when Rebel pickets took potshots at his camp, sent his troops charging at an enemy outpost on a rise called Munson's Hill. Although the Yankees soon fell back, the cautious Johnston, fearing a stronger attack, withdrew the hill's small garrison. Examining the spot later, Federal troops found that the supposed strongpoint was merely a collection of small rifle pits and its one cannon nothing more than a black-painted log, a so-called Quaker gun. This news produced hoots of derision among the Republicans in Congress and the more agressive members of the press. What was McClellan waiting for if all the enemy had was log guns?

Still, McClellan, convinced he faced a huge enemy force, refused to move, even demanding that his own army be enlarged to a colossal 300,000 men before he would take the offensive. Haste, he insisted, had caused the debacle at Bull Run. "I intend to be careful," he informed Lincoln. "Don't let them hurry me, is all I ask."

The reluctant general did, however, take one small offensive action in the fall of 1861, at a place called Ball's Bluff. The result was a bloody and mortifying setback that seemed to vindicate McClellan's argument that neither his officers nor his men were ready yet for serious action, let alone a major campaign.

The incident began when McClellan noticed that although Johnston had abandoned Munson's Hill and other outposts, a number of Confederates still held Leesburg, Virginia, 35 miles up the Potomac from Washington. Thinking a show of force would "shake the enemy out of Leesburg," McClellan on October 19 ordered Brigadier General George A. McCall to march his 13,000-man division northwest toward Dranesville, about 15 miles from Leesburg. The next day McClellan instructed Brigadier General Charles P. Stone,

whose division had been training in camps near Poolesville on the Maryland side of the Potomac, to move toward Leesburg and see if McCall's approach was having the intended effect of nudging the Rebels out of the town.

Stone, a 37-year-old West Pointer, quickly obeyed McClellan's order, marching his division to the Potomac, then sending a 20-man patrol from the 15th Massachusetts under Captain Charles Philbrick to scout ahead.

The patrol, crossing the Potomac in small boats on the night of October 20, landed at the foot of a steep declivity—Ball's Bluff—located about three miles upstream from the ferry. Scrambling up the rocky, 100-foot-high cliff via an old cow path, the men set off inland in the dark. In an hour or so Philbrick saw ahead what seemed a Confederate camp—about 30 tents perched on a ridge. Prudently hurrying his men back down the bluff, he sent word of the apparently unguarded enemy camp to General Stone at Edwards Ferry.

With far less prudence, Stone decided to exceed his orders and attack the camp. Stone himself led several companies of men across the Potomac at Edwards Ferry, then sent Colonel Charles Devens, commander of the 15th Massachusetts, across the river with a larger force at Ball's Bluff.

Devens, a militia officer and Boston lawyer, had 400 troops across the river by dawn the next day. Once atop the bluff, about 300 of them, Devens in the lead, set off to locate and

destroy the camp spotted by Captain Philbrick the evening before. The camp, however, was nowhere to be found—for the good reason that it did not exist. The tents had been optical illusions caused by moonlight shining through some trees. Undeterred, Colonel Devens marched on toward Leesburg, again finding no sign of the enemy.

There were plenty of Confederates nearby, however—a brigade of 2,000 men led by Nathan G. "Shanks" Evans, the hard-drinking and fiercely combative colonel who had rushed to stem the first Federal advance at Manassas back in July and doubtless saved the day for the Confederacy. General Johnston, far from being intimidated into abandoning Leesburg by McCall's move on Dranesville, had dispatched Evans to meet the threat. Now, alerted by pickets he had posted near Ball's Bluff, Evans sent one regiment marching to meet Devens' advance, followed about noon by two more, including Colonel Eppa Hutton's 8th Virginia, described by a Rebel officer as "375 more people in bad temper."

Pressed by the oncoming Confederates, Devens retreated to a large field atop Ball's Bluff. At first it seemed a good idea. Coming up the cow path from the river were hefty reinforcements, two regiments of Union troops led by Colonel Edward D. Baker, a United States senator and old friend of Lincoln's. Eager for the fray, Baker tried to support Devens by deploying his troops in an arc across part of the field.

But the inexperienced Baker failed to send any of his troops to occupy some wooded knolls on the left that commanded the Federal position. It was a fatal mistake. Soon Confederate snipers lurking in the woods began to pick off Baker's men. Then, about 3:00 p.m., the bulk of Evans' Confederates reached the woods and, after firing volleys into the Federal lines, launched a furious attack.

The hard-pressed Union troops threw back the assault, but during the melee Baker himself was shot and killed. Hit also by two musket balls was a Massachusetts lieutenant named Oliver Wendell Holmes Jr. He would recover to fight again, and to serve in years ahead as a distinguished justice of the United States Supreme Court.

Their leader dead, the Federals found themselves in increasingly desperate shape, pressed back almost to the rim of the steep bluff. Finally, as the Confederates launched another attack, panic broke out among the Union troops, many of whom flung themselves over the precipice. Some were killed, hitting rocks as they fell; others were crushed to death as their fellows crashed down on top of them.

As the Federals scrambled away, Confederate riflemen loosed a murderous fire from the top of the bluff, killing dozens as the fleeing troops overloaded and swamped the few boats available or tried desperately to swim the Potomac to a nearby island. "The river was covered by a mass of struggling beings,"

recalled a Rebel soldier, "and we kept up a steady fire upon them as long as the faintest ripple could be seen."

After the shooting stopped, the Confederates rounded up 529 Union prisoners. Added to the 49 dead found on the field, the 100 and more men drowned and 198 wounded, Federal losses amounted to about 50 percent of the 1,700 men engaged, an appalling toll for so small an action and one of so little significance. It had been, said *Frank Leslie's Illustrated Newspaper,* "not a great military blunder, but a great military crime."

The wrath of the newly created congressional Committee for the Conduct of the War fell at first on McClellan, but he escaped responsibility for the fiasco. Unable to cast aspersions on Lincoln's dead friend Baker, the radical Republicans in Congress vented their fury on the unfortunate General Stone, who was arrested on suspicion of having been in league with the enemy and sent to prison for half a year.

Many, however, blamed the army's obvious shortcomings on its aged chief, General Winfield Scott, and this development gave McClellan what he had been angling for all along. Within a week the infirm but canny Scott was forced to retire. On November 1 Lincoln named the Young Napoleon general in chief of all Federal armies.

His own boss now, McClellan still refused to attack the Confederates—until the coming

of winter made the argument moot. As complaints about his performance escalated, McClellan became both arrogant and defensive to an exceeding degree. All of Washington was a "sink of iniquity," he wrote his wife, the politicians "a set of men unscrupulous and false." Lincoln's cabinet contained "some of the greatest geese I have ever seen." As for the president, who had been astonishingly patient with all the delays, McClellan dubbed him "the original gorilla."

Eventually, though, McClellan devised a daring plan of attack. Instead of a direct assault on Johnston's army at Manassas, he would stage an elaborate end run by shipping more than 100,000 men on transports down the Chesapeake Bay to the Rappahannock River and then upstream to land at the tiny village of Urbanna. From there he would march the 60-odd miles to Richmond, capturing the Confederate capital while Johnston's outflanked army was still hurrying from Manassas to give battle.

Before the operation got going, however, word came that the Confederates were on the move. General Johnston, although contemptuous of McClellan for his inertia, was nevertheless a rather cautious commander in his own right. He decided that the outnumbered Rebel force was dangerously exposed. In early March he sent Stonewall Jackson and his brigade marching west to protect the Shenandoah Valley—where much would be heard of them—and then began pulling the bulk of his force from Manassas 60 miles south to the area of Gordonsville on the upper Rappahannock. This move, of course, ruined McClellan's proposed attack, since Johnston's army would now be within an easy march of the landing point at Urbanna.

McClellan had to come up with an alternative scheme. This he did, designing a still larger and more elaborate plan to outflank the Confederates by shipping his army down the Chesapeake all the way to Fort Monroe on the tip of the Virginia Peninsula between the York and James Rivers. From there McClellan would make a 70-mile march, passing Yorktown and crossing the Chickahominy River to assail Richmond from the east.

Lincoln felt the operation was risky and demanded that a considerable force be left behind to give Washington "an entire feeling of security"—a demand that McClellan thought crippled him and further soured his relations with the president. But by March 17, 1862, a vast flotilla of ships had been assembled in the Potomac off Alexandria—113 steamers, 188 schooners, 88 barges, and some 200 other vessels—and the first units of the 121,000-man army were filing aboard for the 200-mile voyage south. On April 2, more than eight months after he had been given command of the army, McClellan himself boarded ship, starting his campaign at last. "Rely upon it," he told Secretary of War Edwin Stanton, "that I will carry this thing through handsomely."

CHRONOLOGY

1861

July 21	*Battle of First Manassas*
July 22	*McClellan takes command of the Division of the Potomac*
October 21	*Battle of Ball's Bluff*
November 1	*McClellan appointed general in chief*

1862

March 8-9	*Naval Battle of Hampton Roads*
March 9	*Johnston evacuates Manassas Junction*
March 11	*McClellan relieved as general in chief; retains command of the Army of the Potomac*
March 17	*Army of the Potomac begins embarkation from Alexandria, Virginia, to the Peninsula*
April 5	*Siege of Yorktown begins*
April 16	*Skirmishes at Lee's Mill and Dam No. 1*
May 3	*Confederates evacuate Yorktown*
May 5	*Battle of Williamsburg*
May 9	*Confederates evacuate Norfolk; CSS Virginia destroyed*
May 15	*Battle of Drewry's Bluff*
May 31-June 1	*Battle of Seven Pines (Fair Oaks)*

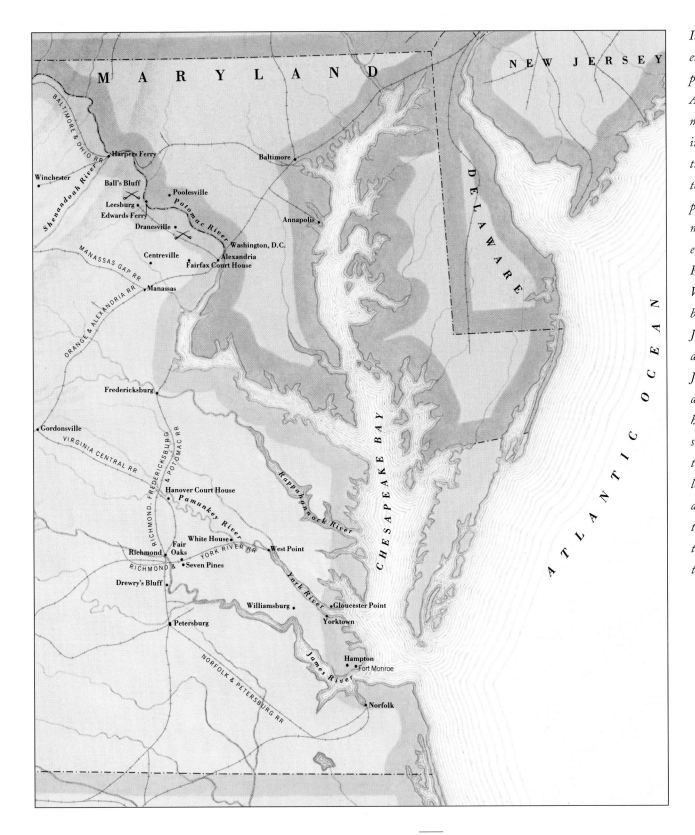

In the spring of 1862, General McClellan, newly appointed commander of the Army of the Potomac, formulated a daring plan to invade Virginia and capture the Confederate capitol at Richmond. His campaign was delayed by the menacing presence of General Joseph E. Johnston's Rebel army in northern Virginia. After a series of battles and skirmishes, Johnston evacuated the area around Manassas Junction and withdrew his army behind the Rappahannock River. McClellan shifted his army by water to the Virginia Peninsula, located between the York and James Rivers. This set the stage for a slow advance that took McClellan's forces to the gates of Richmond.

Major General George B. McClellan (center) poses with his top officers after taking over the Army of the Potomac. The enthusiasm and expectations accompanying McClellan's assumption of command were so great that he said in a letter to his wife, "By some strange operation of magic I seem to have become the power of the land."

BOSTON ADVERTISER

Following the crushing rout of the Union army at Bull Run on July 21, 1861, a desperate Abraham Lincoln summoned McClellan to Washington. The dashing, self-assured young general was just the tonic the demoralized Federals needed. He devoted his energies to ensuring that the troops received proper meals and clothing, along with incessant drill and grand reviews like the one described here. The men quickly formed a bond with their new commander, and morale soared.

September 11, 1861
President Lincoln, Secretary Cameron, Governor Curtin and suite visited the Pennsylvania regiments to-day. The President introduced the Governor and Mrs. Curtin, Secretary Cameron and General McClellan, who were received with enthusiastic cheering.

A hand-shaking then took place, General McClellan cordially greeting officers and men. Each man had something cheering to say to the General. One man said, "General, we are anxious to wipe out Bull Run; hope you will allow us to do it soon?" "Very soon, if the enemy does not run," was the response.

At last Captain Barker, of the Chicago cavalry corps, composing the escort, appealed to the troops not to crowd the General too hard, or shake his hand too much, as before he slept he had a long way to travel, and much writing to do with the hand they were shaking. He promised if they would fall back the General would say a few words to them. They instantly complied, when the General, removing his hat, spoke as follows:—

Soldiers: We have had our last retreat. We have seen our last defeat. You stand by me, and I will stand by you, and henceforth victory will crown our efforts.

COLONEL WILLIAM W. AVERELL

3D PENNSYLVANIA CAVALRY

A native of New York, Averell graduated from West Point in 1855. His prewar service included two years of Indian fighting with the U.S. Mounted Rifles on the southwestern frontier, where he was critically wounded. Although placed on the invalid list, Averell applied for and obtained a staff post with General Andrew Porter in 1861. After the Battle of First Manassas he was appointed colonel of the 3d Pennsylvania and would soon rise to the command of a cavalry brigade.

I remember it was a sunny Indian summer morning and the blue haze which haunts the shores of the Potomac in the autumnal season filled the browning woodlands with inviting suggestions of quiet solitudes and dreamy repose. But the spell of this enchanting landscape, which held the eye, was broken soon after I had crossed the Potomac, by the hearing of trumpet calls mingled with the music of military bands at practice from all directions and the rattle of small arms firing in target practice like the patter of heavy rain drops on a roof be-

fore a coming storm. This portentous suggestion was strengthened by the occasional rolling thunder of distant heavy guns testing ranges along the field works and fortifications surrounding Washington. This was the chorus of the titanic forge in which, under the hand of a mastering military genius, a hundred and fifty thousand men were being welded into a loyal, obedient, irresistible engine of destruction which was to become the bulwark of the nation and to make its name, "Army of the Potomac," illustrious and immortal.

I found the companies of the 3d Pennsylvania enjoying a jolly, gypsy sort of life in picturesque bivouacs, well chosen for the comforts of shade and the convenience of the three essentials of a cavalry camp; viz., wood, water and grass. Some of the men were engaged in athletic sports, some with cards and a few with newspapers. The general appearance of the men was very encouraging. They were young, strong and radiant Americans, the majority of whom were from the country towns and farms. Many of them, by their bearing and manners, showed the habits of good associations. But the appearance and behavior of several of the officers were not promising. It was easy to see that some

By fall 1861 military camps dotted Washington and the northern Virginia hills across the Potomac. Here the 1st Connecticut Heavy Artillery is shown in bivouac at Fort Blenker, on the Arlington Heights. The enlisted men's Sibley tents line the company streets at left, while the officers enjoyed the less crowded accommodations at right.

of them should exchange places with some of their men in the ranks for the advantage of the service.

I selected a wide, grassy slope, easily drained, for a camp in Virginia, a mile from the Aqueduct Bridge. The site was convenient to water and to the transportation of supplies and adjacent to broad and rolling fields, well suited for cavalry exercises. With the assistance of a detail from the Provost Guard in Washington, the camp was laid out precisely in accordance with Army Regulations. New Sibley tents, picket lines, ten days' rations and a supply of forage were all brought on the ground on the 30th of October. The field officers' tents were pitched and a large commissary tent supplied with benches and blackboards for a school was set up near the Colonel's tent. A tall flagstaff, with a set of flags, ready for raising, completed the preparations.

MAJOR JOHN W. KIMBALL

15TH MASSACHUSETTS INFANTRY

In October McClellan contrived a minor operation to gain his novice army some practical experience. He ordered Brigadier General Charles P. Stone, camped across the Potomac from Leesburg, to make a "slight demonstration" toward the Rebel outpost there. Kimball poetically describes a furtive night-time crossing, which kicked off a nasty little bloodbath that McClellan never bargained for.

The face of Balls Bluff veiled by the tree tops and rich sombre foliage, bathed in the radiance of the bright October moon, presented a fascinating succession of lunar shadows, amid which exposed bits of rock and greensward stood forth boldly revealed in the soft white glare.

A dark shadow glides across the rippling surface of the Potomac sparkling in the moonlight.

It is a boat conveying Capt. Chase Philbrick and eight or ten stalwart fellows of the Fifteenth and some of the Twentieth, bound upon a most romantic mission—a nocturnal scout to penetrate the mysteries of those gloomy woods beyond the Virginia shore.

Silence reigns supreme.

The boat glides into the shadow of the bluff and is lost to sight.

A winding foot path, blocked here and there with many a moss-grown trunk, ascends a narrow ravine, and thence by a sloping plateau to the crest of the bluff itself. In places it is a stiffish climb over the precipitous rock face.

What will they wake up—up there at the top—pickets?

The men tread lightly on tip-toe, following the Captain. No talking, except for his whispered direction now and then. What strange things one sees in the woods at this weird hour. Every stump has its individual personality.

Hah!

What was that?

Silence! the whole squad.

Was it the gleam of the picket's rifle?

Pshaw! No.

Only the glinting of a moonbeam across a bright bit of hornblende away up there on the cliff.

Whirr! Away flies a frightened covey, startled from their lair by these nocturnal intruders.

Another halt! No response from the pickets. Then they go on. Involuntarily one looks for the tall form of old Leatherstocking stalking there in the advance, as now the dusky figures steal out in the moonlight upon a bare bit of ledge to gaze down upon the silent tree tops below them swaying in the night breeze, and then vanish from sight in impenetrable shadow.

The top was reached, to find no pickets there.

The spell was on the young scouts, as, upon working through the belt of woods back from the bluff, they saw beyond the next clearing, in the interstices of a row of trees upon the ridge, through which the moonbeams glanced weirdly, what each fully believed to be the snowy canvas of the rebel tents surely.

Alas, a ghostly encampment it proved to be, but back came the scouts with their exciting report.

"What strange things one sees in the woods at this weird hour. Every stump has its individual personality."

CAPTAIN WILLIAM F. BARTLETT
20TH MASSACHUSETTS INFANTRY

When Kimball's foray seemed to indicate that the Confederates were in retreat, Stone fatefully ordered a reconnaissance in force. Companies from the 15th and 20th Massachusetts climbed Ball's Bluff on the Virginia shore and moved toward Leesburg. In this letter Bartlett describes the forbidding terrain facing his unit.

We crossed the river . . . under command of Colonel Lee, in all one hundred men, in a whale boat that could carry sixteen, and two small boats holding five and four respectively. I went over first and found a steep bank one hundred and fifty feet high, with thick wood on it. There was not room enough to form ten men, and the banks were so slippery that you could not stand. I formed the men in single file up the path, waiting for the Colonel and the rest of the men.

After they were all over, we wound our way up this precipice and formed on the open space above. The detachment of the Fifteenth, three hundred men, now moved up the road leading from the top of the bank inland. We were to remain there to support them, and cover their retreat. It looked rather dubious. The Fifteenth might get across, but we must check the advance of the enemy and get cut to pieces. We sent out scouts in all directions; three men under a sergeant composed each party.

My first sergeant, Riddle, went out on our right. At this time we did not know how many of the enemy there might be within gunshot of us. It was now about sunrise, when we heard three or four shots in rapid succession on our right. In a few minutes my first sergeant was brought in, shot through the elbow. He was fainting from loss of blood. We tied a hankerchief around his arm and sent him down to the river. It was nearly nine when we heard a splendid volley in the direction of the Fifteenth. We knew we were in for it then! Soon wounded men were brought down the road mentioned. How large a force they had met we

General Stone, a West Pointer who had fought well in Mexico, would unjustly bear the blame for Ball's Bluff and was subsequently imprisoned for six months. Despite later gallant service at Vicksburg, Stone could never clear his record.

did not know, but we learned from the wounded that the volley was from the enemy. We expected now to see the Fifteenth falling back on us. The firing ceased and we were in suspense, thinking that they might have been surrounded, and waiting to see the enemy come down that road and sweep our hundred men into the river. We were then deployed as skirmishers across the road, Company I on the right, Casper on the left, an opening at the road to let the Fifteenth pass through to the river, and then check their pursuers until they could get across. I never expected to see Camp Benton again and I was glad that you little dreamed of our critical position.

PRIVATE GEORGE A. GIBBS
18TH MISSISSIPPI INFANTRY

The 17-year-old Gibbs was a student in Yazoo County, Mississippi, when he enlisted in May 1861. Gibbs' regiment, hurled into action by the ferociously aggressive, hard-drinking Nathan "Shanks" Evans, rushed two miles from Leesburg to Ball's Bluff to come to the aid of beleaguered Virginia and Mississippi skirmishers facing the Federals. Gibbs served in the army until a wound suffered near Petersburg in June 1862 cost him his left leg.

We were all from Mississippi except one small regiment, which was from Virginia. I suppose the enemy marched something over a half mile from the point where they crossed the river, when they met us, advancing to meet them. We had formed a line of battle a few minutes before, and General Evans made us a short speech. I remember he told us to shoot low, "so as to hit them in the stomach." After the general's remarks, we were ordered to load, fix bayonets, then to charge.

From the very beginning we had the best of the battle. We met them at the top of a small hill, and after a bit of hard fighting, almost hand to hand, we drove them down the hill and pressed them steadily back towards the river.

The enemy had a battery on a hill near the river, and it was giving us a good deal of trouble. Our regiment was ordered to capture the battery. In obedience to this order, we had started up the hill, but when it was discovered that we would uncover our right flank, we were halted until the Virginia regiment could come up and join with us on the right. This occupied ten minutes, during which we were under the fire of the battery.

An amusing incident occurred at this time. Our first lieutenant,

Bostick, was a big, fat old man, near-sighted, and hard of hearing. Not hearing the order to halt, he rushed on up the hill by himself, pistol in one hand and sword in the other. We screamed to him to come back, but he did not hear us, and continued to run up the hill. When near the top he was wounded and fell.

CAPTAIN WILLIAM F. BARTLETT
20TH MASSACHUSETTS INFANTRY

Bartlett left Harvard to enlist as a private the day Fort Sumter fell. Here he describes the withering fire that swept through his regiment. Seeing a fellow captain fall wounded, he frankly admitted, "How I envied him at getting off with the loss of an arm. . . . For I knew then that we should either be killed or taken prisoners."

Well the first volley came and the balls flew like hail. You can see from our position on the plan that we were exposed to their full fire. The whizzing of the balls was a new sensation. I had read so much about being under fire and flying bullets that I was curious to experience it. I had a fair chance. An old German soldier told me he had been in many battles, but that he never saw such a concen-

Nathan Evans would win promotion to brigadier general for his actions at Ball's Bluff. A witness to the battle saw Evans on horseback, directing his troops and "imbibing generously. When inspiration was slow in coming from Above, he invoked the aid of his canteen at his side." Later in the war he was court-martialed for drunkenness; he was acquitted, but his career was wrecked.

trated fire before. They fired beautifully too, their balls all coming low, within from one to four feet from the ground. The men now began to drop around me; most of them were lying down in the first of it, being ordered to keep in reserve. Those that were lying down, if they lifted their foot or head it was struck. One poor fellow near me was struck in the hip while lying flat, and rose to go to the rear, when another struck him in the head, and knocked him over. I felt that if I was going to be hit, I should be, whether I stood up or lay down, so I stood up and walked around among the men, stepping over them and talking to them in a joking way, to take their thoughts from the bullets, and keep them more self possessed. I was surprised at first at my own coolness. I never felt better, although I expected of course that I should feel the lead any second, and I was wondering where it would take me. I kept speaking to Little, surprised that he was not hit yet amongst the rain of bullets. I said two or three times, "Why Lit., aren't you hit yet?" I remember Macy was lying where the grass was turned up, and I "roughed" him for getting his coat so awfully dirty. The different companies began to wilt away under this terrible fire. Still there was no terror among the men; they placed implicit confidence in their officers—I refer to our regiment particularly—and you could see that now was the time they respected and looked up to them.

PRIVATE RANDOLPH A. SHOTWELL
8TH VIRGINIA INFANTRY

In August 1861, at the age of 16, Shotwell, the son of an Episcopal minister from Virginia, ran away from his private school in Pennsylvania. After sneaking through Federal lines along the Potomac, he enlisted in the 8th Virginia, the first regiment from his home state that he encountered. Ball's Bluff was his first battle.

Per contra the Virginia regiment had exhausted its ammunition, and no one knew where the wagon trains could be found; war was a new business at that date. Men could be seen crawling about, searching the boxes of the dead or borrowing cartridges of their comrades—to get one more shot. Colonel Hunton dispatched his adjutant to say to General Evans: "My powder is out; what shall I do?" "Fix bayonets and run 'em into the river!" quoth "Old Shanks" (his regular army *soubriquet,*) who had just taken a liquid reinforcement, equivalent to 10,000 men. It was time for some decisive measure, for Colonel Baker had ordered his right wing to advance and flank the little ridge whence came the rebel bullets.

Fortunately for the Confederates, at the moment this movement began, there was heard the pattering footsteps and jingling canteens of the Eighteenth Mississippi double quicking through the brush, then a wild, terror striking yell; then the simultaneous crash of 1,000 muskets, each hurling its leaden contents along the Federal left and centre! The effect was electric. The roar of this sudden, blinding, raking volley was like the crack of doom to the already demoralized Federals, most of whom were under fire for the first time!

General Beauregard presented this silk battle flag, bearing the battle honor "Leesburg," to the 8th Virginia Infantry soon after Ball's Bluff. The other honors were probably added once the flag was retired following the Battle of Antietam.

COLONEL WINFIELD S. FEATHERSTON
17TH MISSISSIPPI INFANTRY

A former congressman and Indian fighter, Featherston led the 17th Mississippi so well at Ball's Bluff that he was soon given a brigade. As his regiment pressed the Yankees back toward the precipice, he ordered fixed bayonets and shouted, "Charge, Mississippians, charge! Drive them into the Potomac or into eternity!"

About 3 o'clock p.m. I was ordered to advance rapidly to the support of these regiments, which were then engaged with a greatly superior force of the enemy, and accordingly we moved at a double-quick a distance of more than 2 miles to the field, when, perceiving that there was an interval of about 200 yards between the two other regiments, I immediately occupied it with my regiment. Learning that Colonel Burt had been dangerously wounded and borne from the field, I conferred with Lieut. Col. T. M. Griffin, commanding the Eighteenth Mississippi Regiment, and formed my regiment on the center of our line, in the edge of the woods, and immediately in front of the enemy, who were drawn up in the woods upon the opposite side of a small field, at the same time requesting Colonel Griffin to form the Eighteenth Regiment upon my right, which he did promptly. One company of the Eighteenth Regiment which was on our left fell into our line and continued to act with us in that position.

While we were forming our line, the Eighth Virginia Regiment, which, together with a detached company from this and one from the Eighteenth Regiment, was engaged with the enemy upon our left, made a gallant charge upon their right wing. At the same time Colonel Hunton, commanding that regiment, informed me that his ammunition was exhausted.

I then ordered the Seventeenth and Eighteenth Mississippi Regiments to advance without firing until they were close to the enemy, and then to fire and charge. This order was gallantly obeyed. The two regiments moved forward slowly and steadily under a heavy fire, but without returning it, until we had crossed the field and penetrated the woods in which the enemy were posted, and to within 40 or 50 yards of their line, when we poured in a close and deadly fire, which drove them back, and continued to advance, loading and firing until the enemy were driven to seek shelter beneath a high bluff immediately upon the brink of the river, and some of them in the river itself.

CAPTAIN FRANCIS G. YOUNG
71ST PENNSYLVANIA INFANTRY

As Young relates, Colonel Edward D. Baker, for all his military ineptitude, was certainly not lacking in personal courage. But his brave death gave scant comfort to a nation reeling from news of this latest disaster. Frank Leslie's Illustrated Newspaper editorialized about Ball's Bluff, saying, "This time military incompetence must accept its own responsibilities." In early January 1862 Young was dismissed from the service for insubordination and an unauthorized absence in Washington.

Colonel Baker fell about 5 o'clock. He was standing near the left of the woods, and it is believed he was shot with a cavalry revolver by a private of the enemy, who, after Colonel Baker fell, crawled on his hands and knees to the body and was attempting to take his sword, when Captain Bieral with 10 of his men rushed up and shot him through the head and rescued the body. At the time Colonel Baker was shot he was looking at a mounted officer, who rode down a few rods into the field from the woods, who, being shot at by one of our men, returned to the woods and appeared to be falling from his horse. Colonel Baker, turning about, said "See, he falls," and immediately fell, receiving four balls, each of which would be fatal. I had but a moment before, standing by his side, been ordered by Colonel Baker to go with all possible dispatch to General Stone for re-enforcements on the left, as there was no transportation across the river for the wants of the hour. There was some confusion on the field, and the officers of the companies of the Fifteenth Massachusetts Regiment ordered their men to retreat. The enemy then for the first time came out of the wood at double-quick, and receiving a double charge of grape-shot from the 12-pounder, broke in disorder and returned to the woods. There were but few of the Federal forces now on the field, having returned to the river side down the steep, but finding no means of escape, some 200

Colonel Edward Baker's death was front-page material in Northern periodicals. A native of England who came to the United States as a child, he practiced law in Illinois and became a friend of Abraham Lincoln's before moving to the West Coast, where he became a U.S. senator from Oregon. It was his impulsive decision early in the Battle of Ball's Bluff to reinforce the Massachusetts regiments rather than withdraw them that precipitated disaster. Baker paid for his mistake with his life but emerged posthumously as a hero. His superior, General Stone, would become the scapegoat.

charged up the hill and poured in a volley, the enemy at this time occupying the field. It was getting dark, and some one tied a white handkerchief to a sword and went forward. Many were taken prisoners at the moment, and some fled into the woods on either side, and many others ran down to the crossing. I got the body of Colonel Baker on the flatboat, at this time partly filled with water, the dead and wounded, and safely reached the island.

sword, I stooped to recover it from the place where I knew it had fallen, and having gathered it up along with a handful of bloody grass, had just regained the perpendicular, when I was seized by Baker with a hand on each shoulder. "What, Wistar, hit again?" "Yes, I am afraid badly this time." Then sheathing for me the sword at my request, he called a soldier: "Here, my man, catch hold of Col. Wistar and get him to the boat somehow, if you have to carry him."

COLONEL ISAAC J. WISTAR
71ST PENNSYLVANIA INFANTRY

Wistar, shown here with his arm still in a sling from the wound he describes below, commanded the Union army's hardest-hit regiment in the debacle at Ball's Bluff. "Of the five hundred and seventy officers and men taken into action," he reported, "the total loss, in killed, wounded, and missing . . . amounts to three hundred and five."

MAJOR HENRY L. ABBOTT
20TH MASSACHUSETTS INFANTRY

Born into a wealthy, politically connected family, the Harvard-educated Abbott proved to be one of the Union's finest soldiers. He first showed his mettle in the harrowing conditions of Ball's Bluff; at dusk he and Captain Bartlett quietly led 80 survivors upstream away from the killing ground until they found a leaky skiff and rowed to safety.

Early in the action I was struck in the jaw by a bullet or a small stone dashed up by one. Though the injury did not eventually amount to much, it caused severe pain and loss of blood which became matted in the beard, and dripping down in front, rendered me a ferocious and unpleasant object to behold, as I have since been assured. Later a bullet passed through my thigh within a short distance of the old arrow wound, suffered years before in the upper Klamath country. This though but a flesh wound, filled my boot with blood so that I was obliged to cut a hole to let it out. Just before dark, while endeavoring to change front with the two left companies to repel a charge on that flank, I was struck in the right elbow by a ball that shattered all three of the bones meeting at that point, causing a momentary mental confusion and even suspension of sight. Though I could not see my

Our company made the last charge. The general was killed, shot by 5 balls; nobody knew who was the senior in command & Col. Lee ordered a retreat. But we were determined to have one more shot. So Frank ordered a charge & we rushed along, followed by all our men without an exception, & by Lieut. Hallowell with about 20 men, making about 60 in all. So we charged across the field about half way, when we saw the enemy in full sight. They had just come out of the wood & had halted at our advance. There they were in their dirty gray clothes, their banner waving, cavalry on the flank. For a moment there was a pause. And then, simultaneously, we fired & there came a murderous discharge from the full rebel force. Of course we retreated, but not a man went faster than a walk.

When we got back to the wood, we found the whole regiment cut to pieces & broken up, all the other forces gone & Col. Lee sitting under a tree, swearing he wouldn't go another step, but had rather be taken prisoner. However, we got him to go & we all started down the bank, every body knowing, however, that there was no chance of an escape. The col. ordered a surrender & had a white flag raised but the rebels fired on us & we were obliged to retreat to the river's edge, the rebels pouring down a murderous fire.

PRIVATE RANDOLPH A. SHOTWELL
8TH VIRGINIA INFANTRY

Shotwell relates with quiet compassion the scene of absolute horror at the foot of Ball's Bluff as darkness fell on October 21. From high above, Confederates poured fire into the panicky Yankees clustered on the riverbank, where boats were in desperately short supply. More than 500 men—in some ways the lucky ones— were taken prisoner, including the grandson of Paul Revere. A more terrible fate awaited many who tried to swim the Potomac; more than 100 drowned.

A kind of shiver ran through the huddled mass upon the brow of the cliff; it gave way; rushed a few steps; then, in one wild, panic-stricken herd, rolled, leaped, tumbled over the precipice! The descent is nearly perpendicular, with ragged, jutting crags, and a water laved base. Screams of pain and terror filled the air. Men seemed suddenly bereft of reason; they leaped over the bluff with muskets still in their clutch, threw themselves into the river without divesting themselves of their heavy accoutrements—hence went to the bottom like lead. Others sprang down upon the heads and bayonets of those below. A gray-haired private of the First California was found with his head mashed between two rocks by the heavy boots of a ponderous "Tammany" man, who had broken his own neck by the fall! The side of the bluff was worn smooth by the number sliding down.

From the beginning of the battle a steady stream of wounded men had been trickling down the zig-zag path leading to the narrow beach, whence the boats were to convey them to the Island. As it happened, the two larger bateaux were just starting with an overload when the torrent of terror-stricken fugitives rolled down the bluffs upon them. Both boats were instantly submerged, and their cargoes of helpless human beings (crippled by wounds) were swept away to unknown graves! The whole surface of the river seemed filled with heads, struggling, scream-

"The whole surface of the river seemed filled with heads, struggling, screaming, fighting, dying!"

ing, fighting, dying! Man clutched at man, and the strong, who might have escaped, were dragged down by the weaker. Voices that strove to shout for help were stifled by the turbid, sullen waters of the swollen river and died away in gurgles. It is strange how persons about to drown turn to their fellows for strength; they may be in mid-ocean, with no hope for any, yet will they grasp one another and sink in pairs.

CAPTAIN WILLIAM F. BARTLETT
20TH MASSACHUSETTS INFANTRY

Bartlett survived Ball's Bluff and went on to forge a remarkable wartime career. He lost a leg at Yorktown the following spring yet was appointed colonel of the 49th Massachusetts and fought at Vicksburg, where he was twice more wounded. In 1864 he sustained yet another wound in the Wilderness, was made a brigadier general, and was taken prisoner at the Battle of the Crater. Later paroled, he ended the war as a major general commanding a division.

I turned back and left the Colonel, to collect the remnant of my company, and when I returned he was gone. I asked for him and they told me that he, the Major, and Adjutant had got into a small boat and gone across safely. I looked and saw a small boat landing on the other side, and took it for granted they were safe. I then, being in command, collected what I could of the regiment, and told those who could swim, and wished to, to take to the water, it was the only means of escape. Nearly all my company could swim, and I made them stop and take off their clothes. We sent over messages and reports by them. Little and I thought it our duty to stay by those men who could not swim. I allowed Macy to go, hoping that one of us might get home to tell the story. Little sent his watch over by Kelly, the bravest boy in our company, and I told him to go to Boston, and go to you and tell you that your son was probably a prisoner.

"The Rebels had now come to the bluffs and commenced poring death and destruction into our number."

LIEUTENANT COLONEL GEORGE H. WARD
15TH MASSACHUSETTS INFANTRY

In a letter that he wrote to his wife and children three days after the battle, Ward talked about having lost his leg. "I really think myself lucky to get off as I did, when so many poor fellows were hurried out of this world," he said. Outfitted with a cork leg, Ward was able to continue fighting with his regiment until he fell mortally wounded at Gettysburg on July 2, 1863.

Captain Alois Babo of the 20th Massachusetts led a company at Ball's Bluff made up of German immigrants. Babo was shot and drowned as he attempted to swim the Potomac without discarding his equipment during the Yankees' frenzied flight.

Every thing was now confusion, every one for himself, and much excitement prevailed. All retreated to the river. The boats were soon loaded, so that they soon sank after leaving the shore. Retreat being now cut off, to swim the river was the alternative. Men threw their guns and equipments into the river and plunged in after. Most of them were undressed or nearly so. The Rebels had now come to the bluffs and commenced poring death and destruction into our number. The river was literally filled with human beings struggling with death for the master. Large numbers were either killed or wounded by the enemy in the river, many were drowned and the rest succeeded in reaching the shore. Lieut Grout of Company D was killed in the river & Capt Gatchel of Company K was either killed or drowned. Large numbers were taken prisoners including Cols Cogswell and Lee. Major & Surgeon Revere, & Capts Rockwood, Bowman and Studley of our Regmt several Lieuts. Some escaped by going up and some by going down the river. It was a complete route and our men were worthy of a more fortunate result. Col Devens and Major Kimball swam the river. Soon after I was taken into the Hospital, the surgeons decided that it would be necessary to amputate my leg. The operation was performed by Dr Nathan Haywood of Roxbury Mass, Surgeon to the 20th Regmt assisted by Dr Haven Asst Surgeon of our Regmt. It was quite dark, and all the light they had was about 2 in of tallow candle stuck in an ink bottle. Dr Bates our Surgeon was not on the Island. He came down to the bank of the river, having got up from a sick bed for the first time where he had been confined from three to four weeks part of the time dangerously sick. He rendered good service in the Brigade Hospital afterwards. I was taken from the Island about 10 1/2 o,cl PM the same night of the battle on a litter and put on a canal boat for Edwards Ferry. The boat was crowded with our wounded, and it was some time before we got under way. The boat moved very slow and we were a long while getting to the Ferry, where I was put into a Hospital wagon driven by a Mr P Kirby of the Mass 20th and formerly of Worcester. The road from that Ferry to camp (5 miles) was very rough and it was necessary to walk the horses all the way. Mr Waters our Commissary Sergt accompanied me from the Island to the Hospital at Poolsville near our camp where we arrived about 5,o,cl in the morning of the 22nd. It was a damp cloudy night raining at times, and I suffered much pain from my wound.

Lieutenant Charles H. Eager commanded Company B, 15th Massachusetts, at Ball's Bluff. He survived, and in November 1863 became the 15th's commanding officer.

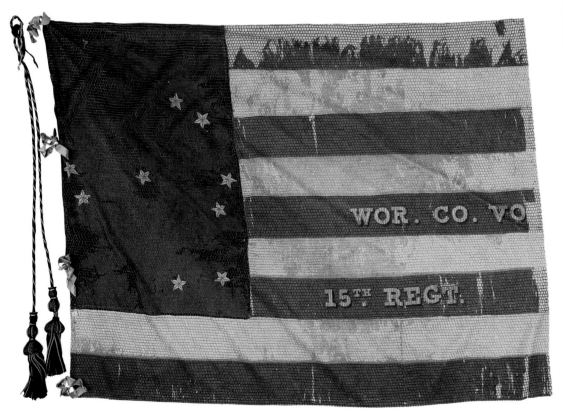

This silk flag was presented to the 15th Massachusetts on August 7, 1861, by the ladies of Worcester. It was saved from capture at Ball's Bluff by Color Sergeant Joshua Freeman, who swam to safety with the flag. It was retired in February 1863, when the regiment received new Federal and state colors.

"The woods in which the enemy were concealed were found thickly strewn with dead and wounded."

MAJOR JOHN W. KIMBALL
15TH MASSACHUSETTS INFANTRY

A manufacturer of farming tools before the war, Kimball had also led a company in the peacetime Massachusetts militia. On the basis of this service he was commissioned a major in August 1861 and later commanded his own regiment, the 53d Massachusetts. After the war he was very active in veterans' affairs, and in an interview conducted by the Boston Journal, vigorously defended General Stone's conduct at Ball's Bluff.

I never saw Gen. Devens more cool. Lieut. C. H. Eager, Frederick H. Sibley, with W. A. Eames, A. A. Simonds and George L. Boss, all of Company B, had a branch of a tree, some 20 feet long, with an ordinary piece of scantling about 12 feet long.

They were supporting themselves upon them in the water, and called to us. "Come, Colonel, come, Major, we will take you across." Devens was an indifferent swimmer; some of the others could not swim. I was a good swimmer. When we got out in the stream we found our load too heavy, and I bade the boys good-by and struck out alone. Three times I went down. The shots were spatting the water all round me, and oh, how numb I was! The water was icy cold and the current swift.

The last time I went down my feet touched bottom, and I remember the supreme effort I made to rise above the surface. I came up beside an upturned stump about eight rods from the shore. From that I waded to land, the water being shallow. I met a soldier on Harrison's Island who immediately went to work on me to restore circulation.

As soon as my blood began to flow naturally I was all right, but I could not have gone much farther. Later I rejoined my comrades, who landed farther down stream than I did.

CAPTAIN HEZEKIAH EASTON
BATTERY A, 1ST PENNSYLVANIA LIGHT ARTILLERY

As the fall of 1861 dragged on, pressure from newspapermen and politicians grew to get the Army of the Potomac out of its camps and into action. But McClellan would not be rushed; he limited operations to patrols and one brigade-sized reconnaissance in force toward Dranesville, Virginia, a few miles downstream from Ball's Bluff. There the probing Federals—including Captain Easton— fought a brief but sharp skirmish with a Confederate brigade.

No appearance of the enemy was visible until we reached Thornton's house, near the junction of the Alexandria and Leesburg turnpike, when a heavy fire of artillery and musketry was suddenly opened from a thick woods on our left, the enemy evidently lying in large force in ambuscade, while their artillery was posted on the Centreville road, leading through the wood and coming into the Alexandria turnpike between Thornton's and Coleman's houses. My guns were immediately put into battery and opened fire. Having nothing to indicate the position of the enemy but the smoke of their guns, I opened a brisk discharge of shells into the woods occupied by the enemy, which was kept up until your order to cease firing. The examination of the ground afterward showed the successful and destructive effects of our artillery fire. The rebel battery, in my opinion, was unmanned by our third fire. They succeeded in drawing off their guns, but I captured one caisson and one limber, and one other was exploded and the horses fatally injured. The woods in which the enemy were concealed were found thickly strewn with dead and wounded. The mangled bodies of the dead showed the terrible execution of our fire. Besides the ordnance captured, a large quantity of clothing, blankets, knapsacks, haversacks, &c., was found, which the enemy had cast off in their hasty and thorough rout.

This engraving shows the action at Dranesville on December 20. A Pennsylvania soldier wrote, "The third brigade . . . found some . . . rebels laying in the woods with a masked battery in front of them. They fought very desperate. . . . We passed three rebel prisoners that our fellows took and they were mighty looking soldiers."

CAPTAIN CHARLES M. BLACKFORD
2D VIRGINIA CAVALRY

A Lynchburg lawyer before the war, Blackford enlisted in May 1861 and was elected captain of Company B in August. A year after the skirmish at Dranesville, he was assigned to Major General James Longstreet's staff as judge advocate, an office he held until hostilities ended. After the war he returned to Lynchburg and his law practice and also became president of a bank. Blackford died in March 1903.

The citizens below here towards Dranesville were in a wild state of excitement and it was reported the enemy was coming up the road towards Leesburg in heavy force. General Hill sent me out to reconnoitre. I took only one man as many of my company were down in that direction on picket already with Lieut. Stratton, with headquarters at Belmont. When I reached Belmont I found Stratton under the impression the enemy were in force at Dranesville, as they had been the day before. I sent him and James T. Smith to reconnoitre the Green Spring road and I went down towards Dranesville. In a short time I met one of my men who had been on outside picket coming back in great haste with the story that the enemy was advancing in two columns, one on the pike, the other on a parallel road; that he had seen them with his own eyes; that one of my men had been captured, but that the outpost at Broad Run would fall back slowly. This was startling news and surely seemed authentic. I made the fellow join me and fairly flew to reinforce the picket at Broad Run, which was composed of some of my best men, who I knew would not give up the bridge without some stand. At the rate I was moving I soon reached Broad Run, meeting people fleeing from the approaching enemy in carts, wagons, afoot, and on horseback, with women, children, and such household goods as they could pick up and carry off. As I passed them they all, with wild gestures, pointed in the direction I was moving, and signalled me to go back, but I had no time to talk and flew by them. When I reached the picket I found them alert and prepared, with several videttes out a mile towards the enemy. They reported it was E. G. Scott who had been captured and that they thought it was only a scouting party of the enemy who had come back to ascertain whether our troops had occupied it. I went down the road with the whole picket, picking up the videttes as we passed them, but strange to say, found no enemy. I went on until I reached Dranesville, which to my surprise I found occupied by a scouting party of Stuart's command, with whom Scott was affiliating instead of being captured. The people in the neighborhood knew the yankees had occupied Dranesville the evening before and seeing troops there in large force the next morning supposed them all yankees and hence the false reports which reached us.

LIEUTENANT ALEXANDER B. SHARPE
7TH PENNSYLVANIA INFANTRY

Sharpe enlisted as a private in the 7th Pennsylvania at Carlisle a few days after Fort Sumter. Commissioned a lieutenant in August, he fought with his regiment at Dranesville. Shortly after the battle, Sharpe was assigned to the staff of General Edward O. C. Ord as an aide. He remained on Ord's staff throughout the war, rising to the rank of colonel and twice receiving brevets for gallantry —at Vicksburg and Petersburg. Sharpe wrote this account of the Dranesville battle for the Wellsboro (Pennsylvania) Agitator in March 1886.

My recollection is that there was a little church on a knoll at the extreme end (the west end) of the village, opposite the one we entered, and that Ord rode rapidly to the top of the knoll. After he had looked over the ground a few moments he asked me for my field-glass, and soon turned it south or a little west of south. In that direction I could see with the naked eye dust and objects moving, but could not tell what the latter were nor their number. I had hardly fixed my gaze steadily on the objects in the direction mentioned when he told me to go out for Jackson's regiment, the one on the left of our column (south) entering Drainsville, and bring it in, and I had just done this and got up to him when he ordered Captain Easton, who was

standing near him with his guns near by, to load with shells. He pronounced shell broadly, as if it was written shall. I can see and hear him now turning and saying to quiet, noble Easton, in a loud tone, "Load with shall."

In the meantime the regiments of Colonel McCalmont, Penrose and Taggart had come up. . . . The movements of the enemy that General Ord had been watching were such that he concluded that an engagement was imminent. He had learned that their approach was on the south side of the Leesburg pike, with artillery and infantry, and that our pickets on that side had been driven in and two of them wounded, and concluded that they would attack on both sides of the pike as we returned eastward. He changed front therefore, facing directly eastward, and our left now became the right and the right our left. Jackson's regiment, which thus became our right, was ordered to flank the road on the right, left in front, and if the enemy showed himself on that side to bring his regiment forward into line, and McCalmont's on the left, in the same order, Kane to cover the road and be supported by Penrose and Taggart, the cavalry to watch any threatened attack from the rear.

Before this disposition was completed a shell, the first I had ever heard, came from the south, whizzing and hissing up the road that intersects at right angles the Leesburg pike at the east end of Drainsville. This is the direct road from Centreville to Drainsville, and into it two other roads on the right and left of it converge and all three pass through two wooded tracts of land separated by a clearing, but they all unite in the woods nearest Drainsville, and in this way the near approach of the enemy and their number were concealed before the firing began. Ord at once concluded that the attack would be made from the south only and not from the south and east, and ordered Easton to place his guns on a rise close to the Leesburg pike, facing the guns of the enemy, which appeared to be about five hundred yards south and in the Centreville road.

This drawing by Alfred R. Waud, sketched after Federal troops had occupied the Manassas area in March 1862, shows a former Confederate camp near Centreville. The soldiers' log huts and an earthen-walled fort overlook the old Manassas battlefield in the distance. General Joseph Johnston's army spent the fall and winter of 1861–1862 in the area, constructing a series of formidable earthwork fortifications connected by rifle pits to guard the approaches to Centreville and the railhead at Manassas Junction. Despite these efforts, the Rebels abandoned the area on March 7 because Johnston felt it could not be safely held.

PRIVATE EDGAR WARFIELD

17TH VIRGINIA INFANTRY

In December 1860, shortly after John Brown's raid on Harpers Ferry, Warfield, an apothecary clerk in Alexandria, helped organize the Old Dominion Rifles, a volunteer militia company. In 1861 he joined his father, a veteran of the Seminole Wars, and his older brother George in the 17th Virginia. George was killed at the Battle of Frayser's Farm in 1862. Edgar fought until Appomattox.

We felt it almost our bounden duty to have a little fight every day at the Peach Orchard on Munson's Hill. While I was on picket here one day, with the enemy in possession of the orchard, a Yankee climbed up on a gate post and began cutting up, going through such antics as twirling his fingers on his nose, shaking his fists, and dancing.

We had with us at this time a volunteer scout from Texas by the name of Fort. He was a fine shot, and it was decided to call him to the front and give him a chance at the fellow on the post. Fort crawled up on him as close as he thought necessary, sighted his Sharpe's rifle for a long-distance shot, and fired. The man fell, and it was some time before any of his comrades ventured to come out and get his body for fear the same marksman was waiting for them.

On another occasion the boys mounted a section of an old stovepipe on two wheels which they had obtained at a wheelwright shop at the crossroads. It was a favorite trick to run it out into the center of the road and go through the motions of loading a gun and pointing it at the enemy, who promptly stampeded, under the impression that we had a piece of artillery with us. General Longstreet in his history makes mention of this incident.

One night when we were occupying an old schoolhouse as quarters for the reserve pickets the lights were ordered out. Then the storm began. The mischievous ones among us commenced throwing shoes, cartridge boxes, haversacks, and anything else they could find within

reach about the room and mixing things up generally in the dark. Then suddenly the pickets outside began firing briskly, the sentinel at the door gave the alarm, the order came to fall in, and what a predicament the company was in! Many of the boys fell in line without shoes, some had belts and cartridge boxes that belonged to others, and confusion reigned supreme. Fortunately our pickets drove back those of the enemy. Order was restored, lights procured, and things put to right, but the incident taught the boys a lesson they never forgot.

PRIVATE FRANKLIN L. RILEY

16TH MISSISSIPPI INFANTRY

Born in rural Lawrence County, the 26-year-old Riley served with Company B of the 16th Mississippi through four years of war. In his diary Riley relates an incident exemplifying the sometimes harsh and summary nature of military justice in the field. After describing the event somewhat dispassionately when it occurs, he reacts to it with dismay and resignation three days later.

Saturday-Monday, Dec. 7-9, 1861. Camp E. K. Smith. Pleasant weather. Ground is thawing. Tues. Frank Gipson was discharged (disability). Sun. at Dress Parade our division (of about 16,000) was ordered to turn out at 9 A.M. Mon. to witness the execution of two privates from the Tiger Rifles, Maj. Wheat's Battalion. From nearby trees, hills, and houses, 50,000 men must have seen the execution. The men were court-martialed for mutiny (refusing to obey orders) and resisting an officer. Accompanied by a priest, they were marched to within a few feet of their graves, by which their coffins had been placed. Then, after they had been tied to stakes placed there for that purpose, they were blindfolded and made to kneel while 28 of their company marched to within 30 paces of where they were. After Army Regulations had been read by one of General Smith's aides, the order was given to fire. In a second it was all over.

Tuesday, Dec. 10, 1861. Camp E. K. Smith.

Horrible! That two of our soldiers could be killed, deliberately, not by Yankees but by their own men. Yet few protest the action, for the soldiers of Wheat's Battalion have a bad reputation. They are brave and they are beautifully uniformed, but clothing doesn't make a man. Nor is bravery necessarily the same as morality. After they had displayed their courage at Manassas, it is said that they sulked around the battlefield robbing the dead, Union and Confederate alike. They are quarrelsome, frequently drunk, and poorly disciplined. Yet it is horrible to see

Southerners killed by Southerners. Ordinarily their punishment would have been light. Apparently the actions of Wheat's Battalion have been so outrageous that examples had to be made.

COLONEL WILLIAM W. AVERELL
3D PENNSYLVANIA CAVALRY

Averell accurately conveys the stirring effect of the grand review and the boundless devotion felt by the men of the Army of the Potomac toward their commander at this stage of the war. McClellan had restored their dignity as individual soldiers and as members of the majestic and seemingly invincible host assembled that day.

The best remembered military event of the winter of 1861-2 was the grand review at Bailey's Crossroads. The field was a broad amphitheatre, favorable at any part for a view of the whole, and the spectacle of a vast, organized host of eighty thousand men in masses of divisions with the artillery and cavalry of each division attached and all its banners floating in the sunlight was the grandest and most inspiring I ever beheld. General McClellan, with his staff, rode rapidly along the fronts of divisions awakening the wildest enthusiasm as he passed. Then the army passed in review before President Lincoln and the Commander-in-Chief; and as the ground trembled under the steady tread of the endless columns of disciplined soldiers and the air throbbed with the music of countless bands, the all pervading feeling was an enthusiastic and ardent admiration for the man who had created the Army of the Potomac.

In the realization of all observers, even the most experienced officers, the army was born that day. Everyone in and around Washington that had felt the throes of a tremendous and vigorous growth going on about them since the first of August and those who had visited the busy camps and attended the inspections and reviews of divisions had formed no adequate conception of the army as a whole. Not one had ever seen an army of over eighteen thousand men together except General McClellan, who had visited and studied the armies of Europe. Out of nothing and with the bleeding and dispirited fragments of McDowell's little command after Bull Run as a nucleus, this splendid army of one hundred and fifty thousand men, together with forty miles of garrisoned fortifications around Washington had been created in six months. The eyes of all spectators, and even of the army itself, were suddenly opened, as were the eyes of the young man who beheld the mountain full of horses and chariots round about the prophet of Israel.

This pencil drawing depicts the construction by the Federals of a rooftop observation post on Upton's Hill, near an advanced line of fortifications guarding the Leesburg pike west of Washington. Beyond the house in the background lies Munson's Hill, where the 17th Virginia Infantry had been encamped during the fall of 1861.

PRIVATE D. AUGUSTUS DICKERT

3D SOUTH CAROLINA INFANTRY

Dickert enlisted at age 17 in Company H, 3d South Carolina. His service up to the retreat from Manassas, which he describes below, was fairly routine; but afterward he was wounded four times in various campaigns and eventually rose to the rank of captain. A friend noted that in the latter stages of the war "he was in command of his regiment acting as colonel without ever receiving his commission as such." After the war he was addressed as Colonel.

On the night of the 9th of March we broke up quarters at Bull Run and commenced our long and tiresome march for the Rappahannock. We were ordered by different routes to facilitate the movement, our wagon trains moving out in the morning along the dirt road and near the railroad. All baggage that the soldiers could not carry had been sent to the rear days before, and the greater part destroyed in the great wreck and conflagration that followed at Manassas on its evacuation. In passing through Manassas the stores, filled to the very tops with commissary stores, sutler's goods, clothing, shoes, private boxes,

and whiskey, were thrown open for the soldiers to help themselves. What a feast for the troops! There seemed everything at hand to tempt him to eat, drink, or wear, but it was a verification of the adage, "When it rains much you have no spoon." We had no way of transporting these goods, now piled high on every hand, but to carry them on our backs, and we were already overloaded for a march of any distance. Whiskey flowed like water. Barrels were knocked open and canteens filled. Kegs, jugs, and bottles seemed to be everywhere. One stalwart man of my company shouldered a ten gallon keg and proposed to hold on to it as long as possible, and it is a fact that a few men carried this keg by reliefs all night and next day. This was the case in other companies. When we got out of the town and on the railroad, the men were completely overloaded. All night we marched along the railroad at a slow, steady gait, but all order and discipline were abandoned. About midnight we saw in our rear great sheets of flame shooting up from the burning buildings, that illuminated the country for miles around. Manassas was on fire! Some of the buildings had caught fire by accident or carelessness of the soldiers, for the firing was not to begin until next day, after the withdrawal of the cavalry. The people in the surrounding

The rail yard at Manassas Junction, 25 miles west of Washington, changed hands several times in the first year and a half of the war. On each occasion, the rolling stock and warehouses were destroyed and the rails ripped up by the retreating army, only to be rebuilt by the new occupiers. This photograph shows the devastation wrought by Johnston's Confederate troops before they evacuated in March 1862.

country had been invited to come in and get whatever they wished, but I doubt if any came in time to save much from the burning mass. A great meat curing establishment at Thoroughfare Gap, that contained millions of pounds of beef and pork, was also destroyed. We could hear the bursting of bombs as the flames reached the magazines, as well as the explosion of thousands of small arm cartridges. The whole sounded like the raging of a great battle. Manassas had become endeared to the soldiers by its many memories, and when the word went along the line, "Manassas is burning," it put a melancholy feeling upon all. Some of the happiest recollections of the soldiers that composed Kershaw's Brigade, as well as all of Johnston's Army, were centred around Manassas. It was here they had experienced their first sensations of the soldier, Manassas was the field of their first victory, and there they had spent their first winter. It seemed to connect the soldiers of the Confederacy with those of Washington at Valley Forge and Trenton, the winter quarters of the army of the patriots. It gave the recollection of rest, a contrast with the many marches, the hard fought battles, trials, and hardships.

The next day it began to rain, and a continual down-pour continued for days and nights. Blankets were taken from knapsacks to cover over the men as they marched, but they soon filled with water, and had to be thrown aside. Both sides of the railroad were strewn with blankets, shawls, overcoats, and clothing of every description, the men finding it impossible to bear up under such loads. The slippery ground and the unevenness of the railroad track made marching very disagreeable to soldiers unaccustomed to it. Some took the dirt road, while others kept the railroad track, and in this way all organizations were lost sight of, but at night they collected together in regiments, joined the wagon trains, and bivouaced for the night. Sometimes it would be midnight before the last of the stragglers came up. We crossed the Rappahannock on the railroad bridge, which had been laid with plank to accommodate the passage of wagon trains, on the 11th and remained until the 19th.

Johnston's retreat from Manassas (below) provoked the wrath of President Jefferson Davis, with whom there was bad blood of long standing. Davis challenged Johnston's assertion that Manassas was untenable, but the general would not be swayed. Moreover, he did not inform Davis of the evacuation until three days afterward.

SURGEON WILLIAM CHILD
5TH NEW HAMPSHIRE INFANTRY

McClellan seemed surprised to find that Johnston's fortifications at Manassas had been abandoned, even though it was said that the smell of cooked bacon from the burning Confederate storehouses permeated the countryside for miles around. Here Child displays a fine appreciation of an enlisted man's cynically humorous observations on the empty Rebel encampments and adds his own tacit commentary by comparing them with an officer's opinion of the same facilities.

On the 12th the division moved early, marched to Union Mills and encamped four miles from Manassas Junction, one mile from Bull Run battle-field. A squad of men from the Fifth, with Corporal Gove, guarded a wagon train to Fairfax Station. Beyond and around this region were found the first fortifications. Here it was first known that these had been abandoned by the enemy. They were judiciously situated on a range of high hills. They consisted of rifle-pits, ditches, breastworks and redoubts. Here was found much abandoned property.

On the 13th the division and regiment remained here. Small parties went foraging, bringing in much abandoned property.

Here we will give the words and opinions of a colonel and a corporal respecting the condition of affairs in the now abandoned Confederate camps and fortifications. Says Corporal Gove's diary: "They had excellent barracks made of logs and plastered with clay. I do not think the soldiers were half starved and frozen."

Colonel Cross, in his personal journal, says: "I examined the works. They were chiefly located on a long ridge, there being nine strong redoubts, each pierced for from six to nine guns, some for twelve; and so located as to control the country for miles around. Fine ways of timber—some open, some covered—ran from redoubt to redoubt; fine rifle-pits and abattis in abundance. Behind these were a second series of works equally elaborate, excellent and powerful. Evidences were abundant that more than 50,000 men had been here during the winter. The quarters were of the most substantial and comfortable character, and the troops must have had abundant provisions and supplies of all kinds." Here wooden guns were found.

PRIVATE FRANKLIN L. RILEY
16TH MISSISSIPPI INFANTRY

McClellan declined to pursue the retreating Confederate army beyond Manassas, deciding that the heavy rains and destruction of the rail lines, described here by Riley, would have slowed his massive force down to a snail's pace. Instead he opted for his waterborne end run up the peninsula between the James and York Rivers. Riley was wounded at Antietam in September 1862 and recovered to serve with the 16th Mississippi until captured near Petersburg on April 2, 1865.

Received further orders (Sat.) to reduce our baggage. Marked, then sent our packages by Co. C to the Miss. depot at the RR. This morning the regiment marched to Manassas Junction. The road was so muddy and crowded with troops that we didn't arrive until afternoon. At the Junction we saw huge piles of supplies and baggage (some broken into and looted) which we were told will be burned to-morrow. (Ours included?) Some of the camps near the Junction already have been burned. After dark we marched down the track of the O&A RR to a point near Bristoe Station. We have left most of our equipment—tents, extra blankets, clothing, cooking utensils. We have only what we can carry. Halted near midnight. Either we are moving east, where our lines have been broken, or we are withdrawing. We probably are withdrawing, 'tis said to Gordonsville.

Monday-Tuesday, March 10-11, 1862. Enroute.

Rained most of the day. Cleared in the evening. Weather continues pleasant. Buds are swelling. We have gathered bushels of wild onions to eat. Mon. we bivouacked 5-6 miles from the Rappahannock. To-day we crossed the river and camped on low ground a mile from the O&A bridge. 5-6 miles isn't a long march, but we stopped to tear up the RR and burn the bridges. Numerous stragglers. The farther we marched the more we threw away from our knapsacks. From Warrenton to the river we piled wood on the bridges but did not actually set them on fire. Perhaps the 15th Ala. or some other unit will do this. At the river our brigade drew up in line to await the attack of the enemy but McClellan refused the challenge.

Wednesday, March 12, 1862. Rappahannock Station.

Occasional rain. Our division (Ewell's) is stationed near the bridge, guarding the fords up to Warrenton Station. Actually we have fallen back only 35 miles—not a very serious withdrawal, for we are still less than 50 miles from Alexandria. So far the enemy has scarcely moved.

Thursday-Saturday, March 13-15, 1862. Rappahannock Station.

Rain. Thurs., bands braying and bayonets glinting, McClellan's army moved forward only to find smoking and deserted camps. All of our troops, except for some still on picket, have crossed the river safely. From Rappahannock Station our regiment was ordered forward Sat. to reinforce the pickets at Warrenton Station, where the Yankees appeared Fri. in force. We double-quicked to Cedar Run where, after a brief skirmish, the enemy retreated. At the Station we burned several RR cars but took no prisoners. Darkness and high water prevented pursuit of the enemy.

PRIVATE HENRY E. HANDERSON
9TH LOUISIANA INFANTRY

After growing up in Ohio and attending college in New York, Handerson in 1859 took a job as a tutor to a plantation owner's family in Louisiana. Though he felt secession was "unwise and dangerous," he nevertheless volunteered in his adopted state and served throughout the war. Afterward, he returned to the North and became a well-respected physician.

The rain had fallen almost incessantly during our march, and our camps along the Rappahannock were converted into shallow lakes by the standing water, which prevented comfortable rest by night or day. After a week or more of such experience, thoroughly worn out by want of sleep, I determined one rainy evening to slip quietly out of camp and seek some shelter where I might rest comfortably for one night at least. Accordingly soon after sunset I stole away in the drizzling gloom, and avoiding the sentinels wandered off at hazard in search of shelter. After a walk of perhaps half an hour I descried upon a hill a short distance from me an old church, which seemed to offer protection from the increasing storm, and hastening my steps toward it I was both surprised and somewhat startled as I drew near to observe through the windows the reflection of lights which indicated that the building was already inhabited. However, we have the testimony of Horace that *Vacuus viator cantabit coram latrone*, and I felt desperate enough to face almost anything for the chance of securing shelter.

Opening the door carefully and peering within, a novel sight met my eye. Most of the pews were already occupied by soldiers who had fled to the sacred building for shelter, each of them having preempted his own position and spread his blanket upon the seat. A large fire had been started in the stove, upon the surface of which numerous slices of bacon were cooking and diffusing an appetizing odor throughout the building. Some were eating their suppers, some smoking and chatting together, while others had already yielded to sleep. The high, old-fashioned pulpit was occupied by a New Orleans prize-fighter, Tom Jennings, whose face was familiar among the "Tigers," and his legs hung gracefully over the sides as he lounged upon the seat and smoked his pipe with an air of solid comfort and unqualified satisfaction. Stealing quietly to a vacant pew near the rear of the church, I ate my frugal supper and in turn drew forth my pipe and amused myself by watching the scene.

Most of my neighbors, having now finished their meal and betaken themselves to their pews and their pipes, the hum of conversation and the sharp jokes and repartee of men of little refinement, but thoroughly good-natured and happy, re-echoed from side to side and occasioned outbursts of hearty laughter. Gradually songs of a familiar kind were heard, and the chorus was taken up by numerous voices until the very rafters resounded with the noisy strains. After a time a vulgar song was sung by some soldier, and received with such laughter that his example seemed on the point of being followed by others, when I was thoroughly surprised to see Tom Jennings rise in the pulpit and address the riotous assembly in the following words: "See here boys! I am just as bad as any of you, I know. But this is a church and I'll be damned if it's right to sing any of your smutty songs in here, and it's got to be stopped." It *was* stopped too. Either tender consciences or Tom's reputation and influence was effective at once, and soon we all dropped off to sleep. Poor Tom Jennings! When next I saw him he was borne off the field of Cold Harbor, writhing with agony from a gunshot wound through the bowels and pale with the pallor of approaching death. I hope the recording angel jotted down poor Tom's protest against obscenity in the little church upon the Rappahannock, and that the entry blotted out many pages of vice and sin.

McClellan's Halting Advance

On March 17, 1862, units of the Army of the Potomac began to embark at Alexandria for the voyage to Fort Monroe at the tip of Virginia's Peninsula. With the reluctant blessing of President Lincoln, General George McClellan's great offensive to conquer Richmond and end the Southern rebellion had finally gotten under way.

For the next three weeks, nearly 400 vessels shuttled back and forth along the 200-mile route, transporting division after division—more than 121,000 men—as well as all the animals, equipment, and supplies needed to sustain the army on its march to the Confederate capital. It was an operation unprecedented in magnitude in military history—as a British observer put it, "the stride of a giant."

The opening phase of McClellan's plan, once he was on land, was to push quickly up the Peninsula and make his base at West Point, at the head of the York River. Then, somewhere between West Point and Richmond, he predicted, "a decisive battle" would be fought. But first he would have to overcome an obstacle: the Confederate fortifications at Yorktown, a formidable collection of earthworks and naval guns that commanded approaches by land and the York River.

On April 4 McClellan began the advance up the Peninsula in two long columns: the III Corps, under Brigadier Samuel P. Heintzelman, headed directly for Yorktown, while the IV Corps, commanded by Brigadier General Erasmus D. Keyes, veered left on a route that would flank the city, passing it four and a half miles to the south.

Hardly a day into their march the Federals discovered that their maps were faulty, failing to show numerous muddy streams that slowed progress. And although McClellan had been told that the Peninsula's roads were passable in all conditions, he discovered otherwise. Rains turned the roads into quagmires that swallowed wagons up to their axles.

On the afternoon of April 5 Heintzelman's troops drew up in front of Yorktown, coming under heavy artillery and musket fire. McClellan had anticipated this. He was prepared to halt and exchange cannonades with the Yorktown defenders while his other column, under Keyes, passed well clear of the Confederate fortifications.

Two abandoned Confederate 32-pounder naval cannons point silently toward the York River following the Federal occupation of Yorktown. The guns had formed part of the Rebels' formidable line of defense against McClellan's advancing army.

But Keyes' column had also been stopped in its tracks that afternoon—by a natural obstacle, the Warwick River, that was not supposed to be there. According to Keyes' maps, the Warwick ran parallel to his march; in reality, it cut squarely across his path. And in recent months the Confederates had built several dams that deepened and widened the river. Now it could be crossed only at the dams, which were well guarded by Rebel batteries and infantry.

Keyes discovered this when he was greeted with heavy fire from a redoubt protecting the Lee's Mill Dam. After a hasty reconnaissance of the Rebel defenses, he sent McClellan a message warning that "no part of the line, so far discovered, can be taken by assault without an enormous waste of human life."

McClellan received Keyes' note around the same time that he got more bad news in the form of a telegram from the war department. The general had been counting on the arrival of his I Corps under General Irvin McDowell—38,000 troops that he would use as a reserve, to be thrown into battle as needed. Now President Lincoln was denying McClellan this corps, insisting that it be held near Fredericksburg in the event it was needed to protect Washington.

McClellan was infuriated by the president's decision. He wrote his wife, somewhat hysterically, that it was "the most infamous thing that history has recorded." And he suspected—as he often did when events turned against him —that political enemies were working behind the scenes to ruin him.

But McClellan did not need additional troops on the afternoon of April 5 to break through the Confederate line. He had 58,000 men facing the Warwick River and nearly as many available at Yorktown or en route—to deal with a Confederate force he himself estimated to number only about 15,000. Ever cautious, though, McClellan,

confronted by a well-entrenched foe, hesitated.

Lincoln, fully aware of his general's numerical superiority, chafed at the delay. He fired off a telegram stating, "I think you had better break the enemy's line from Yorktown to Warwick River at once." But McClellan could not be induced to move. And the longer he dithered, the more his situation seemed to deteriorate. The Rebels across the river appeared to be receiving massive reinforcements.

The Confederate commander opposing McClellan was Major General John Bankhead Magruder. Known in his own army as Prince John for his love of high living, Magruder called on his experience in amateur theatricals to produce his best show ever—a great ruse featuring a cast of 11,000. His bands played, his artillery roared, and along the river his men marched in gigantic circles—out of sight except when they paraded past points in clear view of the Yankees. For hours the Federals watched as gray-clad troops passed, looking for all the world like an endless stream of reinforcements coming to bolster the river line.

McClellan was completely taken in. On April 7 he wrote, "The Warwick River grows worse the more you look at it." He telegraphed Lincoln: "It seems clear that I shall have the whole forces of the enemy on my hands, probably not less than 100,000 men, and possibly more." In his reply Lincoln questioned McClellan's arithmetic and again, in vain, urged him to attack.

Little Mac was now convinced that an infantry assault would only result in the slaughter of his troops. He decided instead to bring up his big guns and obliterate the Yorktown defenses from a safe distance. Seven years before, as an official military observer during the Crimean War, he had been fascinated by the great siege of Sevastopol. Siege warfare, with its methodical preparations and methods, appealed to the engi-

neer in McClellan and to his cautious nature.

When an opportunity arose on the morning of April 16 for an infantry breakthrough, McClellan passed it up. He had ordered a reconnaissance in force at a dam site called Burnt Chimneys, near the middle of the Warwick River line. Following an artillery barrage, some troops of the Vermont brigade forded the river while others charged across the dam. They drove the Rebel defenders away and secured a breach in the line.

If McClellan had thrown large numbers of troops across the river to exploit the breach, the bulk of his army could have passed through and moved toward Richmond, leaving Yorktown isolated in the rear. But he refused to act, and before long the Confederates counterattacked and the Vermonters were withdrawn.

While McClellan prepared for his siege, which was to begin on May 5, the Confederates had ample time to flood the Peninsula with real reinforcements from General Joseph Johnston's army, which had settled in camps on the Rapidan River, 50 miles northwest of Richmond. The Rebel movement was unopposed by McDowell, who had orders from Washington not to leave his position. On April 17 Johnston himself arrived to take charge of the Peninsula's forces. Three of his five divisions had reached the scene, and the others were on their way.

By Saturday, May 3, nearly all the massive Yankee siege guns were in place—114 of them, in addition to the more than 300 pieces of field artillery accompanying the army. Everything was ready for the great bombardment that would pave the way for an irresistible infantry assault.

But Joseph Johnston declined to cooperate. He knew that Yorktown's fortifications could not stand up to McClellan's big guns, and he decided to withdraw. On the night of April 3, after a bombardment of their own, the Confederates quietly pulled out of their

ORDER OF BATTLE   April 30, 1862

ARMY OF NORTHERN VIRGINIA (Confederate)

Johnston 50,000 men

Magruder's Command

McLaws' Division
McLaws' Brigade
Griffith's Brigade
Kershaw's Brigade
Cobb's Brigade

Toombs' Division
Toombs' Brigade
Semmes' Brigade

Ewell's Command at Williamsburg

Longstreet's Command

A. P. Hill's Brigade   *Pickett's Brigade*
R. H. Anderson's Brigade   *Wilcox's Brigade*
Colston's Brigade   *Pryor's Brigade*

D. H. Hill's Command

Early's Division
Early's Brigade
Rodes' Brigade

Rains' Division
Rains' Brigade
Featherston's Brigade

Crump's Command at Gloucester Point

Reserve G. W. Smith

Whiting's Division
Whiting's Brigade
Hood's Brigade
Hampton's Brigade
S. R. Anderson's Brigade
Pettigrew's Brigade

ARMY OF THE POTOMAC (Federal)

McClellan 105,000 men

II Corps Sumner

Sedgwick's Division
Gorman's Brigade
Dana's Brigade
Burns' Brigade

Richardson's Division
Howard's Brigade
Meagher's Brigade
French's Brigade

III Corps Heintzelman

Porter's Division
Martindale's Brigade
Morell's Brigade
Butterfield's Brigade

Hooker's Division
Grover's Brigade
Taylor's Brigade
Starr's Brigade

Kearny's Division
Jameson's Brigade
Birney's Brigade
Berry's Brigade

IV Corps Keyes

Couch's Division
Brigg's Brigade
Peck's Brigade
Graham's Brigade

Smith's Division
Hancock's Brigade
Brooks' Brigade
Davidson's Brigade

Casey's Division
Naglee's Brigade
Keim's Brigade
Palmer's Brigade
Sykes' Brigade

lines and began retreating up the Peninsula toward Williamsburg, 12 miles to the west.

McClellan had won Yorktown as he had hoped, without a fight. "Our success is brilliant," he wrote in a dispatch to Washington. He ordered his cavalry to pursue the Confederates, with the infantry to follow. He also sent four divisions by boat up the York River to West Point in hopes of cutting off the enemy retreat.

Yankee cavalry under Brigadier General George Stoneman caught up with Johnston's rearguard troopers a few miles outside Williamsburg. After a series of running skirmishes, the Confederate horsemen took refuge behind a line of earthworks consisting of 13 redoubts, the largest of which was called Fort Magruder. The line was fronted by rifle pits and bounded by impassable swamps; the guns of Fort Magruder, in the middle of the line, commanded the convergence of the two roads that led up the Peninsula.

On the morning of April 5, a Federal division under Brigadier General William F. Smith pulled up astride the Yorktown road before Fort Magruder to await orders from Brigadier General Edwin V. Sumner, who had been given command of the pursuit.

On the Lee's Mill road, to Smith's left, Brigadier General Joseph Hooker's division approached the Confederate line, and Hooker, spoiling for a fight, did not wait for orders. Covered by an artillery barrage, his troops plunged forward. In a two-hour exchange with the defenders of Fort Magruder, Hooker's men made some headway, but Rebel reinforcements were now pouring into the line.

Johnston had ordered Major General James Longstreet, his most dependable division commander, to countermarch from the main column's position to Fort Magruder and take charge. By noon, Longstreet had his entire division—eight brigades—ready for action. He counterattacked, and Hooker's men began to yield.

By 4:00 p.m., Longstreet's infantrymen, capturing enemy artillery and battle flags as they went, had pushed the Yankees back a mile and a half from Fort Magruder, and a rout seemed in the making. At the last possible moment General Sumner, who unaccountably had failed to commit Smith's idle troops to the fray, awoke to the situation and dispatched another division to support the hard-pressed Hooker.

This force was commanded by one-armed Brigadier General Philip Kearny, a colorful and combative leader who charged into the thick of the fight, clenching the reins in his teeth and waving his saber with his good right arm. "Don't flinch, boys!" he shouted. "Go in gaily!" Infected by their commander's zest, Kearny's fresh troops charged and the tide of battle changed again.

As Kearny's Yankees gradually forced the Rebels back into the clearing before Fort Magruder, a pivotal engagement was unfolding two miles to the north. Earlier that day a Federal reconnaissance had revealed that the two redoubts at the northern end of the Confederate line were unoccupied, and Sumner dispatched troops under Brigadier Winfield Scott Hancock to seize them.

Hancock occupied the redoubts, and from his vantage point on a crest he could see little in the way of opposition on the plain to his front. He was in an excellent position to outflank Fort Magruder and cut Longstreet's line of retreat to Williamsburg, but before advancing farther he needed reinforcements to support his right flank and rear.

But General Sumner, uncertain of the situation, refused Hancock's request for help and later ordered him to withdraw. Hancock stalled and kept sending pleas for support.

Meanwhile, he had lobbed a few shells in the direction of Fort Magruder and had attracted Longstreet's attention.

Longstreet assigned Major General Daniel Harvey Hill, one of his most capable commanders, to silence Hancock's artillery. Hill's regiments swarmed forward, screaming the Rebel yell, and drove back Hancock's skirmishers. Hancock calmly positioned his infantry behind the crest of the ridge and waited until the charging Confederates were 30 paces away. Then his battle line rose and opened fire.

The withering volley cut down scores of Confederates, including Brigadier General Jubal A. Early, who was shot in the shoulder. The storm of lead brought the Rebel charge to a halt, and just at that moment Hancock galloped to the front and yelled, "Forward! Charge!"

The Yankee line surged forward, and Hill's Confederates fell back in rout. Hancock's engagement had ended in triumph, but he was not allowed to follow through. General Sumner, finally alarmed by the battering Hooker's men had taken, ordered Hancock to halt his pursuit and retire to the captured redoubts, and with that the Battle of Williamsburg drew to a close.

General McClellan was jubilant. "Hancock was superb," he wired Washington. From Hancock's reinforced position on the far right, McClellan was ready to crush Fort Magruder the next morning. But the light of dawn revealed that once again the Confederates were on the retreat.

The unplanned clash proved costly to both sides. The Confederates lost 1,603 men killed, wounded, and missing. The Federals suffered even higher casualties: 2,239, including 456 dead. McClellan, however, held the field. His mammoth army had at last been tested in battle and had claimed a victory. The Rebels were on the run, and Richmond was only 50 miles away.

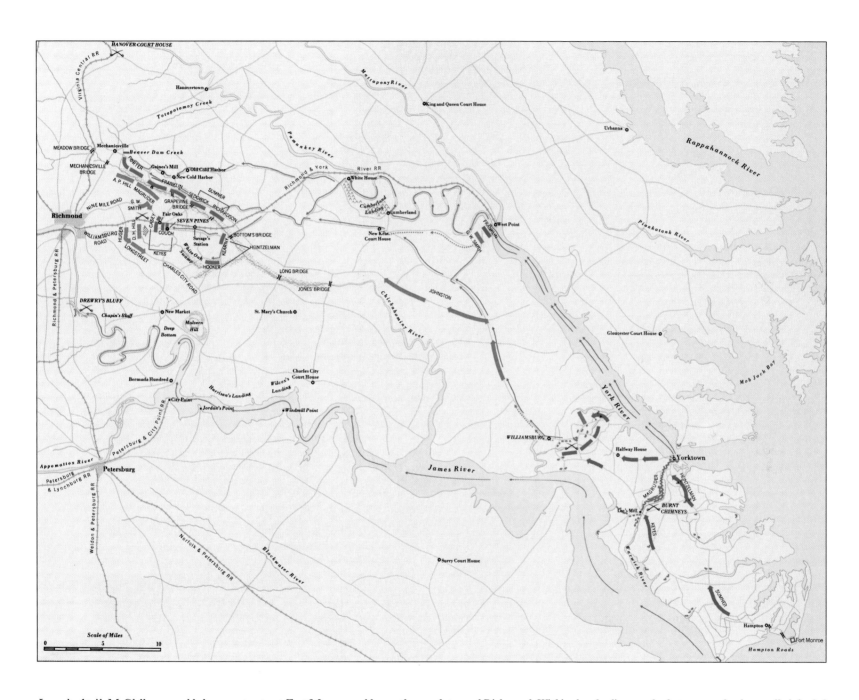

In early April, McClellan assembled 50,000 troops at Fort Monroe and began the march toward Richmond. Within days he discovered what appeared to be a well-defended Confederate line clear across the Peninsula. In fact, the Rebels were cleverly shifting troops from place to place to disguise their inferior strength. After clashes at Lee's Mill and Dam No. 1, McClellan began ponderous siege operations only to find the line evacuated by the Rebels on May 3. While Federal ships steamed toward West Point and White House on the newly opened York River, McClellan dogged Johnston from Williamsburg to Seven Pines. There the Confederates surprised their pursuers with a vigorous counterattack.

Workmen carry lumber aboard the nearly completed CSS Virginia, lying in dry dock at the Gosport Navy Yard in Norfolk. John Brooke, an ordnance expert, William Williamson, a naval engineer, and John Porter, a naval builder, created the 275-foot ironclad from the burned hulk of the USS Merrimac, a 40-gun, three-masted steam frigate torched and scuttled by withdrawing Union sailors when the yard was occupied by Rebels in April 1861.

MIDSHIPMAN HARDIN B. LITTLEPAGE
CSS VIRGINIA

Littlepage was just 10 days shy of his 21st birthday on March 8, 1862, when the Virginia steamed into Hampton Roads to wreak havoc among the blockading Union fleet. In later life he became a respected authority on Confederate naval operations while working as a researcher in the U.S. Naval War Records Bureau in Washington, D.C. This piece is from his memoir, "The Career of the Merrimac-Virginia: With Some Personal History."

At last the fatal day arrived. We had intended going out a few days earlier, but were prevented by stormy weather. The 8th came in calm and peaceful as a May day. We hauled our fires early in the morning, cast off our fastenings, and drew out into the channel, and were soon under way, accompanied by the Raleigh and Beaufort, two little gun boats of one gun each. As we passed along we found the wharves crowded with people, men and women, the women cheering us on our way, and many of the men with serious countenances. One man, I remember, called out to us, "Go on with your old metallic coffin! She will never amount to anything else!" As metallic coffins were becoming popular about that time, his remark was calculated to make one feel a little dubious.

We passed the several batteries along the river, beginning with Hospital Point, Ft. Norfolk; thence through the obstructions; then Pinner's Point, Lambert's Point, Crany Island and Sewell's Point, all of which cheered us lustily, and the soldiers filled the air with their hats. Soon after passing Sewell's Point we came in full view of Fortress Monroe and the frigates lying there. The alarm gun gave warning, and everything was immediately in motion, the mercantile craft getting below the fortress, and the frigates, Minnesota, St. Lawrence and Roanoke, of about 50 guns each, besides various and sundry gun boats carrying from one to six guns each, getting under way and "standing up."

In passing out of Elizabeth River into the Roads we necessarily headed in the direction of Fortress Monroe, and it was hard for them to tell what might be our point of attack. As soon as we reached fair chan-nel way, however, we turned in the direction of Newport News where laid the frigate Congress, of 50 guns, the Cumberland of 24 guns, and some five or six gunboats. Flag Officer Buchanan assembled his officers around him, pointed out to us the situation, and urged us to hurry with the work before us, that is, the destruction of the Cumberland and Congress, as the heaviest of the enemy's ships were following in our wake. He also told us that the Confederates had complained that they were not taken near enough to the enemy, and assured us that there should be no such complaint this time, for he intended to head directly for the Cumberland.

Made from captured wool bunting, this seven-star ensign, representing the Confederate government's first national design, was in the Virginia's flag locker when the ironclad made her epic foray into Hampton Roads. The ship was flying a newer 11-star version at the time.

SEAMAN WILLIAM REBLEN
USS CUMBERLAND

Against his parents' wishes, the 20-year-old Reblen left home in Detroit and en-listed in the navy in July 1861 under the alias George Dennis. Until March 8, 1862, his duty in Hampton Roads was tedious, the most memorable event being the tossing overboard of 96 bags of maggoty hardtack declared unfit to eat. "Plen-ty of gun practice by day and guard rowing by night was our principal occupa-tion," he recalled, "with an occasional run on shore among the soldier boys."

Midshipman Daniel M. Lee (above), son of Confederate navy captain Sidney S. Lee and nephew of General Robert E. Lee, served aboard the CSS Jamestown, one of the James River Squadron gunboats that fought alongside the Virginia.

The 8th of March, 1862, came, and a finer morning I never saw in that southern latitude. The sun came up smiling in all its splen-dor. It was "up hammocks" that morning and then "holystone" and wash decks as usual. After breakfast (it being Saturday) it was "up all bags," and every old tar went through his bag, mending and getting ready for Sunday's muster 'round the capstan. About nine o'clock the Quar-termaster reported a steamer coming out of Norfolk. He was ordered by the Officer of the Deck to keep a strict watch over her and report.

This steamer kept manuvering around about the Horseshoe—so-

"As she came steaming up the river she was a grim-looking monster— like a floating blacksmith-shop, with sloping roof and smokestack."

called by a sandbar which formed a horseshoe near the ship-channel. It seemed that the duty of this steamer was to find out the depth of water. The steamer seemed to be heading up the river toward Newport News. Both the Cumberland and Congress crews were called to quarters, guns were double-shotted and decks were cleared for action. Every hammock and every bag that could be spared were placed around the forward magazine. All at once the steamer turned back, continually sounding with the lead, evidently getting the depth of water within the channel. Our guns were all ready for what might come. The Cumberland had a very heavy battery, 22 9-inch Dahlgrens, one 11-inch pivot forward, and a 6-inch rifle Parrott aft on the spar-deck. Our crew consisted of 376 officers and men. This included the marine corps, if I remember right. Capt. Radford was not aboard on this day, having been detailed as a member for a court of inquiry concerning the loss of the R. B. Forbes. This court convened on board the Roanoke, and so the command of the Cumberland devolved on our First Lieutenant, George U. Morris, and Thomas O. Selfridge became Executive Officer for the time being. . . .

Everybody was ready for a fight—yes, we had been itching for one all Winter. We got all we wanted before 3 p.m. on the 8th of March. About 11 o'clock the Merrimac was reported by the Quartermaster as coming out of Norfolk, and all hands were again called to quarters, everything being in readiness to give her a warm reception. Some delay was caused by the tide not being just right. The Merrimac kept manuvering around the Horseshoe and the mouth of the ship-channel. Flood-tide would serve at 1 o'clock. Our crew was piped to dinner, and told to get through as quick as possible. It was the last dinner eaten by a good many of them. One o'clock came, and with it came also the Merrimac, making a straight wake for the Congress, who laid right ahead of the Cumberland, down the river, about 200 yards. Our crew were at their guns, watching the Merrimac. As she came steaming up the river she was a grim-looking monster—like a floating blacksmith-shop, with sloping roof and smokestack.

MIDSHIPMAN HARDIN B. LITTLEPAGE
CSS VIRGINIA

One of 13 children born to an old Virginia family from King William County, Littlepage was appointed to the U.S. Naval Academy in 1858 but resigned his acting commission the day his home state seceded—April 17, 1861. That November he was assigned to the Virginia, then a work in progress. Littlepage served on the ship throughout her short but dramatic career.

The action now began in earnest. The Virginia exchanged broadsides with the Congress at a distance of about 200 yards. She continued on with all speed, until she reached the Cumberland, and rounding, struck her under her starboard fore-chains with her prow, delivering fire from the bow gun, a 7-inch Brooke rifle with a percussion shell which exploded in her side at the very instant her prow reached her. The Virginia received, at the same time, a tremendous broadside from the Cumberland, cutting one of her guns off at the trunnions, sweeping away her guard howitzers and everything on the outside, and riddling her smokestack. Most of the men the Virginia lost were killed and wounded from this one broadside.

For awhile the Cumberland rested on the stem of the Virginia, and we felt great uneasiness lest she might carry us down with her, as she was filling rapidly. As soon, however, as there became a slight angle of inclination, the Cumberland glided off, and settled rapidly to her topsail yards.

The smoke from the Cumberland's and the Virginia's guns settled over the Virginia, completely hiding her from view. We heard them cheering on the Congress, and naturally supposed they were cheering some of the other frigates into action. We had great difficulty in getting around on account of the shoalness of the water; and as we afterwards learned, the Congress was under the impression that the Cumberland had sunk us. So, of course, the Congress set up a lusty cheering.

This 16-star boat flag was salvaged from the doomed Cumberland, on whose decks 121 of her 376-man crew died. "With plenty of sea room, a breeze, and an English frigate, or two, as our foe, there might have been a chance of victory," a Union sailor lamented. "But when the armored Merrimac steamed out of Norfolk and threaded her way among the shoals toward us, we stood no chance—none whatever. It was iron and steam against a sailing vessel of wood in a dead calm."

MASTER MOSES S. STUYVESANT
USS Cumberland

Stuyvesant describes in vivid detail what the Cumberland suffered in its unequal clash with the Virginia. He saw his old wooden warship as "probably the last thorough representative of the navy of former days, when the people fostered it, when tars were tars, and seamanship had its value." During the fight, Stuyvesant's gun crews fired one of the few shots that damaged the Rebel ironclad—a shell that killed one sailor and blew away part of the muzzle of a broadside gun.

Her first shot at us struck the starboard quarter-rail, throwing the pieces among the guard of marines, wounding several of them. The second shot struck the waterways, under the forward pivot, which was our heaviest gun, and disabled it. Our firing became at once very rapid from the few guns we could bring to bear as

she approached slowly, heading for our starboard bow, where she rammed us under or forward of the fore-chains. The shock of the collision was, of course, perceptible, but was not violent, and was followed by a rapid fire from her forward ports. The report speedily came up from below of large quantities of water pouring through the gap made by the ram, making it very evident that the good ship was certain to go to the bottom.

Meanwhile, the Merrimac was being swung around by the making tide, her ram breaking off in the operation, and was soon in position abreast of us, distant say twenty feet, both vessels firing rapidly, and every gun bearing.

Her shells found nothing to impede them, and passed through the side of our ship, throwing splinters and fragments of iron among our men on the gun deck, and producing, in the course of the half hour ensuing, a scene of carnage and destruction never to be recalled without horror. In that time, our loss was not less than 100 out of about 190 men stationed at the batteries on the gun deck, where occurred most of the fighting and casualties. The wounded were carried below to the surgeon, from time to time, but the dead and their fragments were thrown to the other side of the deck out of the way.

It was a hopeless fight. Our shot, striking the inclined sides of the Merrimac, bounded up and flew over, dropping into the water beyond. The gun captains, observing this, were cool enough—some of them— to reserve fire until the enemy, opening a port to run out their reloaded guns, appeared to present the opportunity of throwing a shell into the casemate. But the openings were narrow and nearly filled with the muzzles of their guns projecting.

The ship, slowly sinking by the head, now had the water up to the gun-trucks, on the gun deck forward, and probably most of the wounded below were drowned at this stage—but the firing continued. At one time, when the current brought the enemy close alongside, we were called away from the guns to board her, but, the two vessels widening the interval again, prevented our getting on her, which was undoubtedly very fortunate. The constructor of the Merrimac has since stated that we could not have penetrated the vessel, as she only had one hatchway into the casemate, and that a very narrow one.

Failing this, the men returned to their guns and continued the action; but the enemy now appeared to consider the matter settled, and dropped astern. During this wonderful combat, there was no sign of flinching, even at the most appalling moments. Young boys, bringing powder, performed their duties attentively from the beginning to the end of the action. We read of decimated regiments. One-third of the

Cumberland's crew are coffined in her. She sank slowly by the head, every man at his post, until the vessel, careening to port in the final throes, the last gun was fired in the air, and the order given to abandon ship.

The wounded below, as before stated, were all drowned. The survivors were mostly able to jump into the boats before the final plunge. Some swam ashore, and a few were taken off the masts and yards later, when the good ship finally rested on the bottom of the river. The Merrimac was lying off in the stream, not over one hundred feet distant, while the survivors were seeking safety from the sinking ship carrying down with it—the flag yet flying at the peak—more than a hundred of brave shipmates. All of the officers of the Merrimac, and most of her crew, had served in our navy. One can imagine that their feelings were not to be envied as they then contemplated the destruction they had wrought.

This panoramic illustration shows the Virginia driving her 1,500-pound cast-iron prow into the listing Cumberland during the March 8 action. "As she came plowing through the water toward our port bow, she looked like a huge, half-submerged crocodile," recalled the Cumberland's pilot, A. B. Smith. The force of the collision ripped open a gaping hole below the Cumberland's water line that an officer aboard the Virginia described as "wide enough to drive in a horse and cart." The Confederate ironclad then attacked the USS Congress, a 50-gun sailing frigate shown here exchanging fire with the Confederate gunboats Jamestown (center) and Beaufort (right).

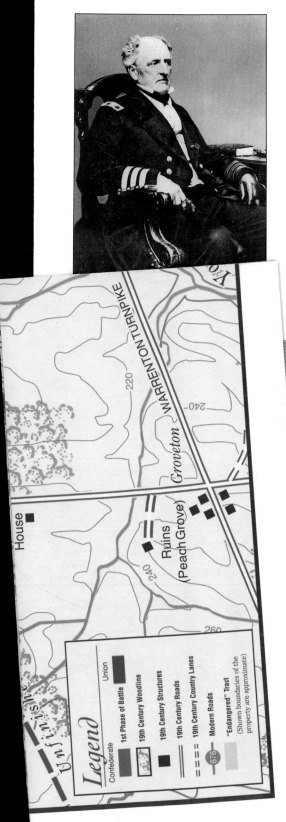

FLAG OFFICER FRANKLIN BUCHANAN
CSS Virginia

Grandson of a signer of the Declaration of Independence and the first superintendent of the U.S. Naval Academy, the 61-year-old Marylander gave up his 46-year navy career to fight for the Confederacy. A Virginia officer called him "one of the grandest men who ever drew a breath of salt air, the beau ideal of a naval officer of the old school."

*H*aving sunk the *Cumberland,* I turned our attention to the *Congress.* We were some time in getting our proper position in consequence of the shoalness of the water and the great difficulty of managing the ship when in or near the mud. To succeed in my object I was obliged to run the ship a short distance above the batteries on James River in order to wind her. During all the time her keel was in the mud; of course she moved but slowly. Thus we were subjected twice to the heavy guns of all the batteries in passing up and down the river, but it could not be avoided. We silenced several of the batteries and did much injury on shore. A large transport steamer alongside of the wharf was blown up, one schooner sunk, and another captured and sent to Norfolk. The loss of life on shore we have no way of ascertaining.

While the *Virginia* was thus engaged in getting her position for attacking the *Congress,* the prisoners state it was believed on board that ship that we had hauled off; the men left their guns and gave three cheers. They were soon sadly undeceived, for a few minutes after we opened upon her again, she having run on shore in shoal water. The carnage, havoc, and dismay caused by our fire compelled them to haul down their colors and to hoist a white flag at their gaff and half-mast and another at the main. The crew instantly took to their boats and landed. Our fire immediately ceased, and the signal was made for the *Beaufort* to come within hail.

CAPTAIN WILLIAM J. MCINTIRE
99th New York Infantry (USS Congress)

McIntire recounts an ugly incident that took place during the surrender of the Congress. His company, consisting of 87 men and two officers, had been loaned to the navy by Major General John E. Wool of Fort Monroe to serve as gunners on the ship. The unit lost nine men killed, 15 wounded, and seven missing. The following day, while the Monitor was engaging the Virginia in the distance, McIntire took two rowboats out to the smoldering wreck in a fruitless search for survivors.

*W*hen the Merrimac was approaching the Cumberland, finding our ship would not swing to her cable, we let it slip, set sail, and ran her aground. The Merrimac, having sunk the Cumberland, was placed in a raking position toward us, about 100 yards from our stern, when she commenced a rapid and most destructive fire with shot and shell upon us, breaking the muzzle on one and dismounting the other of our stern guns; it was only then our commander, Capt.

William Smith, ordered our flag to be lowered. The rebel steamers continuing to fire upon us, we hoisted a white flag to the peak, when in a few minutes the rebel tug Beaufort came alongside; an officer boarded us, ordered the men ashore; said he would take officers and burn the ship, and seemed unwilling to wait for the wounded to be taken out; but, thank God, our troops on shore kept up such a galling fire upon his vessel that he was forced to leave our decks and move his tug off in haste; when she left our side a short distance, notwithstanding our white flag, the Merrimac opened on us again with shot and shell, one shell bursting on our gun deck, killing five or seven, it is said, but so many dead were lying around that it was impossible to tell which number was correct. About the time the rebel officers left our deck, many of the men jumped overboard into the river, and some twenty-odd upon the Beaufort. The latter were the only prisoners taken. The ship's boats being lowered, we commenced active operations to get the wounded and men on shore, and our exertions were not lessened by a knowledge among the officers that the fire was increasing immediately over the powder magazine (and then we could only hope to delay the first progress by covering the hatches, which was done), yet it was in the dusk of the evening when the officers left, the wounded and all the men having been sent on shore. During the whole of this terrible engagement my men behaved with admirable bravery and coolness, and though the ship was on fire several times in different places during the action, and the dead and wounded were falling everywhere, yet all orders were promptly obeyed, and every one kept at his post.

Lieutenant Catesby Jones commanded the Virginia after Flag Officer Buchanan was wounded. Appointed a midshipman in 1836 by Andrew Jackson, Jones saw extensive duty in the U.S. Navy, including a tour on the original Merrimac. He was shot and killed in 1877 by a neighbor in Selma, Alabama, following a quarrel.

LIEUTENANT WILLIAM H. PARKER
CSS BEAUFORT

Parker's failure to effectuate the surrender of the Congress and burn the Federal frigate, described here, infuriated Buchanan, who wrote to navy secretary Stephen R. Mallory complaining that Parker was "unfit to command." Mallory wisely ignored the flag officer's censure. The following year Parker justified Mallory's faith in him by distinguishing himself aboard the ironclad Palmetto State, attacking the Union fleet off Charleston, South Carolina. He was later promoted to captain and asked to organize the Confederate Naval Academy.

When I saw the white flag I immediately lowered a boat, and sent Midshipmen Mallory and Foreman with a boat's crew of three men to take possession of the prize and bring her commander on board the *Beaufort.* As the boat approached the *Congress* a marine at the gangway levelled his piece, and threatened to fire; but Mallory told him he was ordered to board the vessel, and was "bound to do it," and pulled alongside. He and his companions got on board, and Midshipman Foreman hauled down the colors and brought them to me.

The firing having ceased, the *Merrimac* signalled me to come within hail, which I did. Commodore Buchanan then ordered us to "go alongside the *Congress,* to take the officers and wounded men prisoners, to permit the others to escape to the shore, and then to burn the ship." I went alongside her in the *Beaufort,* at the port gangway, and sent an officer to direct her commander to come to me, at the same time sending my men aboard to help to get the wounded men to the *Beaufort.* I did not think it proper to leave my vessel myself as I had but two young and inexperienced midshipmen with me, and I saw an enemy's gunboat not very far off. In a few minutes Lieutenant Austin Pendergrast came down the side of the *Congress* accompanied by an officer whom I took to be the purser or surgeon of the ship. It proved to be Captain William Smith who had been in command until a few days before, when he had been relieved by Lieutenant Joseph B. Smith. Lieutenant Smith had been killed in action, which left Pendergrast in command. Captain Smith was acting as a volunteer; but this I learned afterwards. These two officers landed on the hurricane deck of the *Beaufort* where I was standing, and surrendered the ship. As they were without side-arms, I thought it proper to request them to return to their ship and get them. This they did, though Pendergrast delivered to me a ship's cutlass instead of the regulation sword. I now

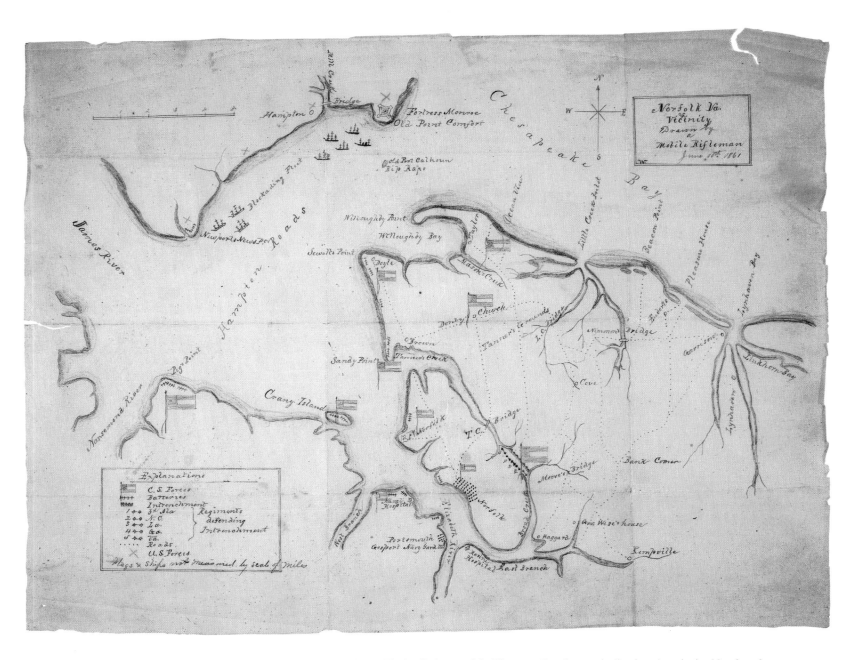

Private Henry F. Wilson of the 3d Alabama Infantry drew this detailed map of the Hampton Roads area, indicating the principal landmarks and deployments—including the site of the battle between the CSS Virginia and Federal warships off Newport News Point. His unit was posted along Broad Creek near Moore's Bridge (marked by the large Confederate flag east of Norfolk), next to regiments from North Carolina, Louisiana, Georgia, and Virginia. After the Confederate evacuation of Norfolk, the 3d Alabama was assigned to a brigade under General William Mahone. On June 1 at Seven Pines Wilson's regiment suffered 175 casualties.

told Pendergrast my orders and asked him to get his officers and wounded men on board as quickly as possible as I wanted to burn the ship. He said there were 60 wounded men on board the frigate and begged me not to burn the vessel. I told him my orders were peremptory. While we were engaged in this conversation the wounded men were being lowered into the *Beaufort,* and just then the *Raleigh* came alongside me. Lieutenant Taylor came on board and said Captain Alexander had sent him to me for orders. I directed him to take the *Raleigh* to the starboard side of the *Congress* and assist in getting off the wounded men. I had scarcely given him the order when a tremendous fire was opened on us from the shore by a regiment of soldiers—Medical Director Shippen says it was the 20th Indiana. The firing was from artillery as well as small arms. At the first discharge every man on the deck of the *Beaufort*—save Captain Smith and Lieutenant Pendergrast—was either killed or wounded. Four bullets passed through my clothing; one of which carried off my cap cover and eye glass, and another slightly wounded me in the left knee, precisely in the spot where my friend Fauntleroy had accidentally wounded me at the siege of Vera Cruz. Lieutenant Pendergrast now begged me to hoist the white flag, saying that all his wounded men would be killed. I called his attention to the fact that they were firing on the white flag which was flying at his mainmast head directly over our heads. I said I would not hoist it on the *Beaufort*; in fact I did not feel authorized to do so without consulting Commodore Buchanan. I said: "Tell your men to stop firing"; he replied: "They are a lot of volunteers and I have no control over them." This was evident. The lieutenant then requested permission to go on board the *Congress* with Captain Smith and assist in getting the wounded down. This I assented to; in the first place, I was glad to have their assistance; and secondly, I would not have been willing to confine them in my cabin at a time when the bullets were going through it like hail—humanity forbade it; I would not have put a dog there.

I now blew the steam-whistle, and my men came tumbling on board. The fire of the enemy still continuing from the shore, I cast off from the *Congress* and steamed ahead so that I could bring my bow gun to bear. I had no idea of being fired at any longer without returning it, and we had several deaths to avenge. We opened fire, but could make little impression with our single gun upon the large number of men firing from intrenchments on shore. The sides and masts of the *Beaufort* looked like the top of a pepper-box from the bullets, which went in one side and out at the other.

DRUMMER JOHN LAWRENCE
USS CONGRESS

As the Virginia bore down on the Congress, Marine Drummer Lawrence beat general quarters and then took his battle station next to the ship's commander, Lieutenant Joseph B. Smith Jr. Moments later, a Confederate shell decapitated Smith and knocked three guns off their mounts. Miraculously, Lawrence escaped with only a bruise from a flying piece of gun carriage.

The fire arose in the steerage, and I was ordered to beat the fire quarters, which I did. The fire spread so rapidly that we had to flood the magazine. The Merrimac came off the flats at this time and lay off from us, then the rebel gunboat Teaser came alongside of us and asked if we had surrendered. The reply was yelled by the crew: "No." In the meantime she captured nine of our men, some of them wounded. The firing commenced between us and the Teaser, and fire was opened on her by the infantry on shore, and she then returned to the Merrimac. It was growing dusk at this time. The Merrimac came up to our stern, and Commander Buchanan, of the Merrimac, hailing us, asked to know if we had surrendered, when one of our marine guard shot and wounded him. She opened fire on us, all the rest of their gunboats firing on us at the same time. The Merrimac backed off, leaving us, as the fire was rapidly spreading. Word was passed to leave the ship, as the magazine would explode shortly and the fire had cut us off from saving our wounded, who were left on the berthdeck at the dispensary.

PRIVATE WILLIAM F. DRAKE
CSS VIRGINIA

Drake saw plenty of action as part of a volunteer detachment from the United Artillery, a Norfolk company that helped man the Virginia's guns. When he died at age 93 on August 13, 1930, at the Confederate Soldiers' Home in Raleigh, North Carolina, he had outlived everyone, whether Confederate or Union, who took part in the historic Hampton Roads battles.

Our guns, which had been in constant action throughout the evening as the enemy came in range in the ever-changing movements of our ironclad, were quiet for a while, when we appeared to be returning toward home. Two of our guns were badly disabled by enemy shot striking their muzzles, but continued to be used at short range. Passing within a quarter of a mile of the Congress, which had been set on fire, as stated, it was observed that it was not burning, so an incendiary shell soon fired it again, burning till it blew up. If was now about sunset and as we moved across the Roads it was growing darker and darker, and we afterwards understood it was the purpose to anchor at Sewell's Point. However, we had a lively time before we anchored for the night, for several enemy war vessels returned and, supposing I presume, that under cover of the darkness they could concentrate such a rain of shot on the Merrimac as would disable her. Vain hope. As the darkness came on the shells began to explode about us, lighting up the expanse of water; both solid shot and shell frequently striking the armored side, to glance high up in the air. Whole shot had passed through the big smokestack, and it was perforated with many fragments. Passing through the storm in safety, the Merrimac anchored at Sewell's Point after darkness had long set in. We had been standing at our guns since 11 o'clock, and you will agree that we deserved supper. All night a sharp lookout was kept up for the approach of the enemy; and though fatigued, the night was passed with little sleep.

PRIVATE WILLIAM H. OSBORNE
29TH MASSACHUSETTS INFANTRY

Osborne watched the explosions that blew up the disabled Congress from Camp Butler on Newport News Point. A little more than four months later, he fought with his regiment at Malvern Hill near Richmond. Wounded and evacuated to the rear, he returned to the fight with another command, until a shell fragment tore through his calf. Captured by the Rebels in the field hospital at Savage's Station, Osborne was paroled and discharged from the service. His recollections were included in the 29th Massachusetts' regimental history, published in 1877. In 1898 he was awarded the Medal of Honor for his gallant conduct.

The frigate "Congress," which lay hard aground on the sandbeach near the camp of the Twentieth Indiana Regiment, had been set on fire late in the afternoon, and the lurid flames now lit up the bay and strand with a brightness rivaling that of the day itself. Many of her guns were still shotted, and as the fire coiled about them, they began to discharge; a shot from one of them, skimming the surface of the water, entered and sank a schooner lying at our wharf. The flames had mounted each mast and spar, and were leaping out at every

"At twelve o'clock, the magazines blew up with a terrific noise. This event had been anticipated by the garrison, and the shores and adjacent camps were crowded with awe-struck gazers."

port with angry tongues. Heaps of shells, which had been brought from the magazines for the afternoon's encounter, lay on the gun-decks; these now began to explode, and ever and anon they would dart up out of the roaring, crackling mass, high into the air, and course in every direction through the heavens.

At twelve o'clock, the magazines blew up with a terrific noise. This event had been anticipated by the garrison, and the shores and adjacent camps were crowded with awe-struck gazers. The whole upper works of the frigate had, hours before, been reduced to ashes by the devouring flames; the masts and spars, blackened and charred, had fallen into and across the burning hull; these were sent high into the air with other *debris,* and as blast succeeded blast, were suddenly arrested in their descent and again sent heavenward. The spectacle thus presented was awfully grand; a column of fire and sulphurous smoke, fifty feet in diameter at its base and not less than two hundred feet high, dividing in its centre into thousands of smaller jets, and falling in myriads of bunches and grains of fire, like the sprays of a gigantic fountain, lighted up the camp and bay for miles.

The yards and rigging of the "Minnesota" and "St. Lawrence" were filled with men armed with fire-buckets lest the falling sparks should ignite the tarred ropes of these vessels, and unite them in one general conflagration. The sides of the hapless "Congress" were thrown open by the last explosion, and the next morning, all that could be seen of the once proud ship were a few blackened ribs, a short distance above the surface of the water.

ASSISTANT PAYMASTER WILLIAM F. KEELER
USS Monitor

Keeler, pictured here with fellow officers on the ironclad's deck (second row, second from left), always insisted that the crew's greatest feat was not confronting the Virginia in Hampton Roads but surviving the harrowing voyage south. "Anyone can fight behind impenetrable armor," he said of the barely seaworthy craft. "The credit, if any is due, is in daring to undertake the trip."

After getting up our anchor we steamed slowly along under the towering side of the *Minnesota*. The men were clambering down into the smaller boats—the guns were being thrown overboard & everything seemed in confusion. Her wooden sides shewed terrible traces of the conflict.

As a light fog lifted from the water it revealed the *Merrimac* with her consorts lying under Sewall's Point. The announcement of breakfast brought also the news that the *Merrimac* was coming & our coffee was forgotten.

Capt. Worden inquired of the *Minnesota* what he intended to do.— "If I cannot lighten my ship off I shall destroy her," Capt. Van Brunt replied.—"I will stand by you to the last if I can help you," said our Capt.—"No Sir, you cannot help me," was the reply.

The idea of assistance or protection being offered to the huge thing by the little pigmy at her side seemed absolutely ridiculous & I have no doubt was so regarded by those on board of her, for the replies came down curt & crispy.

ACTING ASSISTANT ENGINEER ELSBERRY V. WHITE
CSS Virginia

The Georgia-born White wrote this account of the Virginia's first sighting of the Monitor—the moment when the bizarre little ship steamed out from behind the shadow of the frigate Minnesota on the morning of March 9—at the request of a boyhood friend, Robert S. Hudgins II, of the 3d Virginia Cavalry. Hudgins witnessed the duel of the ironclads through field glasses from a meadow overlooking Hampton Roads and asked White for his observations, which included a characterization of the Monitor's appearance that became famous.

When we came out for the second day's fight, thinking we would clean up the *Minnesota, Roanoke,* and *St. Lawrence,* we were not entirely surprised to find the *Monitor,* for, while we did not know exactly what to expect, we knew some kind of craft had come in during the night. However we had no doubt that we could handle her easily. Commodore Buchanan, who had been wounded, had been sent ashore during the night to the hospital in Norfolk. Lt. Catesby Jones took over command, determined to finish the job begun the day before.

As we came in range of the *Minnesota,* a puff of smoke and the whistle of a shot over our heads let us know that she had no intention of striking her colors without a fight. Lt. Jones laid his course directly for her, thinking to bring his rifled guns to bear upon her and quickly finishing the first part of the fight so that he could then engage the *St. Lawrence* and *Roanoke* in turn. But we were to find that before the day ended we would not be able to carry out our plans.

At this time we noticed a volume of smoke coming up from the opposite side of the *Minnesota* and there emerged the queerest looking craft afloat. Through our glasses we could see she was ironclad, sharp at both ends and appeared to be almost awash. Mounted amidships was a turret with ports and, as we looked, the turret began to revolve until her forward gun bore directly on us and, run out, it resembled a cheese box on a raft.

We didn't have long to wait before she fired. Her first shot fell a little short and sent up a geyser of water that fell on our top and rolled off. We then fired our forward rifle and scored a direct hit on her turret, but with no apparent effect. Her next shot was better and caught us amidships with a resounding wham, but while the old boat shuddered, there seemed to be no appreciable damage. By this time we were getting pretty close, and both crafts were firing as fast as the guns could be served. The men were stripped to the waist and were working like mad. Powder smoke filled the entire ship so that we could see but a short distance and its acrid fumes made breathing difficult.

LIEUTENANT S. DANA GREENE
USS MONITOR

Greene was just 22 years old and a recent graduate of the U.S. Naval Academy when he was made executive officer of the Monitor. He was on board when the ironclad was launched in New York harbor on January 30, 1862, and was one of the last men to leave her when she foundered and sank during a nighttime storm off Cape Hatteras on December 30 of that year.

As the engagement continued, the working of the turret was not altogether satisfactory. It was difficult to start it revolving, or, when once started, to stop it, on account of the imperfections of the novel machinery, which was undergoing its first trial. Stimers was an active, muscular man, and did his utmost to control the motion of the turret; but, in spite of his efforts, it was difficult, if not impossible, to secure accurate firing. The conditions were very different from those of an ordinary broadside gun, under which we had been trained on wooden ships. My only view of the world outside of the tower was over the muzzles of the guns, which cleared the ports by only a few inches. When the guns were run in, the portholes were covered by heavy iron pendulums, pierced with small holes to allow the iron rammer and sponge handles to protrude while they were in use. To hoist these pendulums required the entire gun's crew and vastly increased the work inside the turret.

The effect upon one shut up in a revolving drum is perplexing, and it is not a simple matter to keep the bearings. White marks had been placed upon the stationary deck immediately below the turret to indicate the direction of the starboard and port sides, and the bow and stern; but these marks were obliterated early in the action. I would continually ask the captain, How does the *Merrimac* bear? He replied, On the starboard-beam or On the port-quarter as the case might be. Then the difficulty was to determine the direction of the starboard-beam, or port-quarter, or any other bearing. It finally resulted, that when a gun was ready for firing, the turret would be started on its revolving journey in search of the target, because the turret could not be accurately controlled.

The uniforms worn by the Confederate officers aboard the Virginia were blue, like those of their Federal counterparts. The jacket above belonged to Robert D. Minor, Buchanan's flag lieutenant, who was wounded by a Yankee bullet as he rowed toward the Congress to set fire to the sinking frigate.

MIDSHIPMAN HARDIN B. LITTLEPAGE
CSS VIRGINIA

The first shots exchanged between the Monitor and the Virginia, described here by Littlepage, were touched off shortly after 8:00 a.m. on March 9, 1862. A tense four-hour standoff followed. Circling and probing at each other like prizefighters, the ironclads traded fire at ranges varying from a few feet to a half-mile. Although each ship had its moments of peril, neither adversary was able to gain a decisive advantage.

After getting as near to the Minnesota as it was possible to go without grounding, we opened fire upon her. The Ericsson Battery, or "Monitor," as she was afterwards called and is known in history, came directly for us, stopping at a distance of some three or four hundred yards, opened fire on us. Knowing that we had nothing but shells to fight her with, we paid little attention to her as we did not care to develop the situation. When, however, she came nearer we concluded to test our shell upon her, and the action was continued, sometimes at very close quarters, until finally she undertook to run across our bows, and we ran ahead at full speed and struck her, not knowing until then that we had lost our prow the day before in the Cumberland. Her commander, Captain Worden, seeing our object was to ram her, put his helm hard up, causing us to strike her obliquely, which possibly was a very fortunate thing for us, as we were ramming her with our naked stem. We were so close together at one time—in fact, rubbing together, that a man at my gun by the name of Hunt jumped in the port and I ordered him to get back as it was useless to expose himself in that way. He said he wanted to get aboard of the bloody little iron tub, and that he would put his pea-jacket around the pilot-house so she could not tell which way she was going. It would not have been a bad idea, as we realised afterwards, provided he could have gotten back aboard of the Virginia.

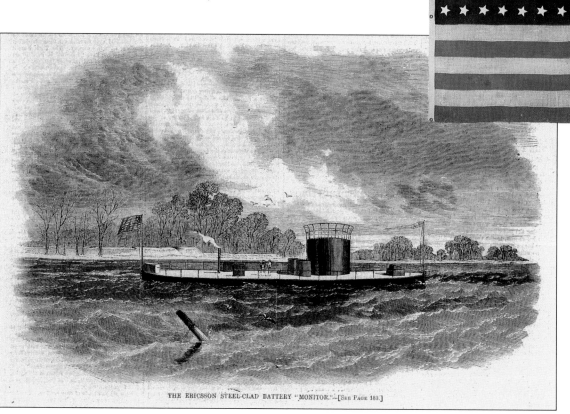

THE ERICSSON STEEL-CLAD BATTERY "MONITOR."—[SEE PAGE 183.]

The Northern public got its first glimpse of the Monitor by means of this out-of-scale illustration published in the March 22, 1862, edition of Harper's Weekly. The artist has exaggerated the height of the revolving turret amidships and shortened the pilothouse near the bow. The innovative craft was the handiwork of the brilliant Swedish-born naval architect John Ericsson. When Ericsson died in 1889, this flag from the Monitor (above) was draped on his coffin.

LIEUTENANT S. DANA GREENE
USS MONITOR

Greene, who commanded the Monitor after Lieutenant John L. Worden was wounded, was later criticized for not pursuing the Virginia when she broke off the engagement. He was subsequently passed over five times for permanent command of the ship. Although he won belated praise—in 1868 Worden wrote that he had "handled the guns with great courage, coolness and skill"—Greene remained a tortured soul. In 1884 he took his own life at the Portsmouth, New Hampshire, Navy Yard.

Soon after noon a shell from the enemy's gun, the muzzle not ten yards distant, struck the forward side of the pilot-house directly in the sight-hole, or slit, and exploded, cracking the second iron log and partly lifting the top, leaving an opening. Worden was standing immediately behind this spot, and received in his face the force of the blow, which partly stunned him, and, filling his eyes with powder, utterly blinded him. The injury was known only to those in the pilot-house and its immediate vicinity. The flood of light rushing through the top of the pilot-house, now partly open, caused Worden, blind as he was, to believe that the pilot-house was seriously injured, if not destroyed; he therefore gave orders to put the helm to starboard and "sheer off." Thus the *Monitor* retired temporarily from the action, in order to ascertain the extent of the injuries she had received. At the same time Worden sent for me, and leaving Stimers the only officer in the turret, I went forward at once, and found him standing at the foot of the ladder leading to the pilot-house.

He was a ghastly sight, with his eyes closed and the blood apparently rushing from every pore in the upper part of his face. He told me that he was seriously wounded, and directed me to take command. I assisted in leading him to a sofa in his cabin, where he was tenderly cared for by Dr. Logue, and then I assumed command. Blind and suffering as he was, Worden's fortitude never forsook him; he frequently asked from his bed of pain of the progress of affairs, and when told that the *Minnesota* was saved, he said, "Then I can die happy."

When I reached my station in the pilot-house, I found that the iron log was fractured and the top partly open; but the steering gear was still intact, and the pilot-house was not totally destroyed, as had been feared. In the confusion of the moment resulting from so serious an injury to the commanding officer, the *Monitor* had been moving without direction. Exactly how much time had elapsed from the moment that Worden was wounded until I had reached the pilot-house and

completed the examination of the injury at that point, and determined what course to pursue in the damaged condition of the vessel, it is impossible to state; but it could hardly have exceeded twenty minutes at the utmost. During this time the *Merrimac*, which was leaking badly, had started in the direction of the Elizabeth River; and, on taking my station in the pilot-house, and turning the vessel's head in the direction of the *Merrimac*, I saw that she was already in retreat. A few shots were fired at the retiring vessel, and she continued on to Norfolk. I returned with the *Monitor* to the side of the *Minnesota*, where preparations were being made to abandon the ship which was still aground. Shortly afterward Worden was transferred to a tug, and that night he was carried to Washington. . . .

My men and myself were perfectly black with smoke and powder. All of my underclothes were perfectly black, and my person was in the same condition. . . . I had been up so long, and had been under such a state of excitement, that my nervous system was completely run down. . . . My nerves and muscles twitched as though electric shocks were continually passing through them. . . . I lay down and tried to sleep—I might as well have tried to fly.

Lieutenant John L. Worden was lionized in the North for saving the Union fleet. After recovering from his wounds and receiving a special vote of thanks from Congress, he joined the South Atlantic Blockading Squadron in command of the monitor Montauk. He took part in the ironclad attack against Charleston on April 7, 1863, and then was assigned to oversee the construction of a new class of ironclads.

Officers of the Monitor examine dents in the turret made by the Virginia's shot and shells. Partially visible in the background is a new, slope-sided pilothouse, built after the original square one was wrecked in the fight. Tactically the duel had ended in a draw. But even the Confederates agreed that the Monitor had won a strategic victory.

"The Monitor continued to maneuver around us, making an effort to run into our propeller, and missed it by only a few yards."

MIDSHIPMAN HARDIN B. LITTLEPAGE
CSS VIRGINIA

As commander of the Confederate Naval Veterans Association after the war, Little-page, shown at left as a midshipman, was determined to argue the Southern point of view concerning the ironclad duel. When Worden petitioned Congress in 1874 to award surviving Monitor crew members $200,000 for saving the Union fleet, Little-page argued that it was the Virginia's deep draft, slow speed, and poor maneuverability that prevented her from achieving her goal. His testimony helped defeat the bill.

The Virginia continued her efforts to get to the Minnesota, paying little attention to the Monitor because she felt satisfied that she could not materially damage an iron-clad with shell. The Monitor continued to maneuver around us, making an effort to run into our propeller, and missed it by only a few yards. If she had succeeded it might have proved a very serious injury. About this time a shell from the Virginia struck the pilot-house of the Monitor and blinded her commander, Captain Worden, who fell back with his face terribly lacerated. The pilot-house was seriously damaged.

I remember perfectly well that as soon as all hands were piped down and the fight considered over, I hurried on deck to get a little fresh air and take in the situation. There lay the Minnesota just as we had left her when we had gotten hard and fast aground trying to get a little near to her, about an hour before I came on deck, but as the tide was flood we succeeded in getting off. Should we have returned to her then and have touched bottom we should have remained there and probably have been destroyed, as it was about high water.

PRIVATE JOHN E. GLEASON
22D MASSACHUSETTS INFANTRY, PORTER'S BRIGADE

Gleason's admiration and affection for Major General George B. McClellan, expressed in this letter to his father, was echoed by nearly every member of the Army of the Potomac's rank and file. The common soldiers appreciated both the pride and professionalism McClellan had instilled in them and the steps he had taken to improve their living conditions, and they were quick to condemn any politician or journalist who dared to criticize him. A schoolteacher from Bedford, Massachusetts, Gleason joined the army in August 1861.

As for "Little Mack," it isn't safe for anyone to utter a word derogatory to *him,* and some of these scarlet faultfinders will find themselves confronted when we get home. If they are so anxious to have him precipitate his battalions upon breastworks which have occupied months in their construction, & needlessly sacrifice thousands of lives as precious, at least, as theirs, let them put on the blue pants and eat "salt horse" and sleep on the ground themselves. When I read some articles in the papers from these ignorant precepitates I think a whole phillippic in a minute & would like to reel it off to them. But the plans of the campaign are daily being developed, and as we see each actor take his place upon the stage in his appointed time we admire the unfolding plot, and believe that God has raised up men for the times. The Richmond papers think a great battle will be fought at the north of that place before anything decisive occurs on the Peninsular. There are reasons for such a belief, and the gates at the north seem to be surely and irresistably closing upon the enemy. Banks & Shields and Fremont (justice overtake his traducers!) & McDowell seem to be following converging lines, & when their forces come near together, the rebels will find hard work to stop their march. Gen. Franklin's Division has crossed to the Gloucester side of York river, his camp fires light up the evening clouds, and are another writing on the wall for the emaciated Jeff. Our mortars and siege guns are rapidly being put in position, & some of our iron Monitors & Galenas will before long give another illustration to the world of Yankee ingenuity, & prove to blustering Old John Bull that his antique wooden navy does not make him "mistress of the seas." This rebellion is full of tests; every day adds a new one. It's well worth being poor to live in these pregnant times.

PRIVATE FREDERICK E. DENNIS
8TH NEW JERSEY INFANTRY, STARR'S BRIGADE

The steamer that carried the 8th New Jersey down to the Virginia Peninsula disembarked from Liverpool Point on the lower Potomac River. After making a leisurely progress to the Peninsula and enjoying some high jinks along the way, Dennis and his comrades soon got their wish for action. Indeed, their first battle, on May 5 at Williamsburg, the old colonial capital, turned out to be far more than they had bargained for: The regiment suffered 215 casualties, including 40 dead.

Many of us were weary of inaction and longed for a slice of active service. We felt stiff and rusty and wanted oiling. We threw loaves of soft bread at one another's heads with unerring aim, took a last fond look at the old camp ground, and to the tap of drum and scream of fife marched down to the pier and embarked on a rickety old steamboat called the Naushon.

Our three months' stay on the old camp ground was spent in comparative comfort, and about the only thing to relieve the monotony was the daily dose of shells from the rebel batteries on the opposite side of the river. They seemed to take fiendish delight in making the racket at just about the time we had stretched ourselves for a good sleep. The only one who seemed determined to sleep through it all was "Old Man Hatch." Above the terrible roar of that battery, the awful, blood-curdling snore of Hatch could be heard, and we gazed at him with envy.

About 400 of the 8th N.J. were huddled on board that old steam scow, and we glided down the Potomac to join the grand army under McClellan, which had sailed ahead of our division and was encamped in the vicinity of the historic field of Yorktown. As we approached the mouth of the river a storm of wind and rain struck the scow, and the Captain, as he listened to the creaking and straining of the hulk, felt nervous about sailing into the Chesapeake Bay, and so we turned into the little Bay of St. Mary's until the storm should subside.

Here is where we had some fun for about two days. Our rations were vanishing like the dew, and by mutual consent and with the fear of God before our eyes we made good use of the sutler, who had a sloop tied to the stern of our tub. In the hold of that sloop were stored heaps of victuals, and I think that cake was by all odds the most plentiful. The boys had not feasted on cake to a very great extent for several months, and we would just this once luxuriate. One meal of cake caused us to feel a slight desire for something more substantial. At about the sixth meal the sight of that cake threw the most of us into convulsions, and silent prayer was indulged in for a little of that bread that we had thrown at one another's heads three days before.

We held a council of war to devise a plan for securing rations that would restore our shattered stomachs to their old-time condition. It was finally resolved to put over to the Maryland shore in a boat and make a desperate dash for beef and hoecake. Three or four boys got in a boat, and we gave them a good send off with a shower of the detestable cake. In about four hours they returned with beef, which they had cooked in salt water. Our troubles were renewed and our hearts sank within us as we tried to sink our teeth in that ancient, vulcanized beef.

Gunners of Battery M, 2d U.S. Artillery, manhandle a 12-pounder Napoleon onto a steamer docked at Alexandria, Virginia, in March. The fieldpiece was part of a mountain of supplies and equipment assembled for the drive up the Peninsula. Shuttling back and forth, nearly 600 vessels moved 121,500 men, 14,592 animals, 1,150 wagons, 44 batteries of artillery, and 74 ambulances, along with pontoon bridges, telegraph wire, and everything else needed to sustain an army.

SERGEANT EDWARD N. BOOTS

101ST PENNSYLVANIA INFANTRY, KEIM'S BRIGADE

A 20-year-old schoolteacher, Boots provided this account of his voyage to Fort Monroe in a letter to his mother. As a quartermaster, he saw little action during the ensuing months but suffered from frequent bouts of fever. Captured in North Carolina in 1864, Boots died at Andersonville prison on September 12, 1864, and is buried at the National Cemetery there.

When we got up it was still raining but we packed up and marched to Pier No 2 Alexandria to embark on board steamers. We had to wait until after dark befor[e] we got aboard. Before we went aboard a storm of lightning, thunder, and rain came up, and in the midst of it we went aboard the steamer Georgia. It was very dark. We could see nothing except by the flash of the lightning, but at last we all got safely aboard . . . , but we were not much better off than on shore, for we were placed between decks, where one side was open to the weather, and when it rained it pelted on us beautifully. In the morning it was found that the Georgia was too heavily loaded and five companies of our Reg't had to go ashore again. We did so and about noon two companies of us were embarked on the Steamer State of Maine. We are placed on the boiler deck. It is rather damp but otherwise is pretty comfortable. There are about fifteen hundred troops on board, so you may be sure that we are pretty well crowded. We have long ago passed the Georgia though she started three hours before us. The remaining three companies will follow on the steamer Herd. Another Steamer the Constitution had about five thousand men aboard. She started yesterday morning, about six hours before we did but we have passed her so I suppose we shall arrive at Fortress Monroe first.

After landing at Hampton, Virginia, two columns of Federal troops march to their camps in this pencil sketch by war illustrator John R. Chapin. "Dense masses of infantry, long trains of artillery and thousands of cavalry, with unnumbered army wagons and mules, were mingled in grand confusion," one soldier wrote of the disembarkation. The first divisions had departed Alexandria on March 17. McClellan himself left on April 1 and arrived at Fort Monroe the next day.

MAJOR JOHN A. FITE
7TH TENNESSEE INFANTRY, S. R. ANDERSON'S BRIGADE

As it gradually became clear to the Confederates that McClellan's target was Richmond, General Joseph E. Johnston began shifting units from his army encamped in northern Virginia to the Peninsula to reinforce General John B. Magruder's forces there. Fite's regiment was one of those that marched to York- town. Although Fite's army career was hazardous in the extreme—he was wounded three times and captured at Gettysburg—he lived to be 93 years old.

After staying at Fredericksberg about a week, we started on to march to Yorktown. It was hot and dry weather. After going some distance we came to a creek or river, and the bridge was down. We cut down some trees on both sides and let them lap over, and made us a sort of a bridge to cross over, but our road wagons could- n't cross. We went on, and about the second day, we hadn't had any- thing to eat, we were marching along the road and stopped to rest by the side of a corn field. The corn was just about in good roasting ear, and there must have been 10 acres in the patch. We got orders to get over in the field and get corn and eat it, and I have no idea there was an ear of corn left there in ten minutes. I got two ears and ate them.

The road was sandy and hot, and we were starved to death for water. Finally we came to the little town of Kent, and there was a well there right on the side of the road, and a trough that we watered our horses in. The trough had been pumped full of water so the fellows would rush up to the trough, stick their hands down into the water and drink and be holding canteens in the water while they were drinking.

We reached Macgruders Army one evening and went into camp. While we were there, I was sent with my Company on picket duty down in a slough that connected with the river. The Yankees were on one side of it, some distance however from the water. It seemed to be a swampy place on the other side.

While we were sitting there on the bank every few minutes an old porpoise would come to the top, then dive down. I had never seen a porpoise before and I was sure it was a Yankee. I took one of the boys gun and told him I was going to kill him. The old thing would come up 50 or 75 yards from me and he'd go down quick so I couldn't shoot him. Colonel Taylor from Kentucky had been there before I was picketing. He came down to where I was and saw me sitting there and asked me what I was doing. I told him there was a damn Yankee out there in the water, had on a diving suit, and I was going to try to kill

him. "O," he said, "You must be mistaken." I said, "No, watch and you'll see directly." About that time old Mr. Porpoise came up and dived again. Taylor was pretty close to me and just rolled over on the ground and said, "You are the damndest fool I ever saw, that's no Yan- kee that's an old porpoise."

PRIVATE OLIVER W. NORTON
83D PENNSYLVANIA INFANTRY, BUTTERFIELD'S BRIGADE

The 83d's nearly unopposed cap- ture of Big Bethel, where Yankees had been beaten the previous year in the war's first battle on Vir- ginia soil, provided the Pennsyl- vanians with their first taste of combat. The easy victory proved illusory; during the rest of the campaign the regiment would lose two-thirds of its original strength.

On Thursday General Porter's division made a reconnoissance two miles beyond Great Bethel. Our brigade with a battery took the lead. It is ten miles from here to the fortifications. The road is perfectly level and sandy all the way. The two regiments of Berdan's sharpshooters are in our division now and a company of them went with us as skirmishers. A spy had reported the rebels two thou- sand strong at the forts. These are a line of earthworks in the edge of a pine woods. In front of these is a large level field of two or three hun- dred acres, and in front of the field an extensive swamp full of wet holes, thickets, briars and vines. The road leads through the middle of this swamp to the field. Here was the place where so many of our brave boys fell last spring. We halted as we came up to the swamp. The colonel came along and told us to watch the colors and stick to them, that Great Bethel would be ours before night. We then commenced to move. The artillery took the road, the Seventeenth and Twelfth New York the swamp on the right, and the Forty-fourth and Eighty-third the left. We had just entered and were forcing our way through when we heard the crack of rifles in the woods ahead. The word was passed along to hurry up. I thought the ball had opened at last. You ought to have seen us go through those thickets then. Pell-mell we went, over bogs and through vines and places I never would have thought a man could get through under ordinary circumstances. As we came out to the field the firing ceased. We formed in line of battle instantly and moved toward the works. I expected to see a line of fire run along their breastworks, but not a sound came from them and not a man could we see. We came up to the front and our color guard leaped the ditch and planted the flag of the Eighty-third on the fortifications so long disgraced by the rebel rag. Great Bethel was ours and not a man hurt. They had pickets there who exchanged shots with our skirmishers as they came in sight and then retreated. We then turned to the left and went

about two miles to another fortification. They had a dam here to fill a ditch in front of the works, and below the dam a bridge. As our skirmishers came out of the woods they saw three men tearing up the planks on this bridge. They fired and shot two of them. Some others ran out of the woods and carried them off, so we don't know whether they were killed or not.

Two Union gunboats in the York River shell Yorktown (below, left) and Gloucester Point (below, right) on April 14. The panoramic scene was drawn by Robert Knox Sneden, cartographer for the U.S. III Corps and an amateur artist. The navy continued the bombardment almost daily for two weeks at the request of McClellan, who wanted the gunboats to "annoy the enemy by firing a few shells by day and night."

SURGEON GEORGE T. STEVENS
77TH NEW YORK INFANTRY, DAVIDSON'S BRIGADE

The son of a minister, Stevens graduated from Castleton Medical College in Vermont and joined the army in October 1861 at age 29. His talents were recognized and he was promoted swiftly, advancing from assistant surgeon to surgeon, chief operating surgeon, chief of surgery and, finally, medical inspector for the VI Corps.

At six o'clock the division was in line and on the road. The morning was indescribably beautiful. The vapors that rose from the broad expanse of waters were tinged with a thousand gorgeous hues as they rolled away, dispersed by the morning sun; and the tall yellow pines were crowned with rich golden coronals of light. The road was perfectly level and dry, and the country delightful. Long rows of locusts and pines lined the sides of the road, and the rich groves of oak just sending forth their foliage, were beautifully interspersed with the holly, with its bright red berries and rich evergreen leaves. Peach orchards in full bloom added to the beauty of the scene, and when at times we could see the lines of troops, two and three miles in extent, their muskets glittering in the bright sunlight, the enthusiasm of the men was unbounded.

All the bridges over the route had been destroyed by the enemy, but pioneers advanced at the head of the column, and as the bridges were all small they were quickly repaired. A march of a few miles brought us in sight of the James river; a noble stream, at least five miles wide at this point. Not far from the shore appeared the masts of the U.S. frigate Cumberland, sunk in the memorable fight with the Merrimac. As our march led us along the banks, the views were charming. On one hand was the noble river, and on the other the orchards and groves. Deserted houses, and gardens blooming with hyacinths and other blossoms of early spring, were passed. On the opposite side of the river lay a rebel gunboat, watching our movements.

Our division, Smith's, had taken the lead on the James river road, while Porter's division had marched upon Great Bethel. After a march of fifteen miles, our division was drawn up in line of battle near Warwick. Porter's division had already reached Great Bethel, on our right, and we could see huge columns of smoke rising in that direction, and hear the roar of artillery. An aid dashed up and informed General Davidson that the enemy were in line of battle ready to receive us. Soon the order came to advance; the line swept onward through the woods and over a cleared field, but found no foe.

LIEUTENANT EDWARD A. ACTON
5TH NEW JERSEY INFANTRY, STARR'S BRIGADE

Against the wishes of his Quaker family, Acton answered Lincoln's first call for volunteers in 1861. He left behind a wife and three children. Wounded in the temple and left hand at Williamsburg, he recovered sufficiently to rejoin his regiment and fight in the Seven Days' Battles. He was killed by a Confederate sharpshooter on August 29, 1862, during the Battle of Second Manassas.

After landing we marched to our camp ground over one of the worse roads I ever saw. It was some two miles distant. On our arrival there we stacked arms, unslung knapsacks, took off our equipments and at once marched back, in fatigue dress, for our commissary stores and baggage—for our teams, which had been loaded on schooners, had not yet arrived and the only way we could get to the camp our food and the officers tents was for us to carry them—after getting these things out our men pitched their tents and we had for that night one of the queerest looking camp grounds thee could ever immagine. We encamped in the pine woods, with a thick undergrowth of bushes, and the company tents were put up so irregularly that at night we could scarcely find our own men.

I think I told thee of our having *shelter tents* furnished us in place of the old tents we had been useing before and gave thee a discription of them. We officers have, before this movement, had two wall tents for our own use, but now we [have] only one; and our accomodations are on the most primitive style. After the tent was put up we went into the wood and cut crotches, or forks and laid poles on them; on these poles we laid short pine branches and boughes—these we *wove* in on the poles and then covered them with Indian Rubber blankets. We all three sleep on this bed and at night, cover our-selves with three woolen blankets. We rested in this way 'till last thirday when we moved where we now are.

Our move was only one-and-a-half miles, but we had to cross the creek. We have now a splendid camping ground but on next second day we will move still further forward. We shall be in the advance and no doubt shall see some very hard work. I do not wish to deceive thee, dear Mollie, the probability is we shall be in a *fight*. Thee can certainly not expect less, but yet thee must try to learn that thy fears so far are far fetched, and too, that thee anticipates resultes much more serious than thee should.

Yesterday I was to the front of our army—the preperation is makeing there for the greatest struggle of the war—and yet I cannot help but think that we shall take Yorktown without much loss of life, for Banks with his army is advanceing on Richmond and McDowell with his army is marching down in the same direction. If the Rebels do make a desperate stand at Yorktown and are defeated (as they will be if they stand) the armies of Burnside, Banks and McDowell will cut off any of their retreat they may attempt to make. Many of our officers think and say that the war of the Revolution was decided at Yorktown, and that the war of the Rebellion will be decided at the same place.

PRIVATE JOHN T. COXE
HAMPTON'S LEGION (SOUTH CAROLINA), HAMPTON'S BRIGADE

In 1861 at age 16, Coxe ran away from the home of his guardian in Greenville, South Carolina, to join Hampton's Legion. The unit fought at Manassas that summer, then camped in northern Virginia until early April 1862, when Johnston ordered it into the Yorktown defense line.

The weather was clear and, in order to save time, some of our cavalrymen were sent on ahead to have placed at different farm houses on the road tubs of water for our accommodation as we rushed along. At noon we reached the small but fine old town of New Kent Courthouse and the intersection of the Richmond and Williamsburg roads. We rested an hour in the old town. Late in the day we got to the confines of Williamsburg and camped.

This city is on a flat plain, so from our camp not much of the city, other than the dome of William and Mary College, could be seen. We marched through the city at an early hour the next morning. The city was clean and very pretty, and the streets were lined with citizens, who heartily welcomed us. From this we marched to Yorktown, twelve miles, reaching there at one o'clock. We marched by General Johnston's headquarters in the suburbs at a time when the General and his staff were returning from a ride along the lines. We sent up a great cheer, which the General acknowledged with a gracious smile. This was the first time I had seen him since First Manassas. We went on and camped in a lovely wood, the same ground occupied by the French army during the siege of Yorktown in the Revolution. The old earthworks and entrenchments of the French were still well preserved, and our thoughts went back and took in with reverence the stirring times of the old days.

Private William Charles Mayson of the 7th Georgia Infantry had been wounded in the thigh the previous summer during the Battle of First Manassas. After hospitalization in Orange County, Virginia, and a furlough back home, he had rejoined his unit. The 38-year-old Mayson was killed instantly by a shell that exploded near Dam No. 1 outside Yorktown on April 16.

PRIVATE WILBUR FISK
2D VERMONT INFANTRY, BROOKS' BRIGADE

Throughout his four years in the army, Fisk wrote about his experiences for The Green Mountain Freeman, a widely read newspaper published at Montpelier, Vermont. He signed his columns with the pen name Anti-Rebel. Here Fisk describes a reconnaissance in force that took place on April 16 at Burnt Chimneys, a dam site near Lee's Mill on the Warwick River. The Vermonters briefly breached the Confederate line, but a fierce counterattack drove them back.

The Second regiment, which during the afternoon, had been marching hither and thither, in the woods towards the right, without, as it seemed to us, any definite purpose in view, received orders about three o'clock to march—somewhere, double-quick, to support the Third. As we emerged into the clearing, the smoke of the battle was rolling up in dense clouds, growing thicker and thicker every moment as our batteries vomited forth from their brazen throats their death dealing missiles to the accursed minions of slavery. We rushed past the batteries in their rear to the left, losing but one man killed, and one wounded by a piece of shell from the enemy. We quickly formed in line of battle, sheltered by a piece of pine woods bordering on the creek which separated us from the enemy. There were other regiments ahead of us, and we were to be their support in case they attempted to charge across the creek. The rebels had ceased firing, and it was unknown whether they were evacuating or playing possum. As the Third and Sixth attempted to cross, they found to their cost that the enemy had a stronghold there, and were determined to hold it. The water, supposed to be about knee deep, was found to be much deeper, and it is thought that the rebels had some way to let in water at will; many of the boys who crossed at the time have assured me that they found

the water had quite perceptibly increased in depth when they returned. When they were in the worst possible situation, the rebels opened fired on them from their rifle-pits, with terrible effect. From where our regiment stood, we could hear the musketry, but could not witness the strife. Our artillery at this juncture opened on them with redoubled fury, and for a few minutes the ground fairly trembled under our feet. Our suspense was painful. In a few minutes squads of men were seen emerging from the woods with their wounded comrades, carrying some of them on their backs, some on stretchers, and others were assisted hobbling along the best way they could; and many, alas! were left that could not be recovered. This confirmed our worst apprehensions. The men were wet to their waists, and of course every cartridge was soaked, and rendered for the time worthless.

Many Federal soldiers purchased brass disks for use as identification tags. This one belonged to Private Daniel Ellis, Company K, 3d Vermont Infantry, who was wounded at Lee's Mill. The reverse side holds an eagle emblem.

LIEUTENANT EDWARD A. ACTON
5TH NEW JERSEY INFANTRY, STARR'S BRIGADE

One of the more hazardous labors assigned to the forces besieging Yorktown was the construction of earthworks for the siege batteries under the guns of the Confederate works. Infantrymen like those in Acton's company were detailed to perform the task under the supervision of engineer officers.

About 10 O'clock in the morning I was ordered to take command of 100 men, with 10 non-commissioned officers and report to the Major of one of the New York Regiments. His name is Lowe. He met us at Gen Hookers Head Quarters, took us nearer the rebels than we have ever before been. We proceeded to within 1000 yds of one of the enemies heaviest batteries and directly in its front. We were in a narrow strip of woods just in rear of our advance line of pickets. As soon as we arrived we quietly commenced work. Our object was to throw up a battery to command theirs. It was a daingerous operation for their guns could easily have shelled us from our position. One discharge of grape or schrapnel would have swept us out entirely. We were not more than 20 yds from the edge of woods. Through the bushes we could see their guns looking threateningly down on us and their sentries watchfully paceing to and fro, but all unconscious of our close proximity. We scarcely spoke. There was not a loud stroke of the axe, nor a heavey fall of a clod, but 400 men (300 had joined us) worked steadily, quietly and with earnest will 'till nightfall, when 400 men

more relived us or took our places. The work still goes on and we are undiscovered. By to-morrow morning if we are not discovered before, the battery will be finished and the guns mounted ready for work. There will be 6 heavy seige guns on it. This is the way McClelland is working and in a few days his plans will be compleated and the enemy not only, but the whole North will be astonished at the amount of work he has accomplished. We shall have probably a bloody battle, but we shall gain a victory surely more brilliant than any that has been won during the war.

Sentries guard the five 100-pounder Parrotts of Battery No. 1, one of 14 heavy-artillery emplacements built by the Federals in front of Yorktown and the only one to fire at the town before the Confederates evacuated it. Made of earth reinforced with gabions—wicker baskets filled with dirt—and sandbags, Battery No. 1 was completed in three days. The big guns were hauled in by teams of horses on roads that were corduroyed—made of logs laid crosswise—over nearly four miles of swampland.

PRIVATE FREDERICK K. FOWLER

5TH NEW YORK INFANTRY, ARTILLERY RESERVE

A gilder by trade, Fowler enlisted in 1861. His service ended on August 30, 1862, at Second Manassas, when bullets struck him in both arms, both legs, his left ankle, and between his heart and lungs. Left for dead on the battlefield for 60 hours, Fowler miraculously survived but remained an invalid for the rest of his life.

When Col. Warren informed Gen. Barry, the chief of Artillery, that we could handle a siege gun as well as a musket we were by Gen. McClellan's order detached from our brigade and detailed to build and man the batteries in front of Yorktown. We built N.1 which shelled the rebels so effectively, No. 6 and 11 both mortar batteries were also built by us, the rest were built by other reg'ts and would have done good service.

The most important of all the works was a continuous line of defense within 1200 yards of the enemy, the rebel fortifications. There were 5 batteries protected by entrenchments and 3 parallels in which 5000 troops could be placed to cover the men at the guns or repel a sortie. One of these batteries no. 15 was in the most exposed situation being directly in front of their heavy guns, in fact it was the position of honor and was given to Co. B and Co. E. We would have put down all the necessary fixings in way of gun beds etc. and opened a correspondence with them but the knaves left, much to our chagrin. God only knows what slaughter there would have been for we had 7 4 1/2 in. rifles, 32 lb. Rodmen guns and 3 100 lb. parrots seige pets and it was confidently expected at the first fire we would have burst their earthworks which would have opened the way for the forlorn hope and given our light artillery a chance to take a part in the contest. . . .

Now suppose I tell you about the dangers to which I have been exposed lately. I had heard many exaggerated accounts of the terrific shelling N. 10 got but would hardly believe it, so it was with a feeling of awe and patriotism that I stood guard over some Co. property in the battalion one morning, sat quietly smoking my merschaum and thinking of you, the times of yore, when bang, whir and a 32 lb. shell exploded within a foot of me. I was so much amused looking at the men tumbling head over heels that I did not think of my danger until it was all over. This was the opening of hostilities on their part and the way they rattled shot, shell, grape and canister about our heads was a caution. They had excellent gunners and their solid 64 plowed up our embankment in a manner amusing to behold.

PRIVATE WILLIAM H. ANDREWS

1ST REGIMENT GEORGIA REGULARS, TOOMBS' BRIGADE

On April 28, the day after the anecdote recounted here occurred, shrapnel from an exploding shell struck Andrews above the left knee. The blast killed a friend lying next to him. Two months later, near the end of the Seven Days' Battles, Andrews was standing beside his brother when the brother was mortally wounded by a Yankee bullet. Another brother in the army died of disease. Andrews surrendered at Greensboro, North Carolina, on April 26, 1865.

Many nights while below the dam, we would sit with water up to our knees and sleep under the inspiring music of the frogs. Whoever thought there was music in the hollering and croaking of the frogs? Under certain circumstances there is. It is a well-known fact that frogs will not holler when the water is disturbed, and in that fact lay the music. As long as they kept up their music, we knew that the yankees were not crossing the swamp.

From some cause, I never knew what, there would be false alarms on the lines at night. Starting on the James River to our right, coming like a flash up the line, but when it would strike the Regulars would pass over and start on the other side. Don't think there was ever a gun fired in our regiment. The firing would usually draw the enemy's artillery fire for a few rounds. Then quiet would again reign supreme on the line. During the false alarm our pickets would have to get on the opposite side of the trees. One night, during a false alarm, the Regulars were stationed behind the heavy works. There was a large force of Negroes throwing up works in our front. They worked by details, one-half on duty, the others off. Sometime during the night the relief off duty lay down among the soldiers and went to sleep, but few soldiers being aware of their presence. During the night there was a false alarm. The Negroes to a man broke to the rear, and most of the soldiers with them, who on coming to their senses returned to the works, but the darkies did not return until the next night. One of them speaking to a soldier said, "Boss, I thought I could do some tall running, but that white-headed man there left me out of sight." He had reference to Pvt. Carolen of Company M who run about two miles before he could stop himself. Sgt. Garrett run 75 yards before he knew what he was doing and then made his way back faster than he went off. Don't think he got over his run for six months or more. The sergeant did not like the idea of acting the coward, even if he was asleep.

McClellan established his headquarters on the lower Peninsula close by this abandoned farmhouse, built beside a branch of Wormley's Creek not far from its conjunction with the York River. The house was photographed by G. H. Houghton of Brattleboro, Vermont, who had traveled to Virginia to compile a pictorial record of the Vermont troops fighting there.

LIEUTENANT ROBERT H. MILLER
14TH LOUISIANA INFANTRY, PRYOR'S BRIGADE

On April 9, when Miller wrote to his mother back home in Concordia Parish, Louisiana, the 14th was camped at Wynn's Mill on the Warwick River defense line. The regiment had moved there on March 27 after the Yankees had driven it away from Ship Point, a strip of land projecting into the mouth of the Poquoson River. Miller lost his life on August 29, 1862, at Second Manassas.

On this line we are now stationed, two miles and a half from Yorktown, and are to guard a place across a creek called Dam No. 1, which is a narrow pathway of dirt the same as a line to make the water above it too deep to cross. Our Reg. is strung along each side of this Dam for the space of three hundred yards on each side in one rank—we have dug Rifle pits, and are compelled to eat—sleep and stand in them from day to night and from night to day. Three days ago, ended the pleasure and novelty for then the April sunshine changed to rain, and the heavens have been weeping bitter *bitter-cold* tears ever since perhaps for the prospect of blasted human happiness that is so soon to follow.

On the last day of the fine weather the Federals having put their batteries in order commenced the Ball, at some points with Artillery at others with musket and bayonet, and our army gave them back as good as they sent, and better, we have better artillerists than the Yankees, and guns equally as good. They were repulsed by our infantry and their batteries silenced by ours, but it was a long Twenty-four hours to us. We had one little six pounder to aid us but we thought so little of it that we did not use it atall preferring to keep it in mock until they should approach it. So we sat quietly in our rifle pits until they should cease firing their shells at us. But away over behind us on a little elevation we had a splendid Parrott Gun, and this gun, struck with a Shrapnell Shot the carraige of one the enemies finest pieces (32 lb. dr.) and tore it all to pieces.

The shell they threw at us, and which (though we were in the woods) fell in the midst of us were "Schrapnell Shot" that is an iron case containing upwards of a hundred ounce lead balls and inside *powder*. I saw one go through a large pine tree 2 ft. thick and burst on the opposite side without appearing to have met with any more resistance than if the tree had been a pillar of smoke. It is utterly surprising how any of them escape killing some one but out of the number that were thrown at us (I should think Three Hundred) only one Lieut. and two privates were hurt.

It is pretty generally known here that Gen. McClellan, Heintzelman, and McDowell, of the Yankees are on the Peninsula with an army of 150,000 men, as all their Grand army has been brought from the Potomac. We have received already ten thousand reinforcements, from the army of Manassas, and they are still coming in. Before you receive this letter you will have heard how the "battle of Yorktown" has gone and I doubt not that this one will be as memorable in history as its predecessor. And I think too it will end the war like the last one did. For here have the heads of Departments *met*—Mr. Lincoln on one side going to Richmond, Mr. Davis on the other going to Washington. What a crash there will be when these trains meet!! And how many lives lost by the accident!! War looks a great deal better in the Newspapers, than any where else, but I think the most unpleasant remembrances of the Strife are these same *schrapnell shot*. They get to us some seconds before the report of the powder that sent them so that the first thing we know of them a shrill whistle unlike any thing you or I ever heard, before, then the sharp bell-like crack of the bomb—the whistle of the little balls like bumble-bees—then the report of the Gun—but it all comes so nearly at the same time that it takes a very *fine ear* to distinguish which is first.

PRIVATE OLIVER W. NORTON
83D PENNSYLVANIA INFANTRY, BUTTERFIELD'S BRIGADE

As a colorbearer and bugler, Norton was usually at the elbow of an officer and thus in a better position than most privates to see the larger picture of the campaign. In this letter to his sister he describes the digging of earthworks in front of Yorktown. Hard duty on the Peninsula caused Norton's weight to drop from 135 to 117 pounds, but he assured his family that his health was fine.

I have nothing more to do to-day, but it is not so with all the regiment. I can hear them calling the roll in some of the other companies, and one company just passed armed with "Irish spoons," going out to work in the trenches. Six of our companies, including K, went out at daylight yesterday and worked all day in the rain. It was a very disagreeable day and we came back at night soaked through, cold and hungry, but as merry a lot of fellows as you ever saw. You won't understand the thing very well unless I describe it particularly. I think I told you about there being a large field in front of the forts. A trench four feet deep and twelve feet wide and over a mile long is to be dug on

Reconnaissance in force by Genl Gorman before Yorktown.
Rebel Battery only three hundred yards distant behind the woods

Federal troops stop for a rest during one of their numerous probes of the Confederate lines in front of Yorktown in this sketch by Winslow Homer, then a 26-year-old freelance artist commissioned by Harper's Weekly to record life at the front. Homer spent part of each year between 1861 and 1865 recording military scenes with his pencil, pen, and paintbrush. Altogether he produced 180 wartime sketches, wood engravings, watercolors, and oils.

this side of the field just in front of the woods. We followed a road up one of the ravines till we came to our pickets and then one by one crept cautiously up into the ditch. A ditch two or three feet deep and wide enough to walk in had been dug during the night and dirt thrown up in front so that by stooping down we were concealed. One thousand men filed in there the whole length of the ditch and then each one laying his gun on the bank within reach, commenced picking or shoveling the dirt up on to the bank. The rebel forts were in plain sight and their sharpshooters were within thirty rods of us, hidden in rifle pits, so that, if a fellow got his head above the bank, he might get a bullet in his cap.

We soon got a bank high enough to stand up behind and then it would have done you good to see the dirt go out of that ditch. Many hands make light work, and I tell you our regiment and the Sixty-second handled a pile of dirt. We had two reliefs—I went in at 6 o'clock and worked till noon and then the other relief worked till night. Last night there were 10,000 men at work all night and as many more to-day, so you may guess there is something going on here. George says that when he gets ready, he will throw one hundred and thirty shells per minute into each of those forts. I think there will be lively dodging there if nobody is hurt. Oh, we are gaining on them slowly but surely.

CORPORAL VALERIUS C. GILES
4TH TEXAS INFANTRY, HOOD'S BRIGADE

Giles recounts one of the amusing events he and his comrades experienced on the Peninsula. The 4th Texas's bivouac was close to the spot where George Washington's Continental army had camped in 1781 before its climactic victory over Charles, Lord Cornwallis' British Redcoats, ending the Revolutionary War. "Many amusing things happened while we were at Yorktown," Giles recalled. "Fun and misery went with us everywhere, and if we were merry today we were sad tomorrow."

The Little Warwick River separated the two picket lines down at Dam No. 1 and Dam No. 2. Dam No. 1 had backed the water until the lake or pond was nearly 200 yards wide above it. On our side the breastworks were built of logs, and the men were quite safe and comfortable after they got behind them. The picket guard was always relieved at night so as to prevent the enemy from seeing, and they practiced the same tactics.

Just across the pond, opposite one section of our works, a two-story house had been burned, leaving nothing but the two old brick chimneys standing. They stood there in the solitude, charred relics of grim-visaged war. One of those energetic Yankee sharpshooters located himself behind the chimney that stood nearest the water, and by some means secured a footing that brought his body up to the fireplace in the second story. Then he removed a brick making a porthole big enough to poke his gun barrel through. That gave him a down pull on our breastworks, and he paralyzed section No. 4, which was immediately in front of him.

The boys located him by the smoke from his rifle and blazed away at the old chimney, but it did no good. He appeared to be there to stay. A novel and original idea struck some of the soldiers, and I think it was Sergeant Dick Skinner who crawled out and hunted up old Captain Riley, who commanded the field battery attached to the Texas Brigade. He enlisted the sympathy of that gruff old Irishman, who volunteered to take one of his Napoleon guns down and fix Mr. Yank right.

He concealed his cannon in the thick brush a little back from our position and went at his work very deliberately, cutting away the boughs that obstructed his view and sighting his gun with care. While he was getting things arranged to suit him, Mr. Yank was amusing himself by shooting holes through old hats held a little above the logs on the ends of ramrods. Finally, old Riley turned his Napoleon loose with a roar that rippled the water in the little lake and filled the woods with black smoke.

The shell struck the old chimney center about six feet from the

Equipped with a four-power telescopic sight, this .45-caliber, 14-pound James target rifle delivered accurate fire at ranges up to 500 yards. The weapon was used by Berdan's Sharpshooters to pick off Confederates manning the earthworks at Yorktown. The expert riflemen were organized by Hiram Berdan, an amateur target shooter from New York who was recognized in 1861 as America's foremost marksman. Before accepting a volunteer, Berdan required him to pass an exacting test— placing 10 consecutive shots on a target 10 inches in diameter from a distance of 200 yards. The sharpshooters wore forest green uniforms for camouflage.

ground. Brick, mortar and dust filled the air and the lot came tumbling over our way. That smart alec of a Yankee came sailing through space, his coat tails standing in the breeze like the latter end of a comet. Arms spread out wing fashion, hatless and without a gun, he fell in the mud, but fell running.

Wet as a beaver, he scrambled up the sleek bank and was exposed to our fire for more than fifty yards. It was a run for life, with whoops, yells, bullets and laughter following him. We could hear the Yankees shouting and holloaing "Go it!" while the Johnny Rebs took at least fifty wing shots at him, but he made good his escape. Old Captain Riley was so elated with the fine shot he made and the fun it created that he laughed until the tears rolled down his wrinkled old cheeks.

Private George W. King of Hinds County, Mississippi, died of disease while serving in the Warwick River defenses in front of Yorktown on April 12, 1862. He was 20 years old. He had been mustered into the 12th Mississippi Infantry on April 30, 1861, at Corinth, and his regiment had yet to experience combat.

LIEUTENANT CHARLES H. BREWSTER
10TH MASSACHUSETTS INFANTRY, DEVENS' BRIGADE

Virginia was an exotic new world to the 27-year-old New Englander, and not just because of the annoying wood ticks he describes here. "This country is a constant wonder," he wrote. "To think that we are in the oldest settled part of the United States and yet the country is almost all forest, and the houses are miles apart."

This part of their works is on the bank of a creek and before them is an open field and our men have thrown up earthworks nearer and nearer every night until they have got within 400 yards of the enemys works and behind them are posted Berdans sharpshooters, and they can hit the size of a man's head or hand at this distance every time and they have killed quantities of them so that they have not fired a big gun at our side for two days, for the moment a gunner shows himself to load a piece that minute dies. . . . I went up there twice yesterday, and there was not a living thing to be seen about the rebel works they dare not show so much as a coat tail.

I suppose when all things are ready we shall have to make a grand charge over them and take those batteries. I wish some of the grumblers at the north that are in such a hurry to have a fight could come down here and try it on. I am willing to exchange my share of this life with them, without any compensation to boot. we get to sleep at night jump up three or four times in the night and form line of battle, find it a false alarm and lie down again, get up in the morning and strip off our clothes and go to digging Wood Ticks out of our flesh, then wash all over, and as likely as not have to perform the same operation again before noon. we are all covered with little sores caused by these wretches and there is no help for it. they are as thick as leaves, and thicker for every leaf is occupied by half a dozen of them. they are hard shiny backed fellows and it takes a hammer and chisel to kill one of them.

SERGEANT AUGUST MEYERS
2D U.S. INFANTRY, SYKES' BRIGADE

Meyers' regiment supplied a portion of the 80,000 men at Yorktown who built roads, dug earthworks and trenches, and transported and mounted siege guns. When the Confederates withdrew on May 3, "there was great cheering in all the camps as they received the news, and the bands played patriotic airs like mad," Meyers recalled. "We seemed to be celebrating a great victory and forgot our tremendous and useless labor during the siege operations."

The first work my regiment did was to assist in building corduroy roads between the camps and Shipping Point on the York river, where the army supply depots were. These roads had to be substantially built for the transportation of heavy siege guns and all kinds of army supplies. This work was severe and frequent cold rains added to our misery; but it had to be done quickly, regardless of weather conditions. Early in the morning a detail of about one-half the regiment, furnished with axes, picks and spades, marched to a part of the Shipping Point road and commenced work. We cut down trees, trimmed them and dragged the logs to their places; we filled in low spots and dug ditches to drain the water from swampy sections, often standing in mud and water to do it. At noon we were allowed an hour's rest to make coffee and eat our rations. About sundown we quit work and returned to camp, very tired and glad that we could rest all of the next day, while the other half of the regiment was at work.

The sick list increased while this work went on, but it was soon finished and then we furnished detachments to work on trenches which were a part of the siege operations of the investment of Yorktown, consisting of ditches and earth breastworks running in long zigzag lines, constantly approaching the enemy's works. New lines were always begun in the night, but strong works for mounting siege guns and batteries were hurried along night and day, in spite of the enemy's frequent shelling, which was answered by our gun-boats in the York river; and generally they were soon silenced by them. After sundown the soldiers who had been detailed for work on the trenches during the night formed ranks and marched to a place where picks and shovels were furnished us; then we neared the place where the work was to be done and concealed ourselves in the woods, which were abundant in the vicinity of Yorktown, and awaited very quietly until darkness had set in. We were then led out into the open fields in front of the Rebel works, where we found pegs driven and lines put up by the engineers, indicating the direction in which the new line of trenches was to be dug. We were cautioned to make as little noise as possible with our tools and no talking was allowed, for the Rebel pickets might be near. The men began digging a wide trench, throwing the dirt in front of them to form a breastwork; and they worked very hard indeed until they had dug a hole deep enough to lie down in, then they took it easier.

As a non-commissioned officer I did not have to do any of the digging; I superintended my section and kept them at work, but the nights were still cold and raw and I often relieved a tired private for a while to warm up; besides I was as much interested as any of them to make a hole in the ground deep enough to protect me when the enemy fired at us.

All through the night, at almost regular intervals of about fifteen minutes, a single gun in the forts at Yorktown fired a shell in our direc-

tion, which passed over us and exploded or buried itself in the ground somewhere behind us. On the half-dozen occasions when I was on such a detail I can recall only one shell bursting over us which severely wounded two men of a regiment working next to ours. When the gun was fired at Yorktown a mile or more away, there was a flash in the sky and a sergeant on watch called out "Lie down!" when we immediately dropped flat on the ground or into the trench. About the time we heard the report of the gun, the shell was passing over us. The interval of time between seeing the flash of the gun and hearing the report was just about sufficient for us to drop for protection. Occasionally the Union gunboats in the river fired a few rounds in the direction of the Rebel gun which was annoying us and had the effect of silencing it for an hour or two. At the first streak of daybreak we ceased digging and returned to camp, depositing our entrenching tools where we had received them.

Armed with axes instead of muskets, soldiers of a Federal infantry company perform the arduous duty of laying corduroy, a surface of cut logs laid across the roadbed. In the spring rains the roads of Virginia's Peninsula, cut through poorly drained, sandy soil and intended for relatively light rural civilian traffic, quickly turned to quagmires under the weight of marching armies.

SERGEANT J. J. MCDANIEL
7TH SOUTH CAROLINA INFANTRY, KERSHAW'S BRIGADE

After employing a variety of stratagems to slow McClellan down, Johnston's and Magruder's forces, collectively known as the Army of Northern Virginia, began their difficult, mud-hampered retreat from Yorktown on May 3 toward a new defensive line nearer Richmond. By March 1863 the 7th South Carolina was so worn down from fighting that McDaniel was commanding a company, a post he held until wounded during a skirmish on July 20 of that year.

It having been determined to fall back, we found it necessary to make a feint to cover the retreat, and while the wagon trains and main army were being hurried off, the 7th and 3d S.C. regiments were sent down to Land's End, junction of Warwick and James rivers. We went down 30th April; on the opposite side of the river the Yankees were thrown into activity at our approach. We were strung out, and built large camp fires through the woods, making the appearance of a large force. About dark, with our fires lighting up the whole face of the heavens, we were silently withdrawn, and ordered back to camps. We had scarcely left our illuminated camps when the enemy began to shell them furiously, which occasioned many a merry laugh. But now, though escaping the enemy's missiles, we were severely tested; we are near eight miles from camp—very dark and raining—the road is about impassable to wagons, in places *belly* deep. Coming down we could see and leave the main track, but not so now; it is with difficulty we feel our way through the almost impenetrable darkness and deep mud. Many a soldier measured his length. I saw one fall two or three times in succession, producing the hearty yells of all around. Many stepped into *mudholes*, sinking up the length of their legs. We arrived in squads at camp from midnight till day, begrimed with mud and drenched with rain.

THE REBEL HEADQUARTERS in Ravine YORKTOWN Va During the Siege

No breeze disturbs the first national banner of the Confederacy as it hangs outside an artillery officer's quarters at Yorktown. Across the York River lies Gloucester Point, which the Rebels had also fortified with heavy artillery. The Confederacy's command of this narrow stretch of the York prevented Yankee ships from ascending the river until the evacuation of May 3.

Curious Yankees inspect a captured Rebel battery heavily damaged by the fire of Union flag officer Louis M. Goldsborough's gunboats. The ground is littered with material from destroyed cotton bales the gunners had used in place of sandbags.

PRIVATE J. W. MINNICH
DeGournay's Battalion, Louisiana Artillery, Rains' Brigade

From devilish modern "torpedoes"—artillery shells rigged with pressure detonators and buried as antipersonnel land mines—to archaic pikes, the Confederate army used a wide array of weaponry during the Peninsula campaign. Though the torpedoes planted at Yorktown came from the mind of Confederate brigadier general Gabriel J. Rains, many Southerners frowned upon their use, considering them dishonorable and cowardly weapons.

We did not receive the order to open up a "slow, steady fire" until near sunset of the evening before the evacuation; and then the whole line, from Peyton's nine-inch Dahlgrens on the river bluff to Magruder, opened up a slow, continuous fire, ours being the last heavy gun on the line. . . . We fired the last shot after midnight. Before

that hour we in our battery realized that we were to move out before day, whatever the rest of the army may have thought. Whether we did any damage or not we never knew, but it was a grand sight to see the shells, flaming fuses, flying through the clear, starlit night and the flashings of bursting shells in the direction of the enemy's lines. Whether any one else knew it or not, we knew we were throwing away ammunition.

Gradually, toward midnight, the firing slackened, and then finally ceased, and we marched out and took our way to and through Yorktown, under the guidance of a lieutenant of General Rains's staff, to enable us to avoid the torpedoes which General Rains had caused to be planted in the road inside the works in Yorktown. After leading us to the upper part of the town, the lieutenant, telling us we were out of any danger from torpedoes, disappeared. . . .

. . . About a mile from Yorktown we found a troop of cavalry drawn up beside the road, and when asked, "What command is this?" they promptly answered: "The Jeff Davis Legion." It was about this time, when light was appearing in the east, that we heard explosions at short intervals in Yorktown and were convinced they were the torpedoes planted in the road, according to our guide. But from some cause they soon ceased. We thought, of course, the Federals caused the explosions in their early pursuit of the Confederates; . . . But we did not hurry our steps because of that; we felt assured that they would not overtake us with the advance we had and the bad roads. Besides, we had the "Jeff Davis Legion" behind us, and we had our trusty steel-pointed pikes to repel them with.

A word about those pikes may not be out of place here. When the Zouave battalion was organized, we were sent to Pensacola and were armed with the converted Springfield muskets and drilled with them, Zouave drill and tactics, which differed somewhat from the "Upton" and "Hardee Tactics and Manual." The latter had been adopted by the Confederate government and was more strenuous than either and [had] more complicated maneuverings. When my Company was detached at Yorktown and merged into the heavy artillery, we still retained our muskets. But there was a shortage of small arms in the Confederacy with which to arm the new regiments being formed, and in their place were issued pikes to the heavy artillerists designed to "repel boarders," as a couple of old tars in our company expressed it, and in which theory we as a whole put little faith. But we were most thoroughly drilled in their use as "Lancers afoot," or foot lancers. Fortunately, or otherwise, we were never called upon to use them, either offensively or defensively, though they would have proved quite an effective barrier in a narrow road against a cavalry charge. The pikes were eight feet long and stout, with most villainous two by twelve inch long double-edged knife blades fixed to the business end. General Rains was the genius who evolved the idea, unless I err.

At any rate, we continued our route across country, and about 4 P.M. passed through Williamsburg, marching heads up and pikes at a right "carry arms," and were reviewed by "Grand Old Jo," who stood on the stoop of the main or principal hostelry of the town and watched us with an approving smile, wondering, no doubt, if we had not leaped full armed from the shades of the Middle Ages.

CHAPLAIN NICHOLAS A. DAVIS
4TH TEXAS INFANTRY, HOOD'S BRIGADE

During their westward retreat from Yorktown, the Rebel columns could average scarcely more than one mile in an hour through the hard rain and the deep, sticky mud of the Peninsula's poorly drained roads. This colorful account of the march comes from Davis' history of the 4th Texas, printed by the Presbyterian Committee of Publication of the Confederate States. It was printed in 1863, which made it one of the earliest regimental histories published by either side.

About noon on ——, we decamped, and, though constantly in motion, only reached the Chickahominy, *about six miles*, by 1 o'clock at night. This was owing to the fact, that the road was blocked up by the rear of our artillery and baggage train, and not daring to lie down or rest, we could only "mark time" in the rain and mud until the hour above mentioned, when all others having passed over, we reached the bridge. Here we found several Generals, with their attendant aids and couriers, all exhorting us to "close up," and for God's sake to hurry. This was more easily said, than done, for the roads had been cut by artillery and wagons, until a perfect mortar had been formed from one to three feet deep, and through this below, and a heavy soaking rain above, the men floundered on. At length, losing all patience, General Whiting dashed upon the bridge. "Hurry up, men, hurry up, don't mind a little mud." "D'ye call this a *little mud!* s'pose you git down and try it, stranger; I'll hold your horse." "Do you know whom you address, sir? I am General Whiting." "General ——, don't you reckon I know a *General* from a long-tongued courier?" says the fellow, as he disappeared in the darkness. This, repeated with sundry variations several times, at length discouraged the General, and leav-

ing the Texans, whose spirits he had threatened to subdue, to cross as best they might, he rode away. Finally all were safely landed on this side the Chickahominy, and without waiting to eat or build fires, the men threw themselves upon the muddy ground, and slept soundly until morning.

PRIVATE J. W. MINNICH
DEGOURNAY'S BATTALION, LOUISIANA ARTILLERY, RAINS' BRIGADE

After abandoning the Yorktown defenses, Minnich and a companion, Ed Kelly, spent the night in Williamsburg. Awakened by the sound of artillery fire from Fort Magruder on the morning of May 5, the two Louisianans found that they had been left behind by their unit and promptly set out for Richmond through driving rain. They still carried their pikes, which, Minnich recalled, made them look as if they had "leaped full armed from the shades of the Middle Ages."

Turning our backs to the firing, Kelly and I started up the road on the sixty-mile tramp to Richmond through mud and water. There had been a lull in the rainfall, but scarcely had we left the town when it began again and in volume appeared desirous of making up for lost time. A mile or so out from the town the water came down in torrents for a while. It was then that we came upon Rodes's brigade, waiting by the roadside in the woods, while Kelly and I plodded along through mud and water almost knee deep in the old sunken road. Under other circumstances we probably would have been subject to some chaffing by the infantry, but they were too miserable themselves to indulge in any verbal gymnastics. Besides, General Rodes himself was not beyond earshot. Standing by the roadside with his arms folded under the cape of his great coat, he was listening to the sounds of battle in our rear. I never have forgotten the picture he made. . . . We stopped and saluted, . . . he smiled his slow, genial smile, and asked: "And what did you expect to do with your pikes?" That was a poser; I had never thought about what a ridiculous figure we would have presented among infantry on the firing line. I told him frankly that I had never thought about that. Saluting again, we trudged on, the water getting deeper until it came almost to our knees.

Two Mexican War-era 32-pounder cannons of a Confederate battery situated on the York River just below Yorktown shimmer under a relentless Virginia sun in this photograph taken after the Federals occupied the city. For a month the Union's naval forces had been held at bay by such antiquated artillery.

BRIGADIER GENERAL WILLIAM F. BARRY
CHIEF OF ARTILLERY, ARMY OF THE POTOMAC

A veteran of the Mexican and Seminole Wars, Barry was picked by McClellan to organize the Army of the Potomac's artillery force. In 1864, after commanding the heavy ordnance that defended Washington, D.C., Barry served as Sherman's chief of artillery during the Atlanta campaign and the subsequent march to the sea.

When it was believed at daybreak May 4, 1862, that the enemy had evacuated Yorktown and its defenses, our pickets and skirmishers and subsequently larger bodies of our troops immediately advanced to occupy the abandoned lines. Before reaching the glacis of the main work, and at the distance of more than 100 yards from it, several of our men were injured by the explosion of what was ascertained to be loaded shells buried in the ground. These shells were the ordinary 8 or 10 inch mortar or columbiad shells, filled with powder, buried a few inches below the surface of the ground, and so arranged with some fulminate, or with the ordinary artillery friction primer, that they exploded by being trod upon or otherwise disturbed. In some cases articles of common use, and which would be most likely to be picked up, such as engineers' wheelbarrows, or pickaxes, or shovels, were laid upon the spot with apparent carelessness. Concealed strings or wires leading from the friction primer of the shell to the superincumbent articles were so arranged that the slightest disturbance would occasion the explosion. These shells were not thus placed on the glacis at the bottom of the ditch, &c., which, in view of an anticipated assault, might possibly be considered a legitimate use of them, but they were basely planted by an enemy who was secretly abandoning his post on common roads, at springs of water, in the shade of trees, at the foot of telegraph poles, and, lastly, quite within the defenses of the place—in the very streets of the town. A number of our men were killed by them before the disgraceful trick was discovered and information of the fact could be given to the troops. Careful examinations were at once made, and sentinels were posted wherever the existence of these infernal machines was ascertained or suspected. Major-General McClellan ordered that the Confederate prisoners taken by us at Yorktown should be made to search for these buried shells and to disinter and destroy them when found. I was myself a witness of the horrible mangling by one of these shells of a cavalryman and his horse outside of the main work upon the Williamsburg road, and also of the cruel murder in the very streets of Yorktown of an intelligent young telegraph operator, who, while in the act of approaching a telegraph pole to reconnect a broken wire, trod upon one of these shells villainously concealed at its foot.

SURGEON GEORGE T. STEVENS
77TH NEW YORK INFANTRY, DAVIDSON'S BRIGADE

Although the 77th would eventually become a hardy veteran regiment that experienced the loss of 273 men to illness and combat during the war, the Peninsula campaign was the unit's first real field service. The enemy's use of land mines incensed the green New Yorkers and quickly disabused them of any romantic notions of war they may have harbored when they enlisted in November 1861. So angry was McClellan at the use of torpedoes, he ordered that Confederate prisoners be forced to dig up and disarm the "infernal machines."

During the night of the evacuation, the roar of artillery exceeded anything that had been heard before. From one end of the line to the other the shells and shot poured into our camps, and the arches of fire that marked the courses of the shells, with flame spouting from the mouths of the guns, created a magnificent pyrotechnic display. But at daylight, orderlies flew from regiment to regiment with the startling intelligence that the beleagured works were deserted, and with orders to occupy them at once. Smith's division hastened to cross over the dam, and we found ourselves in the strongholds that we had so long invested. As the

Seventy-seventh regiment passed along one of the roads leading among the intrenchments, a sharp report like that of a pistol was heard at the feet of those in the center of the column, and directly under the colors. The men scattered, and a piece of old cloth was seen lying on the ground at the point from which the report emanated. Colonel McKean, who was very near, lifted the cloth with the point of his sword, and discovered a torpedo carefully buried in the ground, except a nipple which had been filled with fulminating powder, which was covered by the old cloth. The fuse only had exploded. Had the machine itself exploded, it must have destroyed many of our men, our colonel among them. Other regiments were not so fortunate as we were. Very many men were killed in the streets and intrenchments by these torpedoes, which the enemy had planted in the street at either end of the bridges, about springs, and near the deserted guns. They were concealed beneath the ground with great care, the capped nipple only rising above the surface, and this, covered by an old rag or piece of bark thrown over it, exploded at the slightest touch. These infernal machines were only one feature of the general plan of our enemies to carry on a war by brutal, savage and cowardly means.

Lieutenant Gordon McKay (left) of the 22d Massachusetts Infantry was seriously wounded when he stepped on a buried torpedo as Union soldiers cautiously explored the abandoned fortifications at Yorktown on May 4 after the Confederate withdrawal.

PRIVATE FREDERICK E. DENNIS
8TH NEW JERSEY INFANTRY, STARR'S BRIGADE

A three-year enlistee from Trenton, New Jersey, Dennis writes with irrepressible enthusiasm of the Union army's pursuit of the Rebels after Yorktown. He was later severely wounded at the Battle of Second Manassas on August 29, 1862, left on the field during the Yankee withdrawal, and captured and held by the Rebels until exchanged in December 1862. The crippled soldier then finished out his military service in the Veteran Reserve Corps.

While we were at breakfast on Sunday morning the news spread through the camps like wildfire that the enemy had evacuated his works, and on the heels of that news orders rang along the lines to strike tents and take 100 rounds of ammunition and three days' rations.

The old 8th N.J. was quick to respond in unison with the grand array stretched for miles to the right and left. It was a scene I shall never forget—the drums beating, the bugles blaring, the hurried clatter of mounted officers and their escorts, the rumble of artillery, the din of voices intermingled with the unmusical clatter of tin plates and cups being packed for the march. The sun beat down fiercely on our heads, but what mattered that, for were we not going to catch up with the enemy and "wallop him out of his boots" before he had time to get in line of battle to defend himself?

About noon the order was given to move, and with light hearts and heavy knapsacks we plunged ahead with beating drums to overtake the fleeing rebels. Across the plain with flying colors we tramped toward the frowning battlements, now silent, and the ugly looking cannon pointed at us, but spiked and made useless by the enemy. As we entered the breastworks we were warned to beware of torpedoes and other infernal machines. Here and there were iron rods and sticks driven into the ground to denote the dangerous spots, and we trod with

While chasing the Rebels west of Yorktown, Union artillerymen carefully pick their way across the Warwick River on the narrow dam at Lee's Mill, one of the river's few crossing points. Just a few weeks earlier, Vermont soldiers on a reconnaissance sortie to this location had been subjected to a withering fire from Confederate troops posted in the earthworks visible on the far side of the river.

extreme caution about those dangerous signals. It behooved us to move with care, for several of the boys had "monkeyed" around in their anxiety to see how the old thing worked, and the results were disastrous.

The terrible dust and the intense heat were almost unendurable, and our love of country and its flag began to wane. Some of us dearly wished that the fleeing rebels would turn back and kindly allow us to wallop them. Our halts were frequent, caused by the obstructions thrown in our path, and which the Pioneer Corps was forced to remove. Very late came the order to halt for the night, and all of us wondered what the following day would bring forth.

MAJOR CHARLES S. WAINWRIGHT

CHIEF OF ARTILLERY, HOOKER'S DIVISION

During the opening stages of the Battle of Williamsburg, Wainwright tried to position Battery H, 1st U.S. Artillery, to support the advance of the infantry. The gunners fled in terror at the first hint of Rebel fire, causing Wainwright to order volunteer artillerymen to man the cannon so disgracefully abandoned by the regulars.

The rain was coming down in torrents, making all objects at any distance very indistinct. The road by which we had come up lay through a heavy wood for half a mile or more behind us; some hundred yards inside this wood it made a thorough cut of say thirty yards in length, the bank being six to eight feet high on either side. On both sides of the road the rebs had felled a large amount of the timber as it debouches into the plain in front of Williamsburg. Directly up the road, about eight hundred yards from where we stood at the outer edge of the felled timber, was a large redoubt from which they were firing quite lively. To the right and left of this one we could see a number of other earthworks in the distance; on our left there seemed to be a field battery behind the crest of a knoll (have since found that it was in a small redoubt built in a hollow so that the top of the parapet was about

on a level with the top of the crest). On our side of the plain I could see nothing but woods on either hand with a heavy slashing of felled trees in front. The road was the only way to get on to the plain, and that would be ugly enough for some five hundred yards; the rebel redoubt, Fort Magruder, having a raging fire down it. Still I thought the open plain the proper place, and told the General so; but he said he could not support the batteries out there, his pickets only being at the outer edge of the slashing. On our left the slashing extended up the road about three hundred yards farther than it did on the right, a large triangular field having been lately cleared there, and planted in corn last year. Not being able to go out on to the plain, I told the General that the only place left one was this fallow lot; but I might get a couple of guns in the road. "Get them in then as quick as you can," were his orders.

Going back to the edge of the woods, where Captain Webber had halted his battery, I directed him to put his first piece out at the farthest corner of the slashing in the road; his second also in the road but some twenty yards to the rear, a slight bend in the road here placing them thus in echelon; and the other two sections in the newly cleared field to the right of the road: leaving his caissons in the wood. He at once moved out himself with the first section, while I directed the posting of the other two. Gaps in the fence were pulled down, and after a great deal of trouble from bad drivers and balky horses I got them all in. Almost before the first piece had turned into the field, Lieutenant Eakin fell at my feet terribly wounded in the shoulder. We were both of us on foot, he standing about four feet in front of me. A shell struck the road half a dozen yards from us and burst as it fell, a piece of it entering his left shoulder just below the collar bone; he fell against me, and at once called out that he was a dead man. I got a couple of men to carry him off, but had full occupation myself driving the horses of the guns up to the pulling point. At last, I had all four guns posted; when looking around what was my horror, on seeing that nearly all the limber had cleared off under shelter of the woods, and that there was not more than one or two men near each gun. This was an awful beginning for one's first battle, and knowing what a wretched battery this was, I reproached myself with having so far yielded to Webber's claims as senior officer as to have given him the advance instead of Bramhall.

Rushing back to the road, where the men had hid themselves behind the large felled trees, I met Webber, without his hat, covered with mud and almost wild. "Major," says he, "Lieutenant Pike and two men have been hit and I cannot get the others up to their guns." Though we slammed at them with our sabres, and poked them out with the point, it was no good; drive two or three to a gun, and by the time you got some more up the first had hid again. Never in my life was I so mortified, never so excited, never so mad. It had at any rate the good effect of making me forget my own danger, and the place was an awful hot one there in the road.

"The road was the only way to get on to the plain, and that would be ugly enough for some five hundred yards."

"ON TO RICHMOND".—GREAT BATTLE OF WILLIAMSBURG, VA., ON THE PENINSULA BETWEEN YORK AND JAMES RIVERS, MAY 6.—FROM A SKETCH BY OUR SPECIAL ARTIST WITH GEN. McCLELLAN'S ARMY.—SEE PAGE 105.

Battle lines of Brigadier General Joseph Hooker's division press toward the Confederate strongpoint of Fort Magruder in this engraving printed in Frank Leslie's Illustrated Newspaper. During the Battle of Williamsburg on May 5, General James Longstreet's division turned and counterattacked to slow the Yankee advance, abetted by mismanagement among the Union high command that prevented the Federals from bringing their superior numbers to bear on the stubborn Rebel rear guard.

SERGEANT A. R. WALKER
2D NEW HAMPSHIRE INFANTRY, GROVER'S BRIGADE

Ordered to the front by General Hooker to provide support for Wainwright's beleaguered artillery, Walker and his comrades had to struggle through a large "slashing" of trees the Confederates had cut down for defensive purposes. The 2d's colonel, Gilman Marston, bitterly reported that the regiment then lay exposed to a heavy fire of musketry from the "rebel barbarian[s]" that cost his unit 82 men killed or wounded.

About 5 o'clock the next morning we started again, and after marching about two miles we came out of the woods, and the "hummingbirds" (as we called the rifle-balls) began to whistle past our ears, and the brigade was immediately drawn up in line of battle with the 2d New Hampshire and 11th Massachusetts, on the right of the road, and the 1st Massachusetts and 26th Pennsylvania on the left. We had one company (B) that was armed with Sharp's rifles, and Gen. Grover, commanding the brigade, rode up and said: "I want that New Hampshire company with patent rifles; where are they?" So companies B and E were detached and deployed as skirmishers. An abatis of felled timber was in front of us for several rods, through which our skirmishers advanced, driving the enemy's pickets before them. We made our way through as best we could, and when we reached the edge of the slashing covered ourselves and awaited developments. A broad plain lay before us, across which we could see the spires and buildings of the city of Williamsburg. The enemy were posted behind a line of strong earthworks. Fort Magruder, mounting several heavy guns, was directly in front of us. On either side were thirteen smaller redoubts reaching across the peninsula. The plain in front was dotted with rifle-pits, each occupied by a sharpshooter. For three weary hours did our solitary brigade hold this position with a wet, drizzling rain pouring down upon us, and wondering where the balance of the army was.

PRIVATE EDMUND D. PATTERSON
9TH ALABAMA INFANTRY, WILCOX'S BRIGADE

Wilcox's brigade spearheaded a hard-driving counterattack through the slashing that drove back Hooker's men. Patterson, an Ohioan by birth, was later captured at Gettysburg and endured a forced return to the Buckeye State when he was incarcerated at the Johnson's Island prisoner of war camp in Lake Erie.

Early in the morning we heard heavy firing not more than a mile and a half from town, and could see from the smoke that our artillery was replying gallantly to that of the enemy. I was not much surprised when we were ordered to "fall in" and were marched back through the streets of Williamsburg. Women were to be seen everywhere, some with water for the soldiers, others offering to take care of blankets, while others still, who had relatives in the army, wept and wrung their hands in agony. We marched hurriedly through the town and in the direction of the firing. After getting out of town we stopped a few minutes in the wheat field and were ordered to load our pieces. In front of us and to our right the artillery thundered forth death,—the day dark and gloomy and the rain falling steadily. The smoke settled down over the hills and valleys and added to the general gloom. I can never forget my thoughts as I stood there and looked around, though they were *feelings* rather than thoughts, for they were undefinable. It was the first time that I had ever been called upon to face death. I felt that in a few moments some of us standing here, vainly trying to jest and appear careless, would be in eternity. Would it be this friend, or that one, or myself? I did not feel at all afraid—the feeling called *fear* did not enter my breast, but it was a painful nervous anxiety, a longing for action, anything to occupy my attention—nerves relaxed and a dull feeling about the chest that made breathing painful. All the energies of my soul seemed concentrated in the one desire for action. We were not kept long in suspense for very soon orders came for us to go forward, to the right of the road; we advanced to the edge of the woods, where we joined our right to the left of the 19th Mississippi regiment, and then changed directions, and advanced in a course at right angles to the one pursued in entering the woods. Our line of battle was soon formed; our brigade on the extreme left of that part of the line and our regiment the extreme left of the brigade; our left was supported or protected by a battery which was engaged with a battery of the enemy's about three fourths of a mile in our front. The woods on our right were so dense that they completely hid from us the operations of the remainder of the brigade, with the exception of the 19th Mississippi, which was the next regiment to us. The place over which we had to pass was what in boyhood days I would have called "slashing."

It had been heavily timbered land, and all had been cut down, letting it fall in every direction, and it formed an almost insurmountable barrier. But we advanced slowly, climbing over logs, stumps, through tangled undergrowth, etc., when the crack of a rifle and the falling of a man announced to us that we were in range of the enemy's sharpshooters. Just as the firing began a mounted officer whom I did not know, but who was, I afterwards learned, Gen'l. Anderson of South Carolina, rode up and said, *"Go forward men, straight forward, don't halt at all."* We continued advancing as fast as we could under the circumstances, though it was impossible to preserve anything like a well formed line, and the Yankees being stationed and posted behind the logs had much the advantage of us, for we had to expose ourselves continually in getting over the logs, while we could but seldom get a shot at them. Among the first wounded in the regiment was June Bynum of my company. He had his gun to his face, and the moment he fired a ball struck him in the arm between the wrist and the elbow, passed through shattering the ulna, and then passed through the fleshy part of the arm near the shoulder. "D——n you," he said, "you have wounded me, but I finished one of you." In moving forward, our left companies were in a more exposed condition and suffered more than the right of the regiment. There was an open space between our regiment and the 19th Mississippi, and I was sent down to the right to ask Col. Mott to move his regiment a little farther to the left, but found that regiment, like our own, without much of a line, and Col. Mott dead. We remedied the difficulty as well as we could, and still advanced driving the Yankees before us for about one half a mile,—then there was a cry from some one, "They are flanking us on the left." And Col. Henry, cowardly, or at least foolishly ordered the regiment to fall back to the ravine, which was nearly a half a mile in our rear. The five left companies obeyed the

command, as perhaps we ought to have done, but we could see that we were leaving the 19th Mississippi exposed to a cross fire; besides the Yankees themselves were ready to run, and in fact were giving way at the time. We saw a battery in our front, and it was determined that we should charge it.

SERGEANT SALEM DUTCHER
7TH VIRGINIA INFANTRY, A. P. HILL'S BRIGADE

Responding to General Wilcox's request for reinforcements, the Virginians of A. P. Hill's command marched forward through a hail of Union artillery fire to pitch in to the action and help thwart the Federals' advance toward Williamsburg. Although Dutcher's entrance into the battle was less than auspicious, his bravery under fire was later noticed by Hill, who praised Dutcher's "efficiency and gallantry" in his report of the engagement.

The battle opened, to me at least, most unexpectedly. I had slipped out of camp and was breakfasting with a young lady, when suddenly the ring of a field-piece clanged close by upon the air. Seizing musket and equipments I bolted out of doors *sans ceremonie* and made for the main street, visions of a court-martial floating before me. The sidewalks were full of infantry at double-quick, and artillery, staff officers, and couriers were coming down the roadway at a gallop. Some one told me Hill was on ahead, and, throwing away my blanket, I ran to the head of the column. The commanding officer could not tell me where my brigade was, and I kept on till I cleared the town. Here a group of staff officers were directing the troops, and in response to my query one of them pointed out a regiment just disappearing behind some pines on the further side of the main road. This road the Federals were shelling, and I began to realize that my little escapade had gotten me into a pretty serious predicament. If I crossed the road I ran the risk of being hit, and if I went back into town so as to work my way around, it was not likely I would find the regiment again, and it would be hard work to satisfactorily explain my absence. A little observation, however, showed that the enemy were firing slowly and would not move more than one or two guns in position, and I determined to try the short cut. Throwing off haversack and jacket, I slipped down the bank into the road and waited for the next discharge. As soon as the shell screamed by I started. There was a shout or cry of warning behind me, but I flew across like a deer, dashed full tilt against the opposite bank, climbed up and soon rejoined the regiment. The men gave me a cheer as I came up, and I felt as fine as a fiddle. We were young then, Horatio, and life was a frolic.

The brigade was soon formed in column of regiments, the Seventh, my own, in front. Behind were the ambulance, litter-carriers, and surgeons—a grisly crew. In front the skirmishers were working their way towards a dense woods. In this they disappeared, and for awhile all was silent. Then a shot rang out, then another, then a sharp rattle, and we were ordered forward by the flank. On reaching the woods we were again put in line of battle and ordered in. Scarcely had we entered before some of our troops came running out. It was a new regiment, which being suddenly fired on had given way. They soon rallied, came up behind us, moved off to the right, and, as I heard, did well the rest of the day. As soon as the fugitives had passed we opened fire. I saw nothing, but banged away, might and main, in the direction in which the balls seemed to come. After about half an hour of pretty sharp firing we were ordered to advance, and plunged into a dense tangle of brush, undergrowth, vines, etc. As we tore through this the enemy seemed to get our range and poured in a heavy fire. The thud! thud! with which the balls bored their way into the trees was venomous. As soon as we reached better ground, we advanced firing. This was most exciting. Everybody was yelling, firing, and advancing. In this advance, I don't know that I did the enemy any harm, but, then, on the other hand, I nearly deprived the Confederacy of a soldier. While in the very act of firing, a big fellow, running up rapidly from behind, got almost in front of the muzzle of my musket, which went off within a few inches of his ear. He bent a most reproachful look upon me, but it was no time for explanation, and on he went and I after him, biting another cartridge and ramming it as I went along. The enemy must have made off before we got within sight of them, for the firing ceased and we were halted along a fence.

By this time we were all pretty well warmed up and ready for business. In coming through the brush I had received a very severe gash from a jagged limb, not to speak of being knocked down and trod on, and was by no means in an angelic humor. I looked around with all my eyes, for something to shoot at, but to the right and in front beheld nothing. To the left oblique I thought I saw men moving about among the trees, and on closer inspection could discern some dark blue uniforms. Presently the presence of the enemy became unmistakable. I could distinctly see company after company march briskly down a sort of woods road, halt, and face towards us. Half a dozen fellows by me

saw the same and raised their guns. I took a rest on a tree, and a long aim, and we fired together. Without stopping to reload I peered forward through the smoke to discern the effect of the shot. There seemed some slight commotion, but it may only have been the officers moving about, as in a moment, as if at the word of command, the whole line brought up their muskets. The long stretch of glittering steel, with a head bent down at the end of each gun-barrel, was a thrilling sight. A huge cloud of smoke hid them from our view, and a tremendous report rang through the forest. Our whole line instantly replied, and the ball opened in dead earnest. As I half-faced to the left to reload I saw our junior second-lieutenant flat upon his back, his jaw convulsively working in the agonies of death. He had never been with us in action before, and his presentiment was realized that he would fall in his first battle. I had known him before we joined the army, and the sight of his death filled me with rage. Half mad with pain and anger I rammed the loads home with all my strength, but aimed carefully each time on the range of my first shot. Other troops were apparently brought up, right and left, on both sides, for the uproar swelled until it became deafening. The ground being impracticable for either cavalry or artillery, it was a fair and square stand-up infantry fight at close range, and most stubbornly contested. The enemy hung staunchly to their work, and our own men fought like demons.

For fully an hour the din kept up without cessation. Then the enemy's fire slackened, and we held up a little in turn. Then they reopened with fresh fury, and at it again we went, hammer and tongs. Those were the days, it will be remembered, of muzzle-loaders and the old-fashioned ball cartridge, the end of which you were obliged to tear off with your teeth. After heavy firing the guns would clog, and presently every piece began to foul. I had to stop, tear up my handkerchief and wipe her out. After awhile it clogged again, and finally the ramrod stuck fast. It would neither come up nor go down, and, in despair, I jammed it, full force, into a tree. That drove that charge home, but, on coming to reload, the rammer was so bent as to be almost useless. A few more loads were worried down, and then the gun became wholly unmanageable, and I threw it down and looked around for another. Behind me was one with a prostrate soldier by it. As I stooped to pick it up, the supposed dead man came to life, stretched out his hand, and shook his head as if to say, don't take it. I gestured back it was no use to him, but he still demurred, and to cut short the pantomine, I snatched the gun away and set her to talking.

Major Charles Flowerree (above), of the 7th Virginia, was wounded during A. P. Hill's attack at Williamsburg. He recovered and later commanded the regiment.

PRIVATE FREDERICK E. DENNIS
8TH NEW JERSEY INFANTRY, STARR'S BRIGADE

The retreat of Hooker's division before Hill's and Wilcox's counterattack morti-fied III Corps commander Brigadier General Samuel P. Heintzelman. Desper-ate to rally his infantry, Heintzelman ordered one group of musicians to play patriotic tunes, crying, "Play, damn it! Play some marching tune! Play 'Yankee Doodle,' or any doodle you can think of, only play something!"

With my eyes straight to the front I paid no attention, and cared less, as to what was occurring around me. Billy Davis had stopped firing, and he perceived that a large portion of the regiment had gone to the rear. He asked me what it meant. I told him I did not know, but if he was willing to retire I would go with him.

As I was gathering myself together for a retrograde movement, old man Hatch was struck and tumbled over against my legs. Hatch implored me to drag him out of the woods. I told him it would be impossible, as the rebels were flanking us, and I would be captured before we could get out. He begged of me, with tears in his eyes, to assist him, and I can see the old man now, with his hands up, stretched on the wet ground. Something hindered my pedal extremities from getting back to the rear with that agility so necessary at that supreme moment. I was quick to discover the difficulty. The buttons were lack-ing on my under-trousers, and they had gracefully slid down to my knees with a reckless disregard of etiquet and in violation of all social rules known to civilized man. My locomotion was anything but lively under this most disastrous and distressing predicament, but I made wide strides, and I had the satisfaction of feeling the garment give way under the desperate plunges to extricate myself. I struck a bee line for my knapsack, with some of the boys on the same hunt. I wanted to secure that knapsack. It contained apparel and 40 rounds of ammuni-tion. It also contained photo pictures of a little brother and the Cap-tain's daughter. My affection for the originals of these pictures was about equally divided in ardor and intensity, but I am willing to swear that there was a slight balance in favor of the little lady. They had been mute companions on the weary march, and there was a grain of solace and comfort in a glance at them now and then. While tumbling over knapsacks the Johnnies had appeared at the edge of the wood and opened a fusillade of bullets, accompanying it with jeers and curses.

Lieut. Lackey stood on a stump laughing at us through the blood that ran down his face from a scalp wound, and a splendid target he was for those Johnnies. I strapped on my knapsack while the bullets zipped around me in a most provoking manner. Scrambling over the timber, I met Tom Gilchrist, who wore the aspect of a very demoralized patriot. That hateful gun still belched its deadly missiles, and Tom expressed a burning desire to charge over the ramparts of that redoubt and choke the life out of the gang that worked the gun. We sat under a tree and debated the question as to whether we were really licked, and how it happened that our flank should be turned so ingloriously.

There was yet no sign of relief, and things looked decidedly squally. Close by us, on a narrow knoll, stood a 12-pounder Napoleon gun that had evidently been in action, but the gunners were not to be seen. One man ran up to the gun and yelled for us to help him load it with grape. We replied that many of the boys were crouching behind the timber, and it would be murder to fire grape. He then retired, and we tried to extract as much comfort as the circumstances would permit. The rain still beat pitilessly, and it seemed as though nature was at war with us and had determined to drown us out.

Back in the rear and advancing up the road we recognized the form of Gen. Heintzelman, who was calling out in stentorian tones through his nose for the band to strike up an air. In a few moments a miserable remnant of the tooters rallied and made a number of sickly efforts at Yankee Doodle with their bazoos, which, instead of infusing courage into our hapless systems, sent a cold chill down our backs and set our teeth aching. Each had one eye gazing toward the rear and the other eye was watching out for shells. To a disinterested spectator looking at them from the top gallery he would have instantly come to the conclusion that they were struggling with the jim-jams. They were not flattered with an encore, and they retired to the rear for repairs.

CAPTAIN SELDEN PAGE
11TH MASSACHUSETTS INFANTRY, GROVER'S BRIGADE

Page was one of the many Yankees who was sickened by the swampy, mosquito-infested Peninsula. Suffering from fever and diarrhea at Williamsburg, he entered a field hospital in early June and was discharged the next month. He suffered from the ailments he contracted on the Peninsula for the rest of his life.

During the hottest of the fight in our immediate front, there appeared a small white flag, and we were called upon to stop firing. We were told that we were firing upon our own men, and immediately Captain Stone, commanding company K, accompanied by some six or eight men, stepped out to investigate, when the flag was unrolled and a battle-flag with a white tip was displayed. The party were charged upon, but were not captured, and at about the same time Sergeant Cram, of company H, "covered" a lieutenant, who ordered him to "hold on," as he was shooting his own men. (We wore a dark-gray overcoat furnished by the State.) Said the sergeant, "Who are you?" "We are the 11th South Carolina," was the reply. "You are just the fellows we are looking for. We are the 11th Massachusetts—take that," said the sergeant discharging his musket, and the lieutenant gave one spring and fell a corpse. I saw his body the next morning.

We held the ground until about 4 p.m., when, our battery having been silenced and our left flank completely turned, we were ordered to fall back, and as we did, so the enemy pressed into the roadway

Captain Richard Lee of the 6th New Jersey, whose photograph and gold-embroidered cap badge appear at left, was captured by soldiers of the 19th Mississippi Infantry during the engagement at Williamsburg. Lee's regiment was roughly handled by the Rebels on May 5, losing 139 men killed, wounded, or captured.

between the two slashings as thick as they could stand; and as I passed a section of artillery that commanded the road, the lieutenant ordered his guns double shotted, and I stopped to see the result on the troops massed for a charge. The first discharge opened a swath through the mass as a farmer's scythe does through the grass in a hayfield, and was accompanied by such a yell of horror as I never heard before or since.

The 1st Massachusetts band was standing at the side of the road, some two or three hundred yards from this artillery, when a man on horseback rode up, and in a peculiar nasal twang called out, "Come boys! play something lively to cheer these boys up." One of the band who didn't know him, called out, "Who are you?" "I'm General Heintzelman, and I am going to win this fight," was the reply. The general soon saw a bugler sitting on his horse, and, riding up to him, said, "Come my man, play something to cheer these boys up." "I can't play anything but the calls," said the bugler. "Well," said the general, "Toot! toot!—you can toot, can't you?" It is useless to add that the band played "something lively" and the bugler "tooted."

In May 1861 members of the Boston City Council bestowed this banner on the 1st Massachusetts after Governor John A. Andrew, disliking its colonel, refused to present colors to the regiment. The battle-worn flag was retired in September 1862.

"There is nobody here capable of commanding, and McClellan is at Yorktown."

Col De Trobriand
ny 55 b

COLONEL PHILIP R. DE TROBRIAND
55TH NEW YORK INFANTRY, PECK'S BRIGADE

A native of France, and a poet and lawyer as well as a respected soldier, the dashing De Trobriand was destined to wear the rank of general and command a division by the close of the war. This account of the confusion present among the Federal high command at Williamsburg is taken from De Trobriand's memoir of his Civil War service.

Soon an aid of General Peck brought me the order to pass by Casey's division, which had halted, I do not know why, in a large open field, near a brick church. The sound of the cannonade did not diminish. At this point, Kearney's division turned to the left to come into line by a crossroad less encumbered.

A little further along, I met Captain Leavit-Hunt, aid of General Heintzelman, who had been ordered to hurry forward reenforcements. He informed me that the conjectures of Kearney, as to Hooker, were correct; that Hooker, strongly opposed by superior forces, had lost ground, after a desperate contest of more than four hours, during which no assistance had been sent to him.

The Prince de Joinville, in his turn, passed by me without stopping, urging me to hurry forward. He was mounted on an English horse and covered with mud from head to foot. He was hurrying to Yorktown to endeavor to bring up General McClellan, who, ignorant of what was passing at Williamsburg, had not yet started.

In the absence of the general-in-chief, General Sumner and General Keyes lost time in consulting as to what was to be done. The former was senior in rank, but the latter alone had any troops within reach, and, between the two, no measure was taken, and Hooker lost not only his position but some of his guns.

When I led my troops out on the farm where that idle conference was going on, the Count de Paris and the Duke de Chartres, recognizing the uniform of the regiment, came on foot to meet me. I did not have time either to stop or to dismount; they did me the honor of accompanying me in this manner for several minutes across the furrows, to explain to me the position of affairs, and to wish me success.

"Everything is going to the devil," said the Duke de Chartres to me. "There is nobody here capable of commanding, and McClellan is at Yorktown. As several aids have not been able to induce him to come, my uncle has gone himself to look for him, knowing well that without him nothing will be done as it should be."

PRIVATE CHARLES T. LOEHR
1ST VIRGINIA INFANTRY, A. P. HILL'S BRIGADE

As the men of the 1st Virginia surged after the retreating bluecoats, they captured the eight guns Major Charles S. Wainwright had posted to support Hooker's infantry. With the guns were two Yankee flags, on one of which the Union cannoneers had supposedly emblazoned the phrase "to hell or Richmond."

A. P. Hill praised colorbearer Tapley Mays of the 7th Virginia (above) for bravely carrying his flag at Williamsburg although it was twice shot from his hand and hit by 27 bullets. Mays was mortally wounded at the Battle of South Mountain in 1862.

Marching through the old capital of Virginia, we left our baggage at one of the private residences, and halted in the rear, and to the right of Fort Magruder, which was occupied by the Richmond Fayette artillery and two guns of the Richmond Howitzers, who were subjected to hot fire from the enemy's guns, loosing a great many men, but holding on to their position, from which the enemy was unable to silence or drive them. After forming in line of battle and halting awhile we were ordered forward into the woods, to the right, where the battle was then raging. Soon after we reached the position, as the regiment became engaged, they got separated, and each regiment, so to say, fought on its own hook. We were ordered to support the Nineteenth Mississippi regiment, which was being forced back by the enemy. Before we could reach them some of the companies broke and ran through our ranks, closely pursued by the enemy, who, getting into the felled timber or abattis, was in turn charged by our regiment and driven off in great confusion. Following them through the felled timber, we came out right into a six-gun battery, which we captured, together with a large United States battle flag, also a small brigade guide flag. It was of blue silk with a golden 3 embroidered thereon. This we carried with us to Richmond. An aide of General Longstreet now came up and requested Colonel Williams to make a detail of 100 men to carry off the guns. This Colonel Williams was unable to do, as he could not spare that force. Subsequently a detail was made from the Nineteenth Virginia regiment, and the guns were safely carried off.

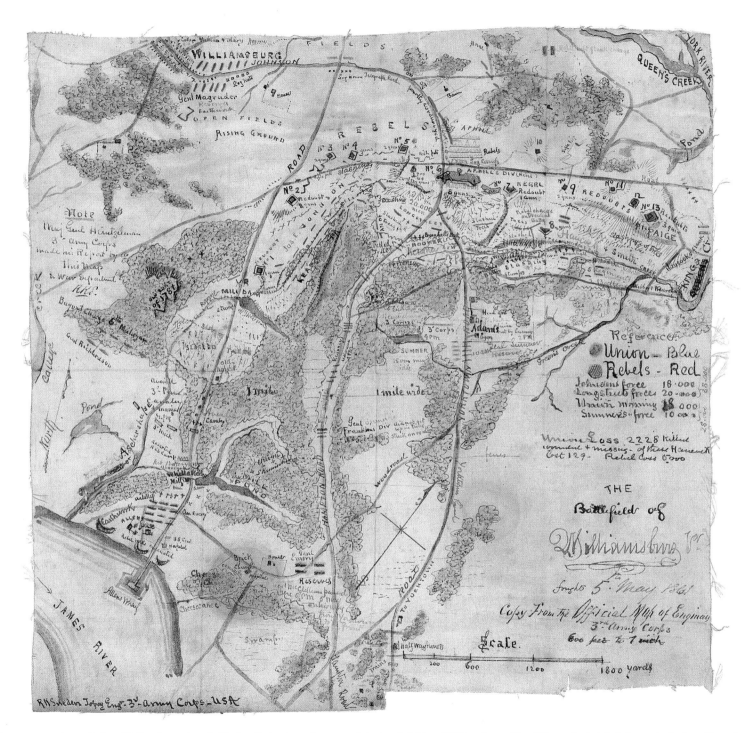

Union army engineer Robert K. Sneden painted this detailed watercolor map of the battlefield at Williamsburg. Fort Magruder is labeled as redoubt "no. 6" on the map, directly astride the main road to Williamsburg. Immediately below the fort, stretching to the east and west, are the fields of slashed timber fought over by the combatants. The line held by Hooker's men and the position of Wainwright's overrun battery can be discerned south of the intersection of the Hampton and Yorktown Roads.

"He rode among his men and cried, 'Floridians, Oh, Floridians, is this the way you meet the enemies of your country?', and fell from his horse dead on the field of honor, his heart pierced by a bullet."

PRIVATE EDMUND D. PATTERSON
9TH ALABAMA INFANTRY, WILCOX'S BRIGADE

In the late afternoon, the 9th Alabama found itself low on ammunition and pinned down on the fringe of a thick wood, in which the Federals were hastily re-forming their lines. The 2d Florida hurried to the Alabamians' aid, but the green Floridians were thrown into confusion by conflicting orders and by the death of their colonel, George Ward. After the battle, Wilcox expressed sadness over the loss of the "gifted and chivalric Ward."

About this time Col. Wilcox came up and complimented us and was loudly cheered. Col. Henry and the remaining companies of the regiment came up, and forming our line again we moved forward to the edge of the woods where we soon became engaged and fired until our ammunition gave out; then we had to lie still, for had we started back we must have gone through an open field, exposed to the enemy's fire; where we were protected by logs and hidden by undergrowth. We remained here for some time, and until the 2nd Florida came to relieve us, which was at 4 o'clock in the evening. They came up in good style, and were to take our places, and to get out as best we could. But when the command was given to our regiment the Florida regiment misunderstood it for all, and they started too; then commenced a scene of wild confusion; both regiments broke in perfect disorder and went running through the field to the rear. I shall never forget the impression made upon me by Col. Ward of the 2nd Fla. He was a brave, gallant man. He rode among his men and cried, "Floridians, Oh, Floridians, is this the way you meet the enemies of your country?", and fell from his horse dead on the field of honor, his heart pierced by a bullet.

The men were now panic stricken, and there was no such thing as stopping them until we had reached some place of protection, for some were falling at every step. After running back a mile or more we reached a ravine, and there stopped and reformed.

MAJOR CHARLES S. WAINWRIGHT
CHIEF OF ARTILLERY, HOOKER'S DIVISION

After his first artillery position was overrun, the indefatigable Wainwright managed to cobble together a reserve line of fieldpieces that momentarily blunted the Rebel attack with blasts of canister. The Confederates regrouped and were once again threatening to overwhelm Wainwright's guns when the fortuitous arrival of Brigadier General Philip Kearny's division from the III Corps stymied the Rebel attack and stabilized the Union line.

By the time I got up the fighting was over. We had lost possession of all the slashing on the left of the road, but held the woods for some distance in that direction. General Heintzelman was there in consultation with Hooker. Osborn had got a dozen or so of his men together, and manned one piece which he had planted in the road just in front of the little thorough cut. So soon as Smith came up, to hurry whom I sent Lieutenant Ames back, I put two of his Parrotts and his section of six-pounders in position on . . . a little knoll, and comparatively open; they had perfect command of the road but nothing more. We did not have to wait many minutes. It was perhaps half an hour after the other guns were captured when the rebs charged in column down the road; my five pieces were all loaded with canister, but I held fire until the head of the column was well down to within about 150 yards of us, and two whole regiments were plainly in view. Three rounds to a gun then blew the whole thing away, except small parties which got into the slashing on the left of the road, and picked off my cannoneers so badly that after trying two or three rounds of canister on them I was obliged to let the men cover themselves behind the trees. Finding no infantry at all near my guns to reply to these fellows, I went back to General Hooker, and asked him to send some, which he promised to do. After waiting ten minutes or so, and finding that the rascals were working up nearer and nearer to me all the time, I again went back and found General Grover, to whom I made the same request, and from whom I received the same promise. Still no supports came. Four of Smith's men had been hit, and I began to be anxious lest another attack should be made, as I could find no infantry within 100 yards to my rear. Going a third time, I found the head of Kearny's column just come up. To Kearny I put my request. This time, instantly he turned to the First Company of a Michigan regiment: "Captain, you will take your company, and put them wherever Major Wainwright here says"—which was done as promptly as it was ordered, and I saw no more of my friends in the slashing.

CAPTAIN JAMES DEARING
LYNCHBURG (VIRGINIA) ARTILLERY, PICKETT'S BRIGADE

From a position near Fort Magruder, Dearing's guns shelled enemy batteries and infantry columns throughout the day before running out of ammunition and retiring toward Williamsburg at dusk. Dearing eventually became a general and was mortally wounded on April 6, 1865, three days before Appomattox.

Captain George W. Mindil (above), chief of staff to brigade commander General David B. Birney of Kearny's division, led a Union counterattack at Williamsburg that outflanked the foremost Confederate battle line, preventing a Union rout. In 1893 Mindil was awarded the Medal of Honor for his act.

I opened immediately on a column of infantry crossing toward the fortifications, and after about ten rounds of shell and spherical case had the gratification [to] find that I had succeeded in turning the column, which filed to the right and disappeared under the brow of a hill. About this time a new battery of the enemy was planted immediately on my right, and enfilading my whole position. I was thus under a most severe cross fire. I, however, continued to fire upon the battery in front, after the infantry disappeared, endeavoring to silence it, but the distance was too great to dismount their pieces with smooth-bore guns, and their guns were of heavier caliber and longer ranged than mine. Among the enemy's battery were two Parrott guns. I therefore turned my attention to the battery on my right, which had my range exactly, and was doing me all the damage, having already wounded one man and killed one horse of mine. I therefore changed my front to the right, and some twenty-five or thirty yards from my first position, and opened on this battery. The first battery was too far, and did not succeed in getting my range sufficiently exact for their enfilading fire to do me any damage. Their shells and case-shot burst beautifully, though not close enough, or rather not at the proper distance to hurt me. I had been firing some time at this second battery, which was between 800 and 900 yards off in a small clearing near the edge of the woods, when Lieutenant Clopton, of the Richmond Fayette Artillery, was ordered by Colonel Jenkins to report to me. I had his two pieces placed in battery on my right. In a short time the enemy's guns ceased firing, and

VIEW of "FORT MAGRUDER". BATTLEFIELD of WILLIAMS

were withdrawn from that point, I suppose, for there was no more firing from that point during the day. Lieutenant Clopton informed me that he had only nine men for his two guns, 4 having been killed and 9 wounded while in the fort, by the enemy's sharpshooters. It was while in this position that I had my junior first lieutenant, T. F. Richardson, killed. He had just aimed a gun at the enemy's battery, and had raised up, when a piece of shell struck him just below the left collar bone, killing him instantly. Here I had two more men wounded, one in the thigh, Private Edward F. Deaton, the other, Private Dillon, in the left leg; also one horse killed. I had sergeants' horses put in the places of those killed and wounded.

The imposing bastion of Fort Magruder, the keystone of the Confederate resistance at Williamsburg, dominates the foreground of yet another meticulous Sneden rendering. From behind the fort's earthen walls, Rebel artillery lobbed shells at the Yankee troops entangled in the slashings, while Confederate infantry used the strongpoint as a staging area for their assaults. On the horizon, the spires of the old Colonial capitol of Williamsburg are visible; smaller infantry redoubts lie scattered in the fields beyond the fort.

...G VIRGINIA. Showing obstructions rifle pits and other REDOUBTS.

sketched MAY 6th 1862

SERGEANT SALEM DUTCHER
7TH VIRGINIA INFANTRY, A. P. HILL'S BRIGADE

By midafternoon both sides were tired and low on ammunition, and an uneasy stalemate settled over the arena. The fighting at this point broke down into sporadic exchanges of gunfire between the Confederates sheltering in the slashing and the Federals hunkered down in the thick woods that covered much of the battlefield. As a noncommissioned officer, Dutcher helped to maintain the 7th's battle line and prevent the regiment's exhausted soldiers from fleeing to the protective confines of Fort Magruder.

We had now been about seven hours in action, some two at this particular point, and the strain was intense. Off on the right one fellow sprang up, dropped his gun to a trail, and made off back into the woods like a quarter-horse. The panic instantly spread, and up and down the line men took to their heels. To tell the honest truth, I gave leg-bail myself, but at the second or third bound a revered and gentle voice, now long silent, whispered reproach, and I wheeled about and caught at the nearest fugitive. He tore loose and half knocked me over. A young officer ran up to the rescue, and as he nailed one man I seized another. They, too, broke away. The officer presented his sword to the next man's breast, and throwing my musket

97

arms-a-port I halted two. For one instant there was a rally; the next they surged over us, and made off as if the devil was behind them. What became of the young officer I know not. I thought I might as well be shot front as rear, and walked back to my tree. Two or three of our men were blazing away. The smoke was lifting a little, and the enemy were preparing to advance. Half a dozen heads had already popped up out of the timber. Back of them their main line was reforming. It was not more than half its original size—had no colors, and otherwise showed marks of the pounding it had received. It seemed very reluctant to advance, and in a few minutes this hesitancy was explained. There was a rousing shout behind; our men had reformed as suddenly as they had run away, and here they came back at a double-quick, yelling vociferously. Down they went again behind the logs, and reopened most vigorously, as if rather refreshed than otherwise by the scare. It makes me laugh now to think of the whoop I gave as they came up. It would have done honor to a Comanche. Hope was almost gone, and the sight once more of these brave men's faces and the cheery ring of their guns was like the breath of life.

Alfred R. Waud's rendering of the mounted General Kearny leading his troops into combat at Williamsburg accurately captures the rainy and overcast atmosphere in which the engagement was fought. A soldier in the 2d Michigan recalled the fiery Kearny exhorting his regiment to attack the Rebels and "drive [the] blackguards to hell at once."

"We then received orders to fall back. This was quite an undertaking for the artillery, as our guns were deep in the mud."

General Kearny's chief of staff, Captain James Wilson (above), was shot down during the crucial Union counterattack engineered by the one-armed general. Kearny later reported that Wilson "had displayed much gallantry" before he fell.

SERGEANT WILLIAM E. WEBSTER
1ST NEW YORK INDEPENDENT LIGHT ARTILLERY, SMITH'S BRIGADE

Cowan's battery was part of a Union force that was led by Brigadier General Winfield Scott Hancock around the unguarded Rebel left and into a position to threaten the Confederate flank. Webster's military service ended when he was severely wounded at the Battle of Cedar Creek, Virginia, in 1864.

*I*n our advance towards the Confederate left we passed a number of small forts, which were vacant. Up to this time not a shot had been fired. In our last position we were to the right of the large fort, and in our front were two small forts similar to the ones we had passed. Our batteries were placed in position and the infantry in line when we observed a double line of infantry advancing from the woods. Their colors were cased, as it was raining. Gen. Hancock remarked:

"I think Hooker has taken the fort and is coming this way." Maj. Curry, one of the staff, rode up, saluted Gen. Hancock and said:

"General, I will find out who they are."

He put spurs to his horse, and rode in amongst the skirmishers, when they fired on him. He turned his horse towards our line and rode like the wind, shouting:

"Fire on them: They are rebels!"

The Major wore a cork leg. It was a great sight to see it swing out. When he was returning to our lines our Captain, Andrew Cowan, shouted: "Battery, Fire!" and the fight was on. This line advanced till they reached the two small forts mentioned, and then divided, a part of them entering the forts. Finally a second line of battle came from the woods, like the first one, but they continued to advance past the forts toward our line. After they had done this the forces in the two forts moved out, formed a line and followed the other into the fight. We then received orders to fall back. This was quite an undertaking for the artillery, as our guns were deep in the mud. It was not a long distance to our second position. On came our misguided brothers, shouting "Bull Run," "Ball's Bluff," etc.

Gen. Hancock's sword fell out of its scabbard and history says he shouted: "Gentlemen, Charge!" but you can't prove it by me. He went in with his men, there was a great crash of musketry, and yells that would make an Indian blush.

COLONEL JOHN BRATTON

6TH SOUTH CAROLINA INFANTRY, R. H. ANDERSON'S BRIGADE

To address the threat on the left, D. H. Hill ordered Jubal Early's brigade to hasten from Williamsburg and hit Hancock. Early's men nearly attacked Bratton's regiment by mistake before haphazardly charging Hancock's 3,400 infantry and two artillery batteries.

The enemy, however, did not advance on me; but late in the evening our friends did—Early's brigade charged my works from the left and rear. Nobody, either officer or scout, had come to the front to reconnoitre, and they did not even know where the enemy were. They charged me (two regiments of them) across the line of the

Winfield Scott Hancock's aggressive flanking maneuver at Williamsburg stood out from the overall Union performance. McClellan later stated that Hancock (above) was "superb" during the fighting. This phrase was picked up by the Northern press, and the accolade Hancock the Superb stayed with the general throughout the war.

enemy, one regiment against each of the works that my troops occupied. I did not know that they were near until they emerged from the wood on the charge, and seeing their mistake I rushed out to stop them and change their direction before they were exposed to the fire of the enemy; but they would not heed, and on they went until they reached my redoubts, when they for the first time learned where the enemy were. Two of Early's regiments were stopped in the wood and proper direction given to them (the Twenty-fourth Virginia and Hoke's North Carolina regiment). The two that charged my works were the Fifth North Carolina and a Virginia regiment commanded by a Lieutenant-Colonel Early—a brother, I was told, of the General. The Fifth North Carolina charged across the entire front of the enemy to the redoubt occupied by my two companies, and on finding it already ours, with scarce a halt, changed direction and advanced most handsomely against the enemy (my two companies joining them in the charge) to within, I think, at least fifty yards of the enemy's line, when they encountered a small fence, partly torn down by the enemy, and unfortunately halted and commenced firing. The Twenty-fourth Virginia had meanwhile emerged from the wood on the left, nearer to the enemy than my redoubt on which Early's regiment charged, and was moving in fine style upon them. Early's regiment never recovered from the confusion into which they were thrown by the taking of my works. They were formed, however, and started forward, but went obliquely to the left to the wood, and I saw no more of them. I met General Early near this redoubt, himself and horse both wounded, and told him that I had checked the enemy, and been there watching him for three or four hours, and asked him to give me a place in the charge. He said, "Certainly, go." I told him that some of my men were in that fort. He said, "Take them and go toward the enemy." I took my men out of the fort and moved them all forward into the gap left by the oblique movement of Early's regiment into the woods. We advanced to within a hundred yards of the enemy, when we were ordered by General D. H. Hill to move by the left flank into the wood. The Fifth North Carolina, on our right, as I said above, unfortunately stopped and commenced firing; I say unfortunately, because from the confused tangling of their muskets I shall ever believe that the enemy were actually broken (their fire, too, almost ceased), and it only required the continued advance of the Fifth North Carolina to complete their route. As it was, the crest of the hill protected the enemy from their fire, and they had time to recover from their panic, and return to the crest, and open fire, which they did, concentrating their overwhelming volleys on the Fifth North Carolina, and almost demolishing it.

Alfred Waud sketched the repulse of the 24th Virginia and 5th North Carolina. In the right foreground, Union artillery prepare for action, while the blue-coated infantry in front of the cannon have already opened fire upon the assaulting Rebels. Waud noted on the back of the sketch that the "enemies dead and wounded [were] covering the field."

MAJOR RICHARD L. MAURY

24TH VIRGINIA INFANTRY, EARLY'S BRIGADE

Half the brigade became entangled in a thick wood, and only the 24th Virginia and the 5th North Carolina were able to confront Hancock's men. As the two regiments tramped across a rain-soaked wheat field toward the enemy, they were swept by a hail of gunfire. Early himself fell when a Union volley put a bullet through his shoulder and knocked out one of his horse's eyes. The brigade lost more than 500 men in this disorganized, fruitless effort.

Yet the advance is maintained; down a slope first, and up again on the further side—still on and on. The regiment soon finds that it is alone; it knows that "some one has blundered," and marvels that the supports are nowhere seen, and that the Major-General, with his part of the brigade, does not appear. Still none falter or cast a look behind. They are pressing the enemy well back, though receiving deadly wounds meantime, for his attention is engrossed by this attack, and the Virginians are drawing his whole fire. Gray-haired old Coltrane, of Carroll, that gallant, staunch old soldier, is well in front, his colors already pierced with many a bullet, and men and officers press quickly on, unchecked by the murderous fire directed upon them. The ground is soft and yielding; the wheat half-knee high, drenched with rain, clings heavily to the legs, and many trip and stumble and sometimes fall. The flag-staff is shattered, but Coltrane grasps the broken staff and cheerily waves the silken folds in front. Away to the right is seen the gallant Fifth North Carolina, coming up at the double-quick to our aid, led by that preux chevalier, Colonel Duncan McRae, his horse briskly trotting in advance. A cheer bursts forth, and all take heart and still press forward. But the Virginians are much nearer the redoubt, and the enemy, regardless of the approaching supports, still concentrated all their fire upon this devoted band, and with terrible effect. Early's horse has been shot, and in another moment he himself receives a wound, the effect of which his bended form showed to his death. Terry, too, that gallant leader, ever in the van of many an after battle, has gotten the first of frequent shots full in the face, and the dauntless Hairston also goes down desperately wounded; so the writer, then but a youth, finds himself, for the first time, in command of his regiment, and the only mounted officer there. His cap has been shot off, and he leads his command, bareheaded and waving a sword just taken from a Federal captain.

But no pause is made. Ten minutes—fifteen—have passed while they cross that field of blood, and every other man is down. But support approaches; not all the rest of the brigade, as was expected—or a part of the division, fresh and in order—but only a single regiment, the gallant Fifth North Carolina, who, seeing what odds the Virginians were fighting, had, as soon as it emerged into the field and found no enemy confronting them, sought leave to march towards the firing, and were now hastening to an awful destruction, in their zeal to share that glorious field. The enemy, too, fall back more quickly as they see reinforcements coming up, and run into and behind the redoubt, to which they have all retreated now. Confusion has seized upon them there, for the Virginians are within twenty yards and show no signs of halting. The fire of the enemy slackens, and as their assailants reach the fence of substantial rails, with a rider, ceases entirely. The order to their artillery to "cease firing" and "limber up" is distinctly heard, and some of the guns are actually run off; the infantry, too, are in great tumult, their bayonets seem tangled and interlocked, some run into the fort, many make off to the rear, and voices calling to others to halt and stand steady are distinctly heard.

George B. Madison, color sergeant of the 5th Wisconsin, was cited by Hancock for "gallant conduct" for carrying this flag throughout the battle, although wounded.

PRIVATE ARTHUR HOLBROOK
5TH WISCONSIN INFANTRY, HANCOCK'S BRIGADE

The soldiers of Holbrook's regiment had initially deployed in an exposed position, in advance of the rest of the brigade. As Early's Rebels approached through the wheat field, the Wisconsin troops began a fighting retreat toward the shelter of the captured enemy redoubt held by their comrades. Exposed to repeated volleys of Rebel musketry during their retrograde movement, the 5th lost 79 men killed and wounded, the largest casualty toll in the brigade.

It was not until the enemy was fairly upon us that Colonel Cobb received the order to retire.

We can never forget the coming of the aide who delivered that order, for he was the only mounted officer in that part of the field, and as the enemy was close at hand and approaching us, he was a fine target for the whole rebel line. The bullets flew about him like hailstones, and he stretched his whole length along the neck and back of his big bay horse. As soon as he was sufficiently near to be heard, he shouted his message to Colonel Cobb, and then retired at breakneck speed.

We then settled slowly back, keeping well together, circling around and around each other, paying little attention to company formation, but standing together as a regiment, each man firing as he came to the front and hotly contesting every inch of ground until we reached the redoubt. There we halted and formed in line and made the final stand, with the enemy directly upon us.

Up to this time the balance of the brigade, which was in the redoubt and in line of battle on each side of it, had been obliged to confine its work to the flanks, for our regiment was masking and preventing them from firing into the main line.

As soon as we gained the crest, and had faced about at the redoubt, and had given them an open field, our gallant comrades of the 6th Maine and the 49th Pennsylvania, who had been watching, waiting, and preparing for their opportunity, commenced work in earnest. At this moment the advance of the enemy was just under the crest, not two hundred feet away, determined to capture our position. The order was given to move forward, and we started toward the advancing enemy.

MAJOR THOMAS W. HYDE
7TH MAINE INFANTRY, DAVIDSON'S BRIGADE

In this photograph Hyde stands between Colonel Edwin C. Mason, on the left, and Lieutenant Colonel Selden Connor. All three were present at Williamsburg. Colonel Mason wrote in amazement after the battle that although 60 soldiers of the 7th "had their clothes pierced with bullets, . . . not a man [was] killed or wounded."

Our advance regiments fell back by General Hancock's order; on the Confederates came, and a fine picture of a charge they made. They were at the double-quick, and were coming over a ploughed field, diagonally across our front, to attack the troops that were retiring. They could not see us as we lay flat on the ground. From my place on the left of the regiment, I saw General Hancock galloping toward us, bare-headed, alone, a magnificent figure; and with a voice hoarse with shouting he gave us the order, "Forward! charge!" The papers had it that he said, "Charge, gentlemen, charge," but he was more emphatic than that: the air was blue all around him. Well, up we started, and the long line of sabre bayonets came down together as if one man swayed them as we crossed the crest, and with a roar of cheers the 7th Maine dashed on. It was an ecstasy of excitement for a moment; but the foe, breathless from their long tug over the heavy ground, seemed to dissolve all at once into a quivering and disintegrating mass and to scatter in all directions. Upon this we halted and opened fire, and the view of it through the smoke was pitiful. They were falling everywhere; white handkerchiefs were held up in token of surrender; no bullets were coming our way except from a clump of a few trees in front of our left. Here a group of men, led by an officer whose horse had just fallen, were trying to keep up the unequal fight, when McK., the crack shot of Company D, ran forward a little and sent a bullet crashing through his brain. This was Lieutenant-Colonel J. C. Bradburn of the

5th North Carolina, and at his fall all opposition ceased. We gathered in some three hundred prisoners before dark. Then the rain came, and though there is nothing specially remarkable about that, for it was always coming down, yet it made much difference with our comfort, and it is one of the trivial facts that will insist on being remembered.

COLONEL DUNCAN K. MCRAE
5TH NORTH CAROLINA INFANTRY, EARLY'S BRIGADE

Although outnumbered, McRae's regiment and the 24th Virginia initially made good progress, forcing the 5th Wisconsin to fall back before their advance. McRae pleaded with Daniel Harvey Hill for reinforcements from the brigade's other regiments, but none were forthcoming, and the two attacking units eventually had to retreat—through a storm of Union lead. After Early's wounding, McRae briefly commanded the brigade, but illness forced him to resign at the end of May.

About this time the enemy's line opened fire upon us, but almost at once became discomposed by our advance, and soon broke into retreat; and what seemed to be one regiment, immediately in our front, was thrown into confusion, which increased until it ran into the extreme left redoubt. While the regiment was passing the first redoubt, I left its line for a few moments to put myself in command of the Twenty-fourth Virginia. I rallied some of its men who were around the redoubt spoken of by Colonel Bratton as that in which he was, and finding the Twenty-fourth prepared, I ordered its advance at the same time—a part of the enemy's line being in some woods in front of it, beyond a narrow field which opened at right angles with the parallelogram I have before spoken of. While all this was going on, I felt much concern because the two remaining regiments of the brigade put in no appearance. I saw that the enemy was disconcerted, and, if pressed with sufficient force, might be routed; but I saw also the hazard of advancing with so small a force against a superior enemy, with one regiment occupying a redoubt and supported by a formidable battery; for although the body of troops which ran into the redoubt was in confusion, and the others of what seemed to be from the flags three other regiments retreated to the rear of it, yet the battery had been retired en echelon with great precision, and there was no such manifest disorder as would justify storming the redoubt. So I hurried my Adjutant to General Hill, with substantially these instructions: "I am pushing the enemy rapidly. He is in confusion. Some of his troops have moved

into a redoubt in seeming disorder. The battery is in full view and is under my fire. But he has a large force outside the works supporting, and I am too weak to go forward alone, and retreat is impossible without great loss. If he will throw out the two regiments to support me, I can capture the redoubt, and perhaps the battery. Tell him by all means to support me, and not to order me to retreat." At this time the Fifth North Carolina had reached the fence about seventy-five yards from the redoubt; and as the enemy had ceased firing, I ordered a halt under cover of the fence—the Twenty-fourth Virginia being at this time in front of the woods. My Adjutant found General Hill with the two regiments in the woods near the opening, and delivered my message; then General Hill said: "Boys, do you hear that? Let us go to Colonel McRae's relief." But in a moment after he said: "No; go and tell him to draw off his men as he best can."

James Edwin Botts (above) of the 5th North Carolina was wounded and captured at Williamsburg. The regiment suffered a dreadful 302 casualties on May 5, giving credence to Hancock's claim that it had been "annihilated."

PRIVATE CHARLES T. LOEHR
1ST VIRGINIA INFANTRY, A. P. HILL'S BRIGADE

As darkness fell and put an end to the fighting, confused and disoriented soldiers of both armies who had become separated from their units in the battlefield's tangled slashings and swampy woodlands began to search for their regiments. Endeavoring to find the 1st Virginia, Loehr nearly fell victim not only to Federal bullets but also to the fire of his own artillery before making his way safely into Williamsburg.

Towards the close of the day I was ordered by Major Palmer to communicate our position to a North Carolina regiment, which was towards the right of our position. Just after reaching this regiment and delivering my instructions to the colonel, the enemy made a fierce attack on this regiment. The men were lying behind the trees, and as they commenced to fire their muskets some of the bullets would come out with a stream of fire, then fall to the ground, the powder having become soaked. However, the enemy was driven off and I started for my command. It was then getting quite dark. Seeing a line of men in my front I thought I could recognize some of my company, but after calling to them and getting closer I found myself within the enemy's line. To turn around and start off in another direction was the next thing. In doing so I was saluted by the Federals with a shower of balls, but I got away, continuing my solitary retreat among the dead and dying in the dark woods, not knowing where to go. I was aroused by hearing some one call out: "Here goes one; shoot him." I now gave myself up for lost. Not knowing what to do and being completely worn out, I shouted back toward the voice, "Don't shoot, I surrender." Then came the query, "What regiment is yours?" To my answer the First Virginia, I was informed that I had come into the line of the Second Mississippi battalion; that the First had passed through them for the rear some time previous. I then started towards the town, coming out in the open field in front of Fort Magruder. Our artillery was hard at work sending its iron messengers towards the Federal lines. I had to cross the field just in front of the batteries, and I tried to do it quickly, but the soft mud was too much for me; so as gun after gun was fired, I had to lay flat down and let the shot pass over before I could get further. Finally I reached the road, and a short walk brought me to the town.

MAJOR CHARLES S. WAINWRIGHT
CHIEF OF ARTILLERY, HOOKER'S DIVISION

After spending a restless night in rain-soaked clothes, Wainwright set out on the morning of May 6 to examine the battlefield and try to locate some of the cannon he feared had been taken by Wilcox's men. In this case, at least, the muddy ground had helped the Federal cause by preventing the Confederates from hauling captured guns to Fort Magruder. Wainwright uses an anecdote about the sad fate of an artillery horse to convey the depth and tenacity of the mud.

I was awfully tired and stiff this morning. The rain had got down inside my rubber cape, and had wet me from head to foot; it was impossible to get dry clothing, so a good part of the night was spent standing over the fire. Soon after I started out this morning, I met Bramhall and his First Lieutenant Martin; I had heard nothing of them, since the capture of their battery, and was more affected at finding them alive and safe than by all the casualties of the day before. On riding up to my position of yesterday, in the fallow field, I found Bramhall's five guns, and one of Webber's Parrotts still stuck in the mud; they had sunk down so deep that the rebs were not able to carry them off. Here too I saw a most wonderful exemplification of the nature of the ground in this field. Shortly before the guns were captured one of the wheel horses of a limber was shot dead. The men did not have time to get the harness off him, and the rebs only carried away the lead and swing teams so that the other wheel horse was left standing in the traces all night. The weight of his dead mate bearing on the pole had caused the live horse to sink in the ground feet-first until it reached halfway up his chest, and suffocated him. When I got there he was quite dead; the surface of the ground coming up to the cantle of the saddle, his tail and rump sunk quite out of sight. The whole of the land hereabouts is underlain by a bed of shell marl which again lies on a subsoil of heavy clay; the soil above the marl is a very light sand, and in places not over a foot or two thick. The immense rains we have had all this spring, sinking directly through the sand and finding no outlet from the marl, have converted it into the consistency of soft mortar; so that when a heavy substance once breaks through the top soil, there is nothing to stop its sinking until it reaches the hard clay.

As I looked over the ground, and saw how thick the cannon balls lay, I was more and more filled with wonder at our small loss in the batteries. I counted thirteen projectiles lying on a piece of ground which could almost be covered by a wall tent. Most of them were six-pounder shell and case with Beauman fuses, not one in ten of which had been cut. The paper fuses did not work well with them or us either, it being almost impossible to drive them without wetting the powder. My own notion, as formed from yesterday's experience, is that the smooth-bore guns are the most accurate within a range suited to them. The firing of my two twelve-pounder howitzers was perfect, and uniform; this may be partly owing to the ammunition for them having been made before the war broke out, when it was manufactured with much more care than now.

LIEUTENANT CHARLES B. HAYDON

2D MICHIGAN INFANTRY, BERRY'S BRIGADE

Williamsburg was Haydon's first real taste of combat, and the carnage he witnessed caused him to conclude that "victory was with us but dearly won." A well-respected and conscientious officer, Haydon rose to the rank of lieutenant colonel but died of pneumonia in February 1864 while headed home on a furlough.

When I went back from the front last night I found the woods & the road side strewed with dead & the moans & cries of the wounded could be heard on all sides. They were scattered around among the logs & brush so that it was almost impossible to get at them if there had been any one to do it. Those who engaged in the battle were so cold & used up that they would not attempt to care for any but themselves. Such as they ran onto they would cover up with blankets, give water to drink & leave as comfortable as possible but they would not turn out of their way to aid them unless they were acquaintances.

Many died through the night who were only slightly wounded & who might under other circumstances have been saved. This m'g several arms & legs were lying on stumps & logs by the road side where they had been amputated. Our men & the enemy were mixed together as the ground was fought over two or three times backward & forward

for the space of half a mile in width & two or three times that length. The dead lay in all postures but most of them on their backs, their heads thrown back, mouth slightly open, elbows on the ground by the sides, with the hands up, folded or lying loosely across the breast or frequently one of them placed over the wound. A few had grass, sticks, dirt or their guns clutched firmly in their hands. Some hands were crossed as in prayer, some stretched up at full length. One I saw standing on his hands & knees with his head shot off. Two men were found lying opposite each other with each his bayonet through the other's body.

PRIVATE RANDOLPH A. SHOTWELL

8TH VIRGINIA INFANTRY, PICKETT'S BRIGADE

Throughout the night of May 5 the Confederate rear guard conducted a furtive withdrawal to rejoin the main body of the army. Although McClellan's forces held the field, the Rebels could also claim a measure of success, for they had checked the Yankees long enough to let their vital supply train pass to safety and had inflicted 2,283 casualties, compared with 1,682 of their own.

So tho' we had captured eight pieces of artillery and several hundred prisoners, and inflicted serious loss,—fully 5,000 men —upon the enemy, we must retire at night. It was not much credit to McClellan's ingenuity as a commander that he didn't see this inevitable conclusion and push us so closely that we could not escape without another day's fighting, which would have been pretty apt to terminate disastrously for us under existing conditions. The waiting for the "marching order," was one of the strangest, saddest episodes of the war to me. As twilight settled down upon the battlefield, the men gathered in little groups and discussed the incidents of the day. Having fought within a dense woods, they had no means of knowing generally how the battle had gone; though there could be no doubt we were holding our own; else Pickett would be withdrawn.

Yet despite the satisfaction of this consciousness the occasion was inexpressibly sombre and depressing. The twilight deepened into a solemn darkness, with nothing audible save the ceaseless patter of the rain, the moaning of the wounded in the thickets, the voices of the litter bearers hunting for comrades that had been left amid the heat of battle, the crackling of the underbrush as an officer came in from the out pickets—or the far-off cry of some poor wretch beseeching "water, water, water!"—

How long the hours seemed after the excitement of the day! How strangely still and solemn seemed the vast forest after all the uproar and clamor of an hour before. And so we waited,—waited,—waited;—a long grey-clad line of men leaning on our muskets, waiting to begin a dismal, fatiguing night march!

It came at length;—the whispered order to slowly, silently, withdraw from the field. No one must speak—, no canteen be allowed to rattle, no sound be made: but stealthily file to the rear like Indian warriors approaching an enemy's camp.

Every one was glad to get in motion, glad to stir his blood, and shake the dripping rain from his clothes; and yet it wasn't a pleasant thought —this turning of backs to the foe for the first time in the history of the army of Virginia. Then, too, the idea of commencing at 10 P.M., an all night march over roads literally knee-deep in soft mud and slush—and with artillery, wagons, ambulances and footmen all jumbled together in the narrow roads—was almost appalling!

The clay and sand of the roads was now worked into a liquid mortar, which overspread their entire surface, hiding the deep holes cut by heavy gun wheels, until man or beast discovered them by stumbling therein. The darkness was intense, rendering it guess work as to where one's foot would land when outstretched. Especially was this the case in the shadow of the woods. Sometimes I caught myself stumbling over a dead horse, and sometimes upon a half living man.

"*Oh don't step on me!*" came imploringly from a bundle of rags, as unwittingly my foot struck against it. "Who are you?" I asked stooping to peer in the darkness. "*I'm from the 9th New Jersey; and I'm bleeding to death. For God sake take off my canteen and give me a drink.*" I hunted about among the man's clothes, getting my hands all daubed with blood, and finally borrowed some water from a passing soldier to give the poor wretch, and then hastened on after my command. This simple act of humanity came near costing me dearly. The regiment had gotten some distance ahead, and as the column of troops plodded on in the very middle of the road, I ran as fast as I could alongside of the road to catch up with my comrades.

Rebel gun thrown into the mill dam and spiked   Grist Mill   Rebel Camp evacuated May 4th on Hill   Whittaker's House   Evacuated 1 gun battery on hill

View of Whittaker's Mill and one gun rebel battery near The Battlefield of Williamsburg Va.
sketched 4th May 1862

Robert Sneden depicted abandoned Confederate camps and earthworks in this watercolor of Whitaker's Mill painted on May 4. Fearing a Confederate flank attack during the Battle of Williamsburg, Heintzelman posted William H. Emory's Reserve Cavalry Brigade and horse artillery around the mill near the James River, less than a mile south of Fort Magruder.

"The repudiated Stars and Stripes are now waving over our Town, and humiliated I feel, we bow our heads to Yankee despotism."

Lieutenant John Donaghy sketched a view of his regiment, the 103d Pennsylvania, as it marched through New Kent Court House on May 14 in pursuit of the Rebels. During the march Donaghy suffered from blisters. When the regiment halted, he bought a battered pair of army brogans. "Ease—not style," he recalled, "was what I was after just then."

HARRIETTE CARY
RESIDENT OF WILLIAMSBURG

Following the Rebel retreat Williamsburg was occupied by thousands of Union soldiers. The sudden presence of an invading army shocked the town's citizenry, as is illustrated in this entry from Cary's wartime diary. After the war Cary made this interesting notation in her journal: "No praise can be too great for George B. McClellan who tried to rob war of its horrors. He was quite a contrast to the savage Grant, Sherman and Sheridan, who believed in making the South 'a barren waste' rather than admit its independence."

The repudiated Stars and Stripes are now waving over our Town, and humiliated I feel, we bow our heads to Yankee despotism. God grant our Southern Patriots may soon relieve us of this degrading yoke. General McClellan's Army took possession this morning about nine o'clock. It seems finely organized and most splendidly equipped—the men robust and well uniformed—especially the officers, yet the utter detestation with which I regard these vandals engenders a disgust which I would not feel for the vilest man on our Southern Soil. A representative of Gen. McClellan's Staff has applied for rooms, but was refused. A fine looking officer with two men very respectfully announced this morning their orders to search, which was but nominal—a glance at each room seemed only necessary—all houses were subjected to the same with more or less scrutiny—I have encountered but one ruffian, who made my blood boil, til sickened with ire and fear. William and Mary College is the head quarters of Gen. Jameson. Gen McClellan is a neighbor of ours—has taken possession of Dr. Vest's house occupied by Gen. Johnston, C.S.A. yesterday. Gen. Porter—the Chancery Office. All is quiet and being assured of protection by two Sentinels placed at our door I shall seek repose, first asking God's blessing on my dear relatives and friends. My heart is sad! God be with the absent ones!

CAPTAIN LOUIS PHILIPPE ALBERT D'ORLEANS, COMTE DE PARIS

AIDE DE CAMP, MAJOR GENERAL GEORGE B. McCLELLAN

The comte de Paris (center), a French nobleman who volunteered to serve on McClellan's staff, was moved by the stoicism of the Confederate wounded. The count was joined in the Army of the Potomac by his brother, the duc de Chartres (far left); their uncle, the prince de Joinville (second from left), accompanied them as an observer.

e reach the College of William and Mary, a large brick building consisting of three pavilions, with pointed roofs supported by arcades. . . . In the middle of the lawn stands an ugly statue blackened by humidity. The pompous inscription announces that this is Lord Botetourt, Governor of Virginia, forgotten by posterity.

This college, apparently destined for quiet and studies, has quite a changed aspect today. The yard is filled with discarded small arms now broken or rusted by the rain. Enemy wounded and prisoners are gathered on the steps beneath the arcade. Many do not have uniforms; those who do wear ash-gray tunics stained by the dust, mud, and blood. They seem indifferent to everything and everyone. Their general expression has a savage quality, their rough and strange faces betray deep humiliation.

We dismount and enter the building. The scene that awaits us inside is one that cannot be forgotten. Whatever one's impression of a dead man, the spectacle of suffering, of the desperate struggles to hold on to life, can be much more moving. These poor people lie in delapidated rooms; most of them received no treatment from the retreating enemy. They lie on a little straw, clothed as during the battle. No one has come to dress their wounds. Many are still on the same stretchers that brought them here. The floor is covered with blood and bits of clothing. A horrible stench lingers everywhere.

A photographer working for Mathew Brady took this photograph of the quiet, sun-baked streets of Yorktown during the Federal occupation of the town. One Northern nurse expressed surprise at how small she found the city. Before the Confederate evacuation, the large dark brick house on the left served as General John Bankhead Magruder's headquarters.

I see a Confederate captain who stands out by the elegance of his uniform. His cap, embroidered in gold, is beside him on the stretcher and inside it are several letters. He died during the night. Other soldiers are in good spirits despite their suffering. In the midst of so much misery I do not hear any complaint. Most of the secesh soldiers are veritable children, some no more than fourteen. One was hit by a ball which struck his brain, yet he continues to live. I have never seen anything more frightful than the mixture of life and death in this unfortunate young man. He no longer has the strength to fight; his rigid hands and face announce that death has taken its prey. Yet the color of youth remains on his cheeks, now more transparent than wax. His chest still rises slowly and regularly as if it belonged to a man peacefully asleep. For two days, whenever I visited the hospital, I would always find this same immobility. Finally, on the last day before leaving Williamsburg, I learned that life had left him. It was a blessing.

In the midst of these wretched scenes I have the pleasure of again meeting Colonel Dwight, an acquaintance from last winter. Wounded in three places during the Excelsior Brigade's combat, he was picked up by the enemy and left at the hospital since they did not think he could be transported. He was not badly hit, however, and never lost the good humor that won for him so many friends.

General McClellan gives the necessary orders to organize the hospital, send for the surgeons and insure the wounded all possible care. Either through indifference or fear the enemy left no doctors behind. As soon as he arrived General Jameson sent a mediator to tell Johnston that any doctor would be received on parole and that our surgeons would do everything possible to help. Leaving the hospital we see a group of officers in gray surrounded by a large escort of our cavalry. A curious crowd soon forms around them: they are the surgeons sent by the enemy. Except for prisoners this is the first time we have come in direct contact with Confederate officers. They seem worried and embarrassed. Finally, while the others remain on horseback with their instrument cases, the first of them dismounts. He introduces himself as Doctor Cullom, chief surgeon of Longstreet's division. He has a soldier's posture and a gentleman's manners. After five minutes, like a true American, he is at ease with everyone. The General asks him for news about all the secesh generals, his classmates and comrades in the army. Soon everyone surrounds him and inquires about a relative or friend in the rebel army. People speak of Joseph Johnston, John B. Magruder, James Longstreet and "Jeb" Stuart as if receiving news of friends after a long absence.

PRIVATE RANDOLPH A. SHOTWELL

8TH VIRGINIA INFANTRY, PICKETT'S BRIGADE

As the Union troops entered Williamsburg, the weary Confederate veterans of the battle continued toward Richmond on a slow and trying march through the mud and rain, whose miseries Shotwell eloquently describes. Shotwell was later commissioned a lieutenant and served with the 8th Virginia until captured on June 27, 1864. He was then confined at the Union prison of Fort Delaware for the remainder of the war.

On the road, about forty feet distant from me, still trudged the long column of weary troops, wading in the reddish *lather* into which the road had been converted by the churning of ten thousand feet, and, as they tramped! tramped! tramped! gave one the idea of a large drove of cattle passing. No pen can describe their discomforts. Wagons were overturned, or broken down, blocking the way; men lost their shoes in the mud; heavy field artillery lurched into holes and had to be pried out; and countless other annoyances occurred. I will give a single instance:

The fences on both sides of the road had been removed to increase the facility for bringing the troops and trains out of town; and in many places the posts of plank fences were pulled up to make fires, leaving deep post-holes unfilled. While I lay back on my comfortable couch with a heavy blanket sheltering my head from the rain, I saw a courier coming from the college-campus, galloping alongside of the troops regardless of the darkness. But when nearly opposite to me an officer grasped his bridle rein, and with an oath, shouted out angrily—*"You shall not ride over my men!"* The courier turned out of the road, and putting spurs started to gallop round the troublesome brigade. Suddenly the poor horse put his foot into one of the fire-lined post holes, and as of course the whole weight of his body descended upon the entrapped leg it snapped like a pipe stem, and with a terrible groan the poor animal lurched against the earth, while the luckless rider was thrown headlong forward into the field. Happily he fell into a puddle of water whose yielding soil, prevented a broken neck, or fractured limb. Tho' himself uninjured, the poor fellow was much cut up at the loss of his horse, and could hardly be persuaded to take the musket which I offered him, and put the groaning beast out of its misery. At length he shouldered his saddle and trudged off manfully through the darkness. "I'm glad I've no despatches to carry in that fashion," thought I, as I again cuddled under my blankets.

HARRIET D. WHETTEN
VOLUNTEER NURSE, U.S. SANITARY COMMISSION

Whetten, who appears above in her nurse's uniform, joined McClellan's forces on May 8 and tended to the wounded of the Army of the Potomac through the end of the Seven Days campaign in July. Whetten's work in taking care of the mangled victims of war was so vastly different from anything she had previously done in her life that she considered the experience one where "everything [was] so strange that nothing [was] strange."

Yesterday afternoon Mrs. Howland and I were ordered on board the *Daniel Webster* to take 200 men, wounded at Williamsburg last Monday, to the hospitals at Fortress Monroe. We went with two of our own surgeons, found three on board, and began to work as soon as we sailed. There were no other women. The men lay about five or six inches apart all over the decks, upper and lower, and on the bul-

warks. Mrs. Howland ordered pails full of soup to be warmed, and tea made—this was served out to them as soon as possible. We in the meantime washed the face and hands of almost every man on board—never while I live shall I forget the uncomplaining fortitude of these men, lying in filth and blood in a state you cannot conceive. They had nearly all been two days or more in the open field in mud and rain. Their gratitude and the comfort they took in their tea and refreshed faces was a rich reward. I could give you little instances of their disinterestedness in favour of their comrades which would bring the tears to your eyes. They were all, not comfortable, but as much so as we could make them before 11 o'clock. The Captain gave us up his state room and we never even heard the explosion of the *Merrimac,* though we saw the fires at Norfolk. This morning busy again serving out breakfast, feeding with a spoon those who could not feed themselves, and giving stimulants to get them strong enough to be carried ashore. We landed them all, poor fellows, by 1/2 past 10. I hope their ghastly wounds are dressed nicely now and that they are comfortabler.

Union soldiers and contrabands relax in the yard of Lafayette's former headquarters in the 1781 siege of Yorktown, one of many local reminders of the Revolutionary War.

Showdown at Seven Pines

On May 6, as George McClellan prepared to resume his march up the Peninsula after his victory at Williamsburg, President Abraham Lincoln arrived at Fort Monroe to conduct a military operation of his own. The goal of this self-appointed mission was to eliminate the menace posed by the Confederate ironclad *Virginia*, which was on the prowl in Hampton Roads.

The *Virginia*'s looming presence not only threatened Federal shipping in the area but also guarded the James River, preventing Union gunboats from steaming upstream to protect McClellan's flank as he advanced on Richmond.

One way to neutralize the *Virginia*, Lincoln knew, would be to deny the vessel its base, the port of Norfolk, across Hampton Roads from Fort Monroe. Norfolk had been bypassed by McClellan and was now isolated in the Federal rear.

Lincoln assigned the capture of the port to Major General John E. Wool, the 78-year-old

- -

Federal soldiers view their encampment at Cumberland Landing in this photograph by James F. Gibson. The massive camp extended two and a half miles along the Pamunkey River, from Cumberland Landing to White House.

commander of Fort Monroe. On the night of May 9, Wool went ashore not far from Norfolk with 5,000 men. They landed without resistance, and the next morning Norfolk's mayor met them on the outskirts of town to report that the Confederate garrison had pulled out.

The *Virginia*, standing offshore, was now a ship without a port—and with nowhere to go. Federal forts barred the vessel's way into the Chesapeake Bay, and it drew too much water to steam up the James to Richmond. On the night of May 10, its captain, Josiah Tattnall, destroyed his ironclad by blowing up its powder magazine.

The James River was now a wide-open avenue to Richmond. At McClellan's urging, a flotilla of Union warships, including the ironclad *Monitor*, was dispatched toward the Confederate capital, about 70 miles away.

Threatened now from both land and water, Richmond went into a panic. The Virginia legislature voted to burn the city rather than see it fall into enemy hands. At a cabinet meeting on May 14, President Jefferson Davis' military adviser, General Robert E. Lee, burst out, "Richmond must not be given up; it shall not be given up!"

As Lee and the others knew, only one obstacle lay in the path of the Federal gunboats—a stronghold at Drewry's Bluff, eight miles below the capital. The bluff, rising 200 feet above the James, commanded a sharp bend in the river. There soldiers and civilians were toiling feverishly to expand the existing defenses and add artillery. Downstream from the bluff, workers scuttled old ships and sank stone-filled log boxes called cribs to close the 120-yard-wide river to vessels seeking to run the stronghold and steam to Richmond.

At dawn on May 15, when the Federal squadron appeared through the mists, the Confederates on the bluff were ready. They opened fire on the lead ship, the ironclad *Galena,* scoring two quick hits. The *Galena*'s captain, Commander John Rodgers, maneuvered the ship so that her guns could bear on the bluff. And then all the Federal ships commenced firing. The roar of cannon, Federal and Confederate, shook the windows in Richmond.

The Rebel gunners took a beating. Shell fragments showered the emplacements, killing seven men. But the Confederates could pour plunging fire down on the *Galena,* penetrating her thin deck armor repeatedly.

The *Monitor* attempted to relieve the *Galena,* but its guns could not be elevated enough to reach the high bluff, and it soon retired downstream. The other ships, outgunned, their wooden hulls vulnerable, did not venture too close to the Rebel batteries.

By 11:00 a.m. the *Galena* had been hit 50 times, her smokestacks riddled, her timbers shattered, her railings shot away. Then a shot tore through the vessel's bow gunport, setting the ship afire. Rodgers gave the order to withdraw. On his decks lay 13 men dead and 11 wounded.

Watching the Federal squadron limp back down the James, the defenders of Drewry's Bluff cheered and tossed their caps aloft. They had saved the city of Richmond—at least for the time being.

Although the waterborne attempt on Richmond had been turned back, McClellan continued his relentless overland advance. By the end of May he had brought his army to the Chickahominy River, a swampy stream that meandered on a southeasterly course from a point just six miles north of Richmond. The general deployed two of his corps on the south bank of the river, basing his left on a crossroads called Seven Pines. He placed his other three corps on the north bank and extended his line up the river for 10 miles to the town of Mechanicsville.

Little Mac had pushed his line to the northeast in anticipation of connecting up with the 38,000 men of Irvin McDowell's corps, who would be marching south from Fredericksburg, President Lincoln having finally agreed to release them. McClellan on May 27 moved to extend his line even farther, sending a division under General Fitz-John Porter to attack the Confederates at Hanover Court House, about 12 miles northwest of Mechanicsville.

The Rebels there—a brigade under former North Carolina congressman Lawrence O'Bryan Branch—were vastly outnumbered and in the ensuing clash lost 200 men dead and wounded and 500 captured. Joseph Johnston regarded the little battle as ominous, for McClellan's sudden move to Hanover Court House seem to portend an imminent linkup between his army and McDowell's. Johnston decided he must attack the Yankee right at Mechanicsville at once to prevent the connection.

But in fact, McDowell was not coming. To McClellan's great disappointment, Lincoln again withheld McDowell's troops, this time specifically to meet a new threat posed by Stonewall Jackson in the Shenandoah Valley. When Johnston was informed by scouts that McDowell was still at Fredericksburg, he changed his plans. He would strike the two

Federal corps isolated south of the Chickahominy with overwhelming force, destroying them before they could be reinforced from across the river.

Three Rebel divisions under General Longstreet would stage the main attack, on May 31, striking east toward Seven Pines along three different routes. To the north, Longstreet's own division would attack down the Nine Mile road, supported by the division of Brigadier General W. H. C. Whiting. In the center, Daniel Harvey Hill was assigned the Williamsburg road and would be supported by Major General Benjamin Huger, who would march by the southern route, the Charles City road.

The timing of the operation depended on Huger. When he got into position on his road, he would signal Hill to begin the assault, and hearing Hill's guns, Longstreet to the north would attack.

It seemed a sound plan, and the weather cooperated on the night before the attack, when a rainstorm turned the Chickahominy into a raging torrent that swamped several of the bridges the Federals had built and further isolated the Yankees south of the river.

But on the morning of May 31 the Confederate plan collapsed when the usually dependable Longstreet, confused about his orders, marched his division south to the Williamsburg road—the wrong road. This meant that Johnston's three-pronged attack was reduced to two. It also meant that the Rebels would miss their scheduled starting time of 8:00 a.m. by many hours, for in moving the wrong way Longstreet's brigades blocked those of Hill and Huger.

It was 1:00 p.m. before Hill attacked. Deployed in thick woods and undergrowth on either side of the road, his men surged forward and shattered the advance line of a Federal division under Brigadier General Silas Casey. The

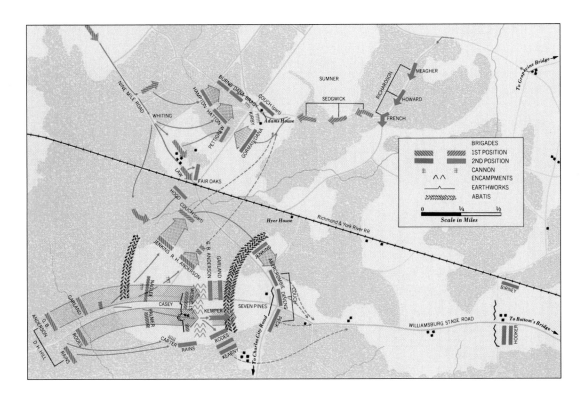

At 1:00 p.m. on the afternoon of May 31 the division of Confederate major general Daniel Harvey Hill routed General Silas Casey's Yankee division from its entrenchments and camps around the hamlet of Seven Pines. But Hill's advance was stalled by a second Union line composed of Darius Couch's division and two brigades under Brigadier General Philip Kearny. A flanking attack against Couch's right by two regiments under Colonel Micah Jenkins along the Nine Mile road finally forced the Federals to withdraw eastward along the Williamsburg road. In a nearly separate battle to the north of the Richmond & York River Railroad, W. H. C. Whiting's Confederates failed to break a Federal line north of Fair Oaks Station.

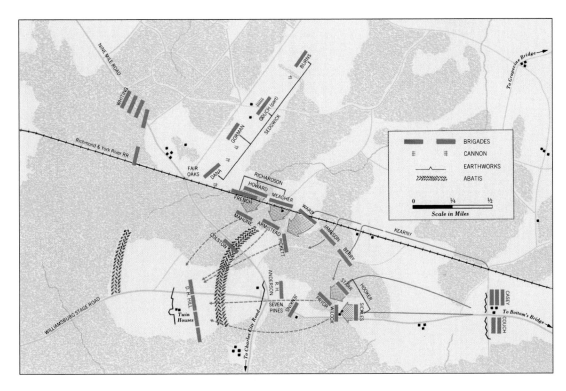

During the night of May 31 the Yankees reorganized their lines north of the railroad grade. Shortly after dawn on June 1, two Confederate brigades advanced westward along the Williamsburg road to reinforce Micah Jenkins and forestall any Federal counterattack, while three more brigades attacked northward toward the railroad. The Rebel attack was stalled with heavy casualties by Israel Richardson's division. When William Mahone's brigade was driven back, the Federals exploited a gap in the Confederate line between the brigades of Armistead and Pickett, forcing them back with heavy casualties. At the same time, Joseph Hooker's division attacked along the Williamsburg road, driving the Confederates back toward Seven Pines. At about 1:00 p.m. D. H. Hill ordered a general Confederate withdrawal, ending the fighting.

Rebels ran into stiffer resistance farther along at Casey's main line—a stretch of earthworks and an earthen fort behind an abatis. But the Yankees were badly outnumbered, and it was not long before they began to abandon their redoubt under withering fire and retreat in confusion.

As Casey's troops streamed back down the Williamsburg road, General Erasmus D. Keyes, IV Corps commander, sent reinforcements—General Darius N. Couch's division and two brigades under Philip Kearny—to shore up the sagging front.

The aggressive Kearny deployed his troops south of the road and launched a flanking counterattack that carried almost to Casey's abandoned camp. Kearny galloped back and forth along his battle line, cheering on his men. When a colonel asked him where to deploy his regiment, Kearny replied, "Oh, anywhere! T'is all the same, Colonel, you'll find lovely fighting along the whole line."

The fresh Federal troops slowed Hill's advance to a crawl, and at about 3:00 p.m. he sent an urgent plea for help to Longstreet, who had remained in the rear. Longstreet, still confused about the battle plan, sent two brigades; one, under Colonel James L. Kemper, marched up to support the Rebel right, opposite Kearny.

The other supporting brigade, commanded by Richard H. Anderson, executed a bold maneuver, attacking northeastward and fighting nearly to the Nine Mile road and Fair Oaks Station on the Richmond & York River Railroad. Then two of Anderson's regiments under Colonel Micah Jenkins circled back southward in a daring attack that took them behind the Federal lines near Seven Pines. Jenkins' thrust forced Kearny to fall back about a mile to protect his threatened flank.

About 4:00 p.m. Joseph Johnston, having realized that his battle plan had been botched,

took personal command of Whiting's division and started it down the Nine Mile road toward Fair Oaks and the battlefield, in hopes that a strike from that direction might salvage the battle.

At first Fair Oaks seemed deserted, but suddenly shells began to fall around Johnston and his officers. The fire came from a lone Yankee battery attached to a handful of Couch's troops that had been cut off from the rest of the division by Micah Jenkins' flanking move.

The Rebels would soon have eliminated this pesky, isolated enemy detachment except for a remarkable turn of events—blue-clad reinforcements began to appear in great numbers. These were troops of General Edwin Sumner's II Corps, who had crossed the flooded Chickahominy on a rickety bridge and marched to the sound of the fighting.

Sumner's lead division, under Brigadier General John Sedgwick, formed a strong line around Couch's position, brought up artillery, and began to pound Whiting's division along the Nine Mile road. At dusk Johnston realized that he faced a formidable force and concluded that he had better recess the battle until the next day.

As Johnston rode forward that evening to inspect his lines, a Federal musket ball hit him in the shoulder, and then a shell fragment slammed into his chest, knocking him from his saddle unconscious. He was carried from the field and taken to Richmond, where he would spend six months recovering.

Command fell to Major General Gustavus W. Smith. After pondering his options, Smith instructed Longstreet to continue the offensive at dawn on June 1 but to swing north from the Williamsburg road to attack toward the railroad—where during the night Federal reinforcements had established a strong defensive line.

At first light Daniel Harvey Hill sent two brigades under Cadmus M. Wilcox and Roger

A. Pryor out the Williamsburg road. There they would relieve Micah Jenkins and spend the morning blocking a counterattack by General Joseph Hooker's Yankees. Then Hill dispatched three brigades—those of George E. Pickett, Lewis A. Armistead, and William Mahone—north through heavy woods toward the railroad.

As they neared the tracks, Mahone's and Armistead's men collided with the Yankees of Brigadier General Israel B. Richardson's division, and vicious, close-in fighting erupted in the dense woods. The commander of Richardson's lead brigade, William H. French, stabilized his line behind the tracks and called for help from General Oliver O. Howard, who personally led two of his regiments through French's line and into the teeth of the Confederate fire, sustaining wounds that would cost him his right arm.

Mahone, outnumbered, committed his regiments one at a time, and each was repulsed by the Federals at the railroad. Finally he was forced to retreat all the way back to the Williamsburg road. Armistead's troops, meanwhile, were holding their own until an error caused their undoing.

Pickett, on the right, lagged behind during the attack, and a gap developed between his brigade and Armistead's to his left. Into the gap poured Colonel J. H. Hobart Ward's Federal troops, who assaulted Armistead's unprotected left flank. The Rebels crumpled before the unexpected onslaught and scrambled for the rear.

Daniel Harvey Hill had seen enough—all morning he had called for reinforcements and had gotten no response. Now he decided that it was futile to continue the attack and ordered his brigades to fall back. About 2:00 p.m. the firing sputtered to a close, and the Battle of Seven Pines was over.

ORDER OF BATTLE   May 31, 1862

ARMY OF NORTHERN VIRGINIA (Confederate)

Johnston 60,000 men

Right Wing Longstreet			Left Wing G. W. Smith
R. H. Anderson's Division	D. H. Hill's Division	Huger's Division	Whiting's Division
Kemper's Brigade	*Garland's Brigade*	*Mahone's Brigade*	*Law's Brigade*
Jenkins' Brigade	*Rodes' Brigade*	*Blanchard's Brigade*	*Hood's Brigade*
Pickett's Brigade	*Rains' Brigade*		*Hampton's Brigade*
Wilcox's Brigade	*G. B. Anderson's Brigade*		*Hatton's Brigade*
Colston's Brigade			*Pettigrew's Brigade*
Pryor's Brigade			

ARMY OF THE POTOMAC (Federal)

McClellan 105,000 men

II Corps Sumner		III Corps Heintzelman	
First Division Richardson	Second Division Sedgwick	Second Division Hooker	Third Division Kearny
Howard's Brigade	*Gorman's Brigade*	*Sickles' Brigade*	*Jameson's Brigade*
Meagher's Brigade	*Burns' Brigade*	*Starr's Brigade*	*Birney's Brigade*
French's Brigade	*Dana's Brigade*		*Berry's Brigade*

IV Corps Keyes		V Corps Porter		
First Division Couch	Second Division Casey	First Division Morell	Second Division Sykes	Third Division McCall
Peck's Brigade	*Naglee's Brigade*	*Martindale's Brigade*	*Buchanan's Brigade*	*Reynolds' Brigade*
Abercrombie's Brigade	*Wessells' Brigade*	*McQuade's Brigade*	*Lovell's Brigade*	*Meade's Brigade*
Devens' Brigade	*Palmer's Brigade*	*Butterfield's Brigade*	*Warren's Brigade*	*Seymour's Brigade*

VI Corps Franklin	
First Division Slocum	Second Division Smith
Taylor's Brigade	*Hancock's Brigade*
Bartlett's Brigade	*Brooks' Brigade*
Newton's Brigade	*Davidson's Brigade*

MAJOR GENERAL GEORGE B. MCCLELLAN

COMMANDER, ARMY OF THE POTOMAC

On May 10 McClellan telegraphed Secretary of War Stanton expressing his fear that the Confederates were massing vast forces for the defense of Richmond. Claiming to be badly outnumbered, he asked for reinforcements before risking battle.

From the information reaching me from every source I regard it as certain that the enemy will meet us with all his force on or near the Chickahominy. They can concentrate many more men than I have, and are collecting troops from all quarters, especially well-disciplined troops from the South. Casualties, sickness, garrisons, and guards have much reduced our numbers, and will continue to do so. I shall fight the rebel army with whatever force I may have, but duty requires me to urge that every effort be made to re-enforce me without delay with all the disposable troops in Eastern Virginia, and that we concentrate all our forces as far as possible to fight the great battle now impending and to make it decisive.

It is possible that the enemy may abandon Richmond without a serious struggle, but I do not believe he will, and it would be unwise to count upon anything but a stubborn and desperate defense—a life-and-death contest. I see no other hope for him than to fight this battle, and we must win it. I shall fight them whatever their force may be, but I ask for every man that the Department can send me. No troops should now be left unemployed. Those who entertain the opinion that the rebels will abandon Richmond without a struggle are in my judgment badly advised, and do not comprehend their situation, which is one requiring desperate measures.

I beg that the President and Secretary will maturely weigh what I say, and leave nothing undone to comply with my request. If I am not re-enforced, it is probable that I will be obliged to fight nearly double my numbers, strongly intrenched. I do not think it will be at all possible for me to bring more than 70,000 men upon the field of battle.

Noting that "every march has been like a little sketching expedition," soldier-artist William McIlvaine Jr. chronicled his service with the 5th New York Zouaves in dozens of on-the-spot drawings and watercolors. On May 13 he depicted the colorfully clad New Yorkers resting near New Kent Court House during a 20-mile march that brought the unit to McClellan's new base of operations at Cumberland Landing on the Pamunkey River.

Laboring in the mosquito-ridden swamp that bordered the Chickahominy River, soldiers of Sumner's II Corps shovel earth atop a corduroy log road spanning the muddy torrent. Sumner's men named the ramshackle crossing Grapevine Bridge after an earlier span destroyed by the Rebels. The name was inspired by the winding nature of the river course and the inch-thick vines that choked its banks.

SURGEON WILLIAM CHILD
5TH NEW HAMPSHIRE INFANTRY, HOWARD'S BRIGADE

Having deployed three of his five corps north of the Chickahominy River for a planned linkup with McDowell's force marching south from Fredericksburg, McClellan was chagrined to learn in late May that McDowell was not coming. Concerned that his corps south of the river were vulnerable, the Federal commander ordered the river bridged at several points. In his 1893 history of the 5th New Hampshire, Child described how his regiment spanned the treacherous stream.

On the 26th of May Colonel Cross received orders to report to General Sumner with his regiment, for fatigue duty. At daybreak next morning, 27th, he reported as ordered, and found that he was to build a bridge, passable for artillery, across the Chickahominy river and swamp. At first view it seemed an impossible undertaking. The First Minnesota Regiment had begun a temporary bridge over the main channel, but the approach to it was a deep morass, into which they had thrown a few logs. Colonel Cross rode into the

swamp, accompanied by Lieutenant Charles Howard, at the risk of the lives of themselves and their horses. They selected a route for the bridge. The channel of the main stream was about forty yards wide, but all through the swamp the water, dark and foul, was from three to six feet deep. The swamp itself was a mass of rank vegetation, huge trees, saplings, bushes, grapevines and creeping plants. Beneath the water lay a soft earth, the consistency of mortar. Here the Fifth was to build a bridge, sufficient to support field guns, in two days. It really was an immense undertaking.

The men stacked arms and were soon divided into gangs—some to chop, some to carry and float timbers and some to build the bridge. Officers were placed over each party, and the work began at each end and in the center. Cross rode into the swamp and personally directed the labors. Cribs of heavy timber were constructed from twenty to twenty-five feet apart and sunk in the water; on these were placed large stringers; and, all being solid, smaller and smooth logs were placed like planks crosswise over these stringers. In some cases the stringers were laid upon stumps or the ground. Where the water was very deep—six feet—two large cribs were sunk instead of one. To do this work the men were obliged to labor in the water—sometimes up to their armpits. Many of the large logs were floated to the bridge from a distance of half a mile or a mile.

On the second day the detail of laborers was increased by two hundred and fifty men from the Sixty-fourth Regiment New York Volunteers, and by one hundred and fifty men from the Irish Brigade. During the night of the 27th the water rose so as to impede operations to a great extent, but they persevered. Of all the party Colonel Cross alone knew of the urgent necessity of having the bridge done as early as might be. About noon, of the second day, General Sumner sent a barrel of whiskey, which was at once issued to the wet and weary men; and the labor went on with renewed vigor until sundown, when the structure was finished.

PRIVATE OLIVER W. NORTON
83D PENNSYLVANIA INFANTRY, BUTTERFIELD'S BRIGADE

After a local civilian reported the presence of a Confederate force at Hanover Court House, McClellan had to deal with the potential threat to his right flank and rear. Norton describes the grueling forced march begun on the morning of May 27 by Porter's V Corps to intercept the enemy. When Porter's column inadvertently passed the concealed Rebels, General Lawrence O'Bryan Branch ordered an attack on the three regiments making up the Federal rear guard.

Last Tuesday morning we were called out at 3:30 o'clock and ordered into line without our knapsacks, taking one blanket and tent, three days' rations, and sixty rounds of cartridges. We had no time to make coffee, and had no breakfast but crackers and water. It was raining heavily and continued to do so till 10 o'clock and then cleared off very hot. The roads were horrible and the artillery was constantly getting stuck and causing delay. We took the road to Hanover Court House, twenty-four miles from camp, and traveled as fast as men could travel except when hindered by the artillery. The bridges were all destroyed but one, and the creeks had to be waded through. It was the severest march we ever had. Officers could not stand it any better than the men, for we had not very heavy loads, and officers and men gave out and lay by the roadside together, utterly unable to go any farther without rest. Captain Austin, Captain Carpenter, Captain Stowe and Captain Graham all gave out, and half the lieutenants in the regiment with scores of the men fell out and lay down to rest.

Saturday P.M., May 31.

A tremendous thunder storm came up yesterday and prevented my finishing my letter. The rain fell in torrents and the lightning was very sharp. A flash struck the quartermaster's tent in the Forty-fourth, about five rods from me, instantly killing him, and stunning twenty others. The bright steel bayonets made excellent lightning rods and a great many in all the camps around were sensibly affected by it.

To go on with my story about the battle. About two miles south of Hanover Court House the Seventeenth New York, which was in front, came upon a North Carolina regiment in the woods. They immediately formed in line of battle in a wheat field and the battery just behind came up and commenced throwing grape into the woods. We followed the battery into the field and took position in time to support it.

LIEUTENANT COLONEL JAMES C. RICE
44TH NEW YORK INFANTRY, BUTTERFIELD'S BRIGADE

A 32-year-old lawyer with strong abolitionist sympathies, Rice took charge of the 44th when its commanding officer unaccountably rode to the rear at the height of the Battle of Hanover Court House. Though engaged in its first fight, the regiment managed to hold its ground, losing 86 men—34 of whom were fatally wounded. Rice's horse was killed beneath him and his sword shot from his side. He described the fierce engagement in his after-action report.

It was unflinching courage alone that gave us the success of the day. The enemy greatly outnumbered us. His fire swept through our ranks like a storm of hail. Our banner was pierced by over forty of the enemy's balls. Four times the colors were struck down, and as soon as they fell they were again raised by volunteer hands. Our cartridges became greatly reduced, and we supplied our necessities by collecting those of the dead and wounded.

Often during the engagement the enemy attempted to leap the fence and embankment in his front, but was repulsed by our deadly fire and the effect of great cheering, which I often caused to be made by our line, to give hope to ourselves and terror to the enemy. Most of the officers during the engagement used the muskets of the dead and wounded with great effect, which added great courage to the men. In the midst of the struggle, when the road was filled with the dead and dying and the enemy seemed to take hope, information was received by me that our cartridges would soon give out. Knowing that we should receive a charge from the enemy and be overpowered if we slackened our fire for a moment, I ordered the men to fix bayonets and be prepared for a charge, determined that no fortune should cause us to lose the day. For the space of one hour the struggle was desperate, our muskets, even, so heated by the continued firing that the soldiers used the water from their canteens to cool them, while many of our arms were shattered by the sweeping cross-fire, and many wounded soldiers loaded muskets through the contest for others to fire.

"Many wounded soldiers loaded muskets through the contest for others to fire."

Alfred Waud's eyewitness sketch shows the vanguard of Porter's corps skirmishing with Confederate troops at Winston's farm, two miles south of Hanover Court House. Troopers of the 6th U.S. Cavalry (foreground) support Captain Henry Benson's battery of the 2d U.S. Artillery, while Porter and his staff, at left, observe the action. The Rebels soon retreated from this field, but Porter called off his pursuit when he received word that his rear guard was under attack.

"As I turned my head, the blow fell on my cheek, the point of the sword cutting to the bone."

PRIVATE ROBERT A. JENKINS
12TH NORTH CAROLINA INFANTRY, BRANCH'S BRIGADE

After launching the 18th North Carolina in a direct assault on the Federal line, Branch ordered the 12th North Carolina to flank the enemy left. In his postwar account of the clash, Jenkins, a former tobacconist, wildly overstates Yankee casualties; the two sides together lost some 300 men.

I was sick and had been for a long while, and was very weak. Dr. Allston told me not to go into the fight, but I thought it best to go. In this fight I was severely cut on my right cheek, the mark of which remains to this day. I had two dead Federal soldiers at my feet, and it was while I was trying to extract my bayonet from the third one, and had my face turned, that Captain Taylor, standing next, shouted to me to look out, and as I turned my head, the blow fell on my cheek, the point of the sword cutting to the bone. With the butt of my gun I knocked my assailant from his horse. About this time we retreated, and the battle ended. The Federal troops had enough for one day and did not follow us. We lost only a few men, but the Federal loss was several thousand. In the retreat, two of my comrades, one on each side, made me put my arms on their shoulders, and in this way took me off the field. I thought then, and still think, what an act of kindness this was; but there were many such happening each day, and very few of them will ever be recorded.

We marched some miles, and as night was then falling, we stopped to take up camp till morning. I and many others were too tired to try to prepare anything to eat; in fact, we had nothing, not even our knapsacks, as we had dropped them when we went into battle, and when we came out in an entirely different place we left them behind; I had broken my gun when I knocked the soldier from his horse, so I had left that also. A slow, drizzling rain had commenced, and before any of us could get any rest, a courier dashed up at great speed to tell the General that the cavalry was in hot pursuit, so we fell in and started on the march again to Richmond.

Colonel Henry S. Lansing of the 17th New York stands behind a 12-pounder field howitzer and limber that his soldiers captured from Latham's Virginia battery in the fight at Hanover Court House. The New Yorkers overran the gun after its team of horses was disabled by a shot from Benson's 2d U.S. Artillery.

PRIVATE HENRY T. CHILDS
1ST TENNESSEE INFANTRY, HATTON'S BRIGADE

Hatton's stirring address, recounted here by Childs, was a prelude to the Rebel attack Johnston planned for Seven Pines, in which Whiting's division—including Hatton's Tennesseans—was to support Longstreet's assault on the enemy line south of the Chickahominy. Hatton's troops set out on the evening of May 30, unaware that Longstreet had taken the wrong road and would not be in position as expected.

About sundown the drum tapped, everybody ran into line, and the brigade took up the line of march, with Colonel Turney in the lead. When the head of the column reached the plank road leading to Seven Pines, the following commands were given: "Halt, front, right dress, order arms, parade rest!" The 7th Tennessee was then marched close in the rear of the 1st Tennessee, and the same commands were given. Then came the 14th Tennessee, close in the rear of the 7th Tennessee, and executed the same commands. Here, then, stood the Tennessee Brigade at parade rest in close column by battalion. General Hatton then swung around on his horse close in front of the colors and made a short speech. I was then a beardless boy, in full life and vigor, and I have always thought that that speech was a flow of eloquence and sublimity never surpassed. It can never be reproduced. I shall only try to give a brief outline: "Boys, before the dawn of another day we will be engaged in deadly conflict with the enemy. We are the only representatives of the gallant little commonwealth of Tennessee upon the soil of Virginia. I appeal to you as Tennesseeans. Show yourselves worthy sons of a noble ancestry. Just in our rear is the capital city of the Confederacy. Around our capital city has been gathered a vandal horde of Yankees. Their object, their aim, their purpose is to plunder and pillage our capital. Shall it be sacked?"

Just then the stentorian voice of Colonel Turney rang out upon the night air: "No, never!" And every boy snatched off his hat, caught up the refrain, and made the welkin ring with the shout of "No, never!"

Lieutenant James B. Washington (at left), an aide to Johnston, was photographed with a fellow former West Pointer, Lieutenant George A. Custer, after he was captured on the morning of May 31 and taken to McClellan's headquarters. Washington had ridden into enemy lines while attempting to locate Longstreet's errant column.

PRIVATE ALBERT MAXFIELD
11TH MAINE INFANTRY, NAGLEE'S BRIGADE

A schoolteacher from Casco, Maine, Maxfield had been in the army less than three months when he witnessed the capture of Lieutenant Washington. Despite his inexperience with battle, Maxfield rightly assumed that the Rebels were massing their forces in the woods west of Seven Pines in preparation for an attack.

The men passed a miserable night, watching in darkness and storm, sheltering themselves as they best could and still remain alert, for all the signs pointed to an early attack on us; the pressure of the enemies skirmish lines, the plain movements of their troops, and the fact that they must either dislodge us or lose Richmond. Towards morning the storm ceased, and the day broke with the promise of clearness. Shortly afterwards Sergeant Brady came out of camp with Private Annis, then a detailed cook, Annis bearing a camp kettle in which he proceeded to prepare coffee, when the men partook of a rough breakfast. Soon Lieutenant Washington, of General Johnston's staff, rode unexpectedly into the line of D, having mistaken a road in carrying orders to some rebel command. Quickly halted, he ruefully yielded himself a prisoner, and under Captain Harvey's pilotage made an unwilling way to General Casey's headquarters. Captain Harvey failing to return, the command of the company devolved upon Second Lieutenant Johnson, as First Lieutenant Stanwood was away sick. The capture of Lieutenant Washington made the pickets doubly alert.

PRIVATE JOHN GEER

98TH NEW YORK INFANTRY, PALMER'S BRIGADE

At 11:00 a.m., hours after the Confederate assault at Seven Pines was to have gotten under way, D. H. Hill impulsively launched his brigades against General Silas Casey's division. Despite earlier warnings, Casey's troops were largely unprepared for the ferocious Rebel onslaught. Some units were quickly broken, while others—like Geer's 98th New York and the 104th Pennsylvania—resolutely stood their ground and inflicted heavy losses on the attackers.

Colonel William W. H. Davis (left) led eight companies of the 104th Pennsylvania in a desperate counterattack against D. H. Hill's troops, buying time to allow a Federal artillery battery to make its escape. Wounded in the left elbow, Davis stood by his embattled soldiers until their isolated position was nearly surrounded, then waged a fighting retreat to the crossroads at Seven Pines. A lawyer and newspaper editor from Doylestown, Pennsylvania, Davis had fought in the Mexican War and briefly served as governor of the New Mexico Territory.

Soon after 1 o'clock, our pickets began to come in sight returning thru the woods and slashing before the enemy. The skirmish line of the enemy pursued them, and we could see both parties jumping over logs and making their way thru the bushes, and hear at intervals the sharp reports of their rifles. A little later a dense mass of men, about two rods wide, headed by half a dozen horsemen, marched toward us on the Williamsburg Road. They moved in quick time, carrying their arms on their shoulders, having flags and banners, and drummers to beat the step.

Our three batteries opened simultaneously with all their power. Our regiment poured its volleys into the slashing and into the column as fast as we could load and fire. The 104th Pa. aimed at the column and at the skirmishers approaching its right front and flank. Unlike us, that regiment had no slashing in its front. The cleared field allowed the enemy to concentrate his fire upon it.

The regiment rushed forward with spirit, jumped a rail fence in its front with a shout and yell, but it was met so resolutely and with such a galling fire by the foe that it fell back in disorder and did not appear on the field as an organization again during the day. Col. Davis was wounded and his "Ringgold Regiment" fought its first battle.

The 104th Pa. falling back cleared the field opposite the advancing column and gave the 98th N.Y. a better opportunity to fire upon it as it moved deliberately on.

The charging mass staggered, stopped and resumed its march again, broke in two, filled up its gaps, but sure and steady, with its flags and banners waving, it moved like the tramp of fate. Thinned, scattered, broken, it passed our right and pressed for the batteries. We poured our volleys into it, and the gaps we made, the swaths we mowed could be seen in the column, for we were only 10 or 15 rods away. The men behind pressed those before, and the head finally reached the redoubt. One of the mounted leaders ascended the parapet and was shot with a pistol by an artillery officer. The whole column staggered and sank to the earth.

Although thrice wounded, Sergeant Hiram W. Purcell of the 104th Pennsylvania saved his unit's flag (above)—a deed that later earned him the Medal of Honor.

LIEUTENANT CHARLES H. BREWSTER
10TH MASSACHUSETTS INFANTRY, DEVENS' BRIGADE

With most of Casey's troops falling back in disorder on Couch's division at Seven Pines, IV Corps commander Erasmus D. Keyes ordered seven companies of the 10th Massachusetts up the Williamsburg road to cover Casey's retreat. Advancing through a field covered with fallen trees and underbrush, the unit formed line of battle but was immediately attacked on the left flank and rear. Two days later Brewster described the chaotic scene in a letter to his mother.

I tried my best to make a face to the rear toward them, and to add to the general confusion it was a matter of great doubt whether they were rebels, or our own men, and we restrained half our fire in that account. the order was immediately given to fall back and form some more fallen brush just behind us, but it was impossible, everything was in confusion and we could not see 3 rods from us in any direction so the order was given to rally on the camp, which we did. Capt Parsons was wounded at the first volley, though I did not know it at the time nor until we formed in front of the camp again, which we did as quick as

The son of six-term Massachusetts congressman and governor George N. Briggs, Colonel Henry S. Briggs (right) of the 10th Massachusetts had also pursued a political career, serving in the state legislature. While trying to extricate his regiment from the deadly cross fire it was taking at Seven Pines, Briggs was severely wounded in both legs and carried to the rear.

Several days after the fight at Seven Pines, James F. Gibson, one of Mathew Brady's cameramen, photographed Federal soldiers reoccupying Casey's redoubt —an earthwork that had been overrun in the initial Rebel assault. Nearly 400 dead were buried behind the buildings in the background. The so-called Twin Houses were originally constructed as two wings of a planned central structure that was never completed.

possible, though with greatly diminished numbers, and were immediately ordered to the left again into the rifle pits where we were before, and here we crossed the field again in a perfect torrent of shot + shell and every other missile of destruction. we lay here for some time again and here we had two or three more wounded.

Pretty soon the firing broke out very hot on the right and we were ordered across the field again to the right. across we went and formed behind a low ridge and faced them, and fought our best, but they turned us again on our right and left, where we had no support. we fell back over another ridge, right in our camp and here we faced them again but twas a hopeless task "a forlorn hope" then Col Briggs fell and was taken up and carried to rear entreating and commanding his bearers to stop, and put him down. he would not leave the field, but they kept on. what few there were of us rallied round the colors and retreated through a strip of woods in which was our camp, but we could not stop to take anything with us as the foe were right on our heels and pouring in a perfect storm of bullets.

General Samuel Garland described his acting chief of staff and fellow VMI graduate, Captain James Lawrence Meem (left), as "a gifted young officer whose conspicuous gallantry won the admiration of all who saw him." More than a third of Garland's 2,000 men fell at Seven Pines, including Meem, who was shot dead from his horse near the close of the battle.

LIEUTENANT WILLIAM H. MORGAN

11TH VIRGINIA INFANTRY, KEMPER'S BRIGADE

After smashing through Casey's position, D. H. Hill's division was stopped by a second Yankee line. With casualties mounting, Hill sent a call for help to Longstreet, whose troops were finally arriving. Colonel James L. Kemper brought up four Virginia regiments at the double-quick. Lieutenant Morgan, who at six feet two inches was one of the tallest men in his unit, recounted Kemper's assault.

Capt. J. Lawrence Meem, of Lynchburg, who, until Garland's promotion was adjutant of the Eleventh Regiment, and was now General Garland's chief of staff, met us with word from the front to "hurry." By this time all were well out of breath, but rushed on at increased speed through mud and water almost knee-deep in some places. Again a messenger is sent from Gen. D. H. Hill to "hurry, it is a critical time at the front; the enemy has been driven from his breastworks and camps, but there are not enough men of the assaulting column left to occupy and hold the works. The men are doing all that mortal men can do, some are falling by the wayside from sheer exhaustion, nothing but the excitement keeps any on their feet." General Kemper said to the messenger, "Tell General Hill I am left in front and would like to change." The messenger replied, "No time to change now, hurry on." Soon the brigade emerged from the woods into the open field, on the

farther side of which the Yankee breastworks and camps were located, but not a living soldier, Yankee or Confederate, was in sight. I have said "living soldier," because as we rushed along by the edge of this field, over which the Confederates had charged, the ground was thickly strewn with dead Confederates close up to the Yankee breastworks and redoubts, where stood their abandoned cannon. Passing beyond these works, Generals Hill and Garland, with their staff officers, were seen waiting, behind a big pile of cord wood, the coming of the brigade, which was directed to file to the right through the Yankee camp, with their small fly-tents still standing, where, facing towards the enemy, the rear rank was in front, but this made little or no difference. Like the English "Fore and Aft," the men fight from front or rear rank just the same. As the brigade filed out through the camp, a terrific fire was opened by the Yankees, who had rallied or been reënforced by fresh troops, a hundred or two yards beyond their camp. The Yankee lines could not be seen on account of the smoke and fog, but the balls flew thick through the air, killing and wounding many. The men lying flat on the ground, returned the fire as best they could. In a short time some one gave the order to fall back to the abandoned Yankee breastworks, some forty or fifty yards in the rear, which afforded protection from the enemy's shots. This order was obeyed in double-quick time, all hurrying over the breastworks, getting on the reverse side, into the ditch half filled with water, preferring the cold water to hot lead.

PRIVATE GEORGE L. KILMER
6TH ALABAMA INFANTRY, RODES' BRIGADE

D. H. Hill intended General Robert E. Rodes' force to advance simultaneously with Garland's brigade, but Rodes was slowed by boggy ground and could commit his regiments only as each one arrived. One of the first units to become engaged, the 6th Alabama was particularly hard hit. Kilmer recounts the increasingly ferocious course of the battle, in which the Alabamians lost 373 men—more than any other Confederate unit and a staggering 59 percent of the regiment's strength.

The butternut trousers of the men were coated quite up to the waist with inky black mud, and they were drenched to the skin from floundering and swimming across White Oak swamp to reach the field on time by a short cut. After crossing the mire they had pushed their way through a thicket grown up with tall briers that scratched and tore their hands and faces, and when at last they got sight of the game that led them such a chase they were in that raspy, nettled, tigrish phase of temper that only finds a vent in biting and hitting back at something or somebody. They were Alabamans—Colonel John B. Gordon's Sixth regiment.

Two of Casey's regiments, the Eighty-first and Eighty-fifth New York, had formed a double line across the stump lot of the clearing, the Eighty-first being partially in the woods between the clearing and the swamp. The fire of the Alabamans being returned by the New Yorkers, the former threw themselves down behind logs and stumps and eased their tempers by a few picked shots where they could count their scores. "I dropped him!" "I saw him fall!" they would exclaim and creep nearer for the next trial. They kept this up, too, when the fight afterward became more exciting, and the victims in Casey's ranks were nearly all hit in the head or chest. In a few minutes the New Yorkers left the stump field for the shelter of the woods and intrenchments. The Sixth Alabama was followed by a brigade line under General Rodes, to which had been given the task of driving Casey's men out of the clearing and intrenchments south of the stage road. A brigade under General Rains was to do the same in the woods between the clearing and the swamp. When Gordon's skirmishers had the game well started, Rodes gave the order to charge the works. Gordon's skirmishers rallied on the colors, and mistaking a word of command faced about and started to the rear. Discovering the error they faced about again, and madder then ever over a blunder that nearly drew upon them the odium of cowardice, charged through the tangled abatis and over the intrenchments without

a halt. The New Yorkers, surprised by the tactics that changed a retreat into a bayonet charge hurried back to a second line at Seven Pines, half a mile in the rear. Gordon's men rushed after them across the clearing until they plunged blindly into another morass two or three feet in depth. There, as else where, the forest had been cut so that the intertwined branches and trunks and the thick growth of briers together formed a trackless labyrinth. Rushing deeper and deeper in, every man for himself, the Alabamans were soon caught like flies in a spider's web. The water in some places ran in currents strong enough to carry a man off his feet, and the heads of the wounded had to be propped up to prevent strangulation.

BRIGADIER GENERAL HENRY M. NAGLEE
BRIGADE COMMANDER, CASEY'S DIVISION

Posted north of the Williamsburg road in advance of the Union earthworks, Naglee's brigade bore the brunt of the Rebel assault and was driven back with heavy losses, as the general recounted in his report. After serving in the Mexican War, Naglee had taken up banking in San Francisco but returned to his native Pennsylvania to fight for the Union.

Gen. Casey gave an order to the 100th N.Y., and 104th Pa., and 11th Maine, to charge, when, as reported by Col. Davis, the regiments sprang forward towards the enemy with a tremendous yell. In our way was a high worm fence which cut our former line of battle, but the boys sprang over it, into the same inclosure with the enemy, where we formed and renewed the fight. The battle now raged with great fury, and the firing was much hotter than before. Spratt's battery during this time had kept up a lively fire in the same direction. At about 3 P.M., the enemy being largely reinforced, pressed us in front and flank, and seeing that we could not hold our position much longer, unless reinforced, I dispatched an officer to Gen. Casey for that purpose. The Colonel of the 100th N.Y. being killed, the Colonel of 104th severely wounded, the Major mortally wounded, the Lieutenant-Colonel absent, half of our men having been killed or wounded, the enemy, ten times our number, within a few feet of us, one of them striking Sergeant Porter, the left guide of the 104th, over the neck with his musket, several of the 11th Maine being bayoneted, and receiving no reinforcements, we were ordered, with "Spratt's" battery, to retire; but, unfortunately, the horse of one of the pieces being killed, we were compelled to abandon that piece.

The enemy endeavored to follow up this success, and was advancing in closed columns, when, our troops having been sufficiently withdrawn, Col. Bailey, of the 1st N.Y. Artillery, at my request, directed the fire of the batteries of Fitch and Bates, situated in and near the redoubt, to be concentrated upon the advancing mass. At every discharge of grape and canister wide gaps were opened in his ranks, which were filled as soon as opened; still he pressed on, until, after many trials, with immense loss, finding that he was "advancing into the very jaws of death," with sullen hesitation he concluded to desist at this point.

A talented 1856 West Point graduate, Colonel Guilford D. Bailey of the 1st New York Artillery (above, right) was shot through the head while defending his guns in Casey's redoubt. "It is as glorious a death as a man can die," Major Charles S. Wainwright noted, "but hard for one so young, with such abilities, and in his first fight. . . . His loss is one that really affects the whole army."

According to one of his subordinates in the 100th New York, Colonel James Malcolm Brown (right) considered General Casey's order to charge "suicidal" but led the attack "with a smile and a hurrah." The colonel died in the assault. A native of Scotland, Brown had served as a military surgeon in the Mexican War and for 18 months shared a tent with his friend Lieutenant U. S. Grant.

PRIVATE MILTON CRAVEN

105TH PENNSYLVANIA INFANTRY, JAMESON'S BRIGADE

At 3:00 p.m. General Philip Kearny was ordered to dispatch one of his brigades to support the embattled IV Corps. Soon afterward Kearny started for the field with the remainder of his division, including two regiments from General Charles Jameson's brigade. Kearny's troops tore into Hill's right flank but soon found their own right under attack. A teenage farmer from western Pennsylvania, Craven lost an arm at the Battle of the Wilderness two years later.

Under cover of a thick second-growth of pine our regiment had approached to within close proximity to the enemy, and then halted for a moment, awaiting orders. Peering out from a curtain of green foliage on a large field to our right, we could see a line of half-finished rifle-pits extending across the Richmond road at right angles. Behind these rifle-pits were posted a line of our troops, apparently awaiting an attack. A short distance to their front was a strip of "slashing" some forty rods wide, separating this from extensive fields beyond. At the farther edge of this abatis was a strong line of the enemy advantageously posted in concealment, while in the open field to their rear the tents were still standing from which Casey's division had just been driven, and a rebel battery crowned the crest of a slight elevation near the Richmond road.

Having received orders, our regiment filed right, and at double-quick entered the field between the rifle pits and the abatis. Instantly, as the right of the regiment emerged from cover, a terrific fire greeted them, answered only by a defiant cheer, and the regiment pressed onward at its utmost speed, moving parallel and within easy musket range of the rebel line, and hence exposed to an incessant, galling fire, while sinking over shoe-top in the miry soil at every step. As a natural consequence, by the time the left had cleared the woods, the regiment was drawn out to nearly twice the proper distance, the right extending beyond the Richmond road. The order was now given, "By the left flank, charge!" and then, under the eagle eye of the impetuous Kearney and the direction of the gallant Jameson, the regiment entered the abatis with a cheer, facing a most furious fire, but pressing forward over logs and tops of fallen trees and through tangled copse, until, panting and ready to sink from exhaustion, broken and decimated, the rebel line was almost reached. It was now manifest to all, that with but little more than a skirmish-line, broken and utterly exhausted with fatigue, an attempt to rout with the bayonet an enemy so vastly superior in numbers, and so compact, fresh, and vigorous could but inevitably result in overwhelming disaster to us. However, a deliberate and well-directed fire was now opened on the enemy at a distance of not more than thirty paces, and, being well supplied with the prepared combustible cartridges, our firing was rapid and destructive. The enemy, thinking, doubtless, to end this sanguinary struggle with a single blow, now in turn attempted a charge, but their close-packed groups, crowded together into narrow open spaces in the tangled abatis, presented a tempting target on which to concentrate with unerring aim a most devastating fire, from which they quickly recoiled, though they continued, as before, a stubborn struggle.

While thus desperately engaged with a vastly superior force in front, many an eye was turned anxiously towards our right and rear, as the terrific roar of musketry and triumphant cheer of the enemy in that direction marked unmistakably their victorious progress. They were sweeping everything before them, like a resistless tidal wave, from the right around to our rear. Our position had now become critical in the extreme.

Sergeant William N. Barr clung to the colors of the 103d Pennsylvania (above) when the unit was swept away in the collapse of Casey's front line. The flag-staff was shot in two, but Barr eluded capture and saved the banner.

MAJOR BRYAN GRIMES

4TH NORTH CAROLINA INFANTRY, G. B. ANDERSON'S BRIGADE

Advancing in the second wave of the Rebel assault, Anderson's brigade reinforced Garland's depleted units and joined in the charge on the Yankee redoubt. Grimes—a wealthy planter and ardent secessionist—was the only officer in the regiment not killed or wounded. By day's end he had only 54 effectives.

The woods were very thick and water deep in ponds from recent rains, in places waist-deep. The enemy, during our advance through the woods, playing upon us with canister and shell, it was impossible to keep an accurate alignment; halted at the edge of the woods, rectified the alignment as near as possible before uncovering my men, and then ordered them to advance, which was through a thick and entangled abatis, formed by felling the trees in opposite directions, which was difficult and tedious to march through. At this time I first saw the redoubt of the enemy about half a mile in front, and somewhat to the right, of my center, which caused me to right-oblique my command. The enemy also had a section of a battery (two pieces) which was dealing destruction to my left wing, while my center and right wing were being mowed down by grape and canister from the redoubt; but the men steadily advanced in admirable order. The enemy fled from the field pieces on my left, and we then concentrated our whole attention to the redoubt. Between this entangled brush-wood and the redoubt was a plowed field, rendered very miry by the late rains, in which the men would mire ankle deep at every step; through this we continued our way. Other regiments at this time were emerging from the thicket both on my right and left, when I gave the order to charge upon the redoubt, which was done by my men in gallant style. When within about 100 yards of the redoubt my horse was killed, catching me under him in his fall. Assistance came and I was extricated uninjured, when we rushed on. When within 30 or 40 yards of the redoubt I saw that we were 200 yards in advance of any other regiment and thought best to fall back to a ditch midway between the redoubt and entangled woods, which I ordered, and the regiment retired in good order; but the

A 19-year-old volunteer in Company E of the 4th North Carolina, Sergeant William A. Cutler (left) was among the 369 casualties the regiment sustained in its intrepid charge— more than half of those who entered the fight. "Their names may not be known to history or to fame," one survivor wrote, "but their comrades knew them and loved them." Wounded in the chest, Cutler recuperated at hospitals in Richmond and North Carolina and in August was detailed as a nurse.

When the 4th North Carolina's color guard was shot down, Major Grimes seized the battle flag (above). A subordinate asked to assume the dangerous responsibility, but Grimes refused, stating, "Lieutenant, your life is worth as much as mine."

color-bearer misunderstanding the order, fell back beyond the ditch to this entangled brush. Those who had taken cover in the ditch then followed the colors, which were then halted, and all ordered to lie down, being still within 250 yards of the redoubt.

About this time our battery arrived and commenced playing upon the enemy. As an evidence of the severity of the fire of the enemy while in front of the battery 46 of my men were found killed within an area of one acre. After allowing my men time to recover from their fatigue, just then I saw my third color-bearer shot down. Captain Simonton and myself rushed up to raise the colors. Captain Simonton, reaching them first, placed them in my hands, raising them aloft, calling upon my men to rally around their standard. It was done with alacrity, and, together with several other regiments, we reached the redoubt, the enemy fleeing.

PRIVATE ALEXANDER HUNTER
17TH VIRGINIA INFANTRY, KEMPER'S BRIGADE

After jogging for a mile and a half at the double-quick, Kemper's Virginians charged into the chaos at Seven Pines with no knowledge of the lay of the land or of the dispositions of the contending forces. Advancing by the left flank, in a column four men abreast, the 17th Virginia followed the 11th Regiment over the earthworks and through the abandoned Yankee camp. Hunter vividly recalled the carnage that resulted from his unit's faulty deployment.

When we reached the vicinity of the woodpile where there was a big barn and several outworks that had been thrown up by the Federals, but which had been captured by our forces, we could see all the camp of Casey's Division not a hundred yards from us. The shelling was now terrific. As we had double-quicked across the field the enemy had plain view of our brigade, and had trained their several batteries, located on the edge of the camp, upon us. Shell, shrapnel and round shot screamed over us, fortunately a few feet too high. Then was the time to form in a line of battle; instead of that we kept on without changing our formation, which was in fours. In other words we pushed towards the enemy like a lance, instead of spreading out in a line. My company was in advance, the lance head of the column. As we advanced close to the woodpile the musketry joined the artillery, and to go into that fire-swept camp seemed like entering the jaws of hell itself. "Why don't we form a line of battle?" was the rank and file cry, as the men began to drop, for in column as we were none could fire. We knew some one had blundered. The onward gait by the column was kept up. "Forward; forward!" cried the officers, waving their swords above their heads: "Don't stop, men, charge in the camp!" Into the camp we went with yells ringing high above the uproar of the guns. As we dashed in we passed a four-gun battery of ours which was deserted, every horse having been killed and the remnant of the men forced to seek shelter by the terrible concentrated fire that swept through the camp like an iron and leaden rain. I saw a little boy hardly sixteen years old, a "powder monkey," as they called him, cowering behind the wheel of one of the guns, his face wearing a look of humble affright, eyes protruding, hands clasped, teeth clenched—a face so white and startling that it haunted me days after, though I but glanced for a second at him.

As we passed the barn and got in among the tents the tempest of war was frightful; every deadly projectile which could take human life and

"To have attempted running the gauntlet across the field in our rear would have been to have rattled dice with death."

maim and disfigure was showered upon us. The air was alive with their coming and shrill and shrieking with their passing. We could see no enemy, but the whole of Casey's Division, of some thousand men, formed around their camp in the shape of a half moon, pouring a converging fire at the attacking column. Had our brigade (commanded by General Kemper) been formed into action, we could probably have swept the enemy away by an irresistible rush, but by the incompetency and ignorance of our commanding officers we were allowed to pour like cattle upon a fortified foe. It sickens me at heart as I write what followed, a result that could not have been otherwise. Mixed up, mingled up, crowded up among the breastworks, barn and woodpile, the brigade got bunched in a hump, lost its organization, became a mob, and that splendid command, of some six hundred muskets, was forced to retreat.

From the half circle on the other side of the camp the enemy rained a constant fire upon the struggling mass. Order disappeared, discipline fled before that tempest. Within five minutes all was over. Men fell in groups; the noise of the Federal bullets ripping through the canvas of the tents added to the horrors of the moment. Men screamed as the balls struck them, the officers shouted out unmeaning cries, the flag went down; Morrill, the color-bearer and the tallest man in the regiment, sank to the earth; Corporal Digges caught the colors and he fell, too. A private grasped them. He raised the staff and in a second he sank face downward with a bullet through his heart. Another gallant private, named Harper, seized the staff from the dead man's hand and bore the colors the rest of the day. In five minutes seventy-four officers and men out of our regiment fell. Then there was a blind rush for shelter. Officers and men scrambled over the breastworks or hurried behind the woodpile. Those rifle-pits, which were built by the Federals to protect their camp, proved now our salvation. But for them none save a few would have escaped alive. To have attempted running the gauntlet across the field in our rear would have been to have rattled dice with death.

CAPTAIN JAMES L. COKER
6TH SOUTH CAROLINA INFANTRY, R. H. ANDERSON'S BRIGADE

As his troops neared the battlefield, Anderson was placed in charge of three brigades and turned his former command over to the dashing young South Carolinian Colonel Micah Jenkins. Jenkins drove northward, smashed through elements of Couch's division, and crossed the Nine Mile road. He then wheeled to the south and with several units—including Coker's 6th South Carolina— swept down upon the right flank and rear of the Federals at Seven Pines.

The first man killed in Company E was Corporal J. L. Kilgore, a shot passing through his brain. His brother Peter, was his file leader. Peter stopped one moment to see his brother's condition, and to remove from his pockets what they contained. Quickly coming up with us again, he continued bravely his duties in the fight. It was only a few minutes before he, too, fell mortally wounded, and the two brothers together as they marched to serve their country, were not parted in their death.

Caleb Tiner was loading and firing where the regiment was lying down in line of battle. He was observing the exact order of drill, and when he rolled over on his back to "tear" and "ram cartridge," a cruel bullet crashed into his forehead and left him stark, the butt of his gun between his feet, and the cartridge in his hand and between his teeth as he was tearing it to load.

Sam Luckey came upon a cavalryman, captured him, and sent him to the rear. He took a Sharp's rifle from the prisoner, and brought it to me, asking me to carry it through the battle, which I did. A few minutes afterwards a bullet brought him down dead on the field.

And so as we passed from point to point on that bloody ground, the leaden hail from the enemy's rifles took from us others of our loved and noble boys, as true and brave as ever stood in battle; Hudson, Dinkins, Dixon, McLendon and Polson.

Standard-bearer John Rabb gallantly advanced ahead of his comrades with this flag of the 6th South Carolina, prompting his commander to write, "Never were the colors borne with a loftier devotion to duty or a quieter disdain of danger."

May the good old State of South Carolina never grow indifferent to the memory of such devoted sons!

In the field near the Nine Mile road, we took possession of some artillery from which the enemy had been driven. This battery had been firing at D. H. Hill's position in the captured works from which he had driven Casey's men at the beginning of the fight. A Confederate battery was now in position there, and taking us for Federals, opened on us when we emerged from the woods.

Adjutant Gaillard was sent back to notify them of their mistake, and they were filled with surprise when told that any Confederates had penetrated so far into the Yankee lines.

While forming a new line in this field, and among the tents of a Pennsylvania regiment, my attention was called by Sam Nettles to a pair of boots showing themselves from under a pile of knapsacks; the suspicious looking boots were taken hold of, and pulled out, and were found to be on the feet of a Yankee Captain. On demand he quickly gave me his sword, and his pistol was found under the cover where he was lying concealed.

CAPTAIN JEREMIAH MCCARTHY
BATTERY C, 1ST PENNSYLVANIA LIGHT ARTILLERY, COUCH'S DIVISION

With Casey's shattered division falling back on the second line of Union earthworks, three batteries of Couch's division came into action near the crossroads, firing their shells over the heads of the retreating infantrymen. Despite the Federal salvos, the Rebels continued to advance, and Confederate artillery opened a heavy counterbattery fire. McCarthy described the duel in his official report.

About 5 o'clock the enemy were pressing on my left with their infantry and at times pouring a most deadly volley into us, but without any serious injury. Fearing that they would charge on us, I ordered the battery to limber to the rear, and took my position about 50 yards to the right and rear. I then ordered the men to fire as rapidly

John R. R. Giles (above) went to war as a lieutenant of the "Tyger Volunteers," which constituted Company D of the 5th South Carolina. In April 1862 he was elected colonel of the regiment but was killed a month later leading a charge at Seven Pines.

as possible at the enemy's battery and the infantry that were supporting it. I would have fired into the woods immediately on my left, but knowing that some of our own regiments were in there, I feared it would be doing more injury than good.

After I was in my last position about fifteen minutes the enemy seemed to concentrate their fire upon my battery, the shells striking my men and horses and breaking rammers, &c. My men by this time were greatly fatigued, nearly all hands working in their shirt-sleeves. I kept my battery there as long as I thought it was safe, the guns being so hot that they burned the thumb-stalls while on the men's thumbs. Several cartridges were also singed whilst they were being put in the pieces. I then limbered three guns to the rear and retreated back to the next field. The fourth gun could not be limbered, on account of the lunette being mashed by one of the enemy's shells.

James F. Gibson photographed these guns of McCarthy's Battery C, 1st Pennsylvania Light Artillery, positioned behind earthworks that were erected following the Battle of Seven Pines. The Confederate offensive on May 31 had encountered far less formidable defenses at this location. Handicapped by a shortage of shovels and axes, General Casey's troops had managed in two and a half days of work to dig some shallow rifle pits and begin the construction of a six-gun redoubt. But, as the army's chief engineer, John G. Barnard, reported, the work "was quite incomplete" when the Rebel attack came.

PRIVATE HENRY T. CHILDS
1ST TENNESSEE INFANTRY, HATTON'S BRIGADE

Childs writes of the heady excitement of going into battle with President Davis and then General Johnston in close attendance. Hatton's Tennessee brigade was marching south on the Nine Mile road when enemy artillery wounded Johnston and revealed the presence of Federal troops on the Confederate left flank. Wheeling to meet the threat, Hatton's men swung into line alongside two other Rebel brigades and charged the Yankee position with fixed bayonets.

As we were passing along the road at a double-quick President Jefferson Davis passed by us with his suite of attendants. Every boy snatched off his hat, and the wild Rebel yell rent the air as a salute to the gallant chieftain of the Confederacy. On we dashed, and at every bound nearer, clearer, deadlier resounded the clash of arms. When we reached a little old schoolhouse on the left side of the road, we were halted. Just beyond the house, on a little mound, was General Johnston, seated upon his big gray horse, with his glasses adjusted, looking at the enemy. Turning around, I heard him ask the question: "What command is this?" General Hatton replied: "Tennessee Brigade." "Put them right in," said General Johnston. General Hatton, turning around to his men, gave the command, "Load!" There was a general rattle of steel as this command was repeated by the company officers down the line. When my gun was loaded, I looked—there was General Johnston's horse, but the saddle was empty. A bomb had burst; Johnston was wounded. . . .

The next command from General Hatton was, "Fix bayonets!" Every old soldier knows what that means. It means that somebody is going to get hurt; it means that in the dreadful tread of a thundering legion, mixed with the wild Rebel yell, something must move. The next command was, "Forward, guide center!" The sons of Tennessee began to move. I have always thought that this was the grandest, sublimest scene I ever saw. The three regiments were moving in perfect line. Above us floated the Stars and Bars, the Cross of St. Andrew, the flag we loved. Our arms were gleaming and glittering and glistening amid the splendors of sunset glow. On we moved toward the sunset with a dreadful tread more terrible than that of Napoleon's thundering legions. Above us and all around us grape and canister and bombs were falling thick and fast, tearing up the earth in front and rear, but the line was never struck. It seemed to me that I was six inches taller than I ever was. When we had gone about one hundred yards, again the sten-

Robert Hatton (above) served in the Tennessee legislature, then lost a bid for governor, but in 1859 was elected to Congress. Though opposed to secession, he accepted command of a Confederate brigade and died leading his troops at Fair Oaks.

torian voice of Colonel Turney rang out above the thunder of the battle: "First Tennessee, change front, forward on first company!" This changed the direction of the 1st Regiment from the west to the north. I glanced back and saw General Hatton going west with the other two regiments, with his hat off, waving them onward. Our regiment, moving north, passed through a skirt of timber where the Yankees had been camped—their tents were stretched; they had been whipped out—and when we had passed through we were ordered to halt and lie down. It was now sunset, and deadly missiles and treetops were falling around us. In the dusk I raised up on my knees to look. Across a little clearing, close to another skirt of woods, I saw the Yankee lines forming. I told the boys they were coming. Soon the company officers passed along the line commanding, "Up, boys!" The boys came to their feet, guns in hand, and the racket of arms began.

Right in the onset everything was enveloped in smoke and darkness. We would shoot at the flash of the enemy's guns, and I suppose they would shoot at the flash of ours. Amid the din and clatter of arms, the boom and thunder of cannon, and the crash of bayonets both sides gave way. It was said that we were engaged three minutes. I know I fired my gun only three times, and I was as calm and deliberate and busy as I could be.

Colonel John Lafayette Riker (above) of the 62d New York was sent with his regiment to the Union right, where he encountered Johnston's advance on Fair Oaks. Riker was killed while leading a bayonet charge in defense of a battery.

PRIVATE DRURY L. ARMISTEAD
STAFF, MAJOR GENERAL JOSEPH E. JOHNSTON

Johnston's advance through Fair Oaks to Seven Pines was thwarted when fresh enemy brigades crossed the Chickahominy and set upon Whiting's division. Lieutenant Edmund Kirby's Federal battery savaged the Rebel columns, and one shell fragment wounded Johnston. Armistead, who five days earlier had been detached from the 3d Virginia Cavalry to serve as a mounted courier on Johnston's staff, described the effort to retrieve the stricken commander's precious sword.

General Johnston and staff rode back about two hundred yards to an elevated position near a small house, which he occupied until he was wounded. The fire of artillery and musketry in our front was then terrific. I being in a few yards of where General Johnston sat on his horse, dismounted and stood with my horse before me. I had an oil cloth strapped on the front of my saddle directly in front of my breast. The minnie balls were flying so very thick I thought I would stoop a little behind my horse, when as I stooped a bullet tore through the oil cloth, just missing the top of my head. It was a powerful close shave. About this time fresh troops going into battle stopped to load their muskets near where I stood, and double-quicked towards the enemy. When the line moved forward after loading, there was an old fellow who had not finished loading, and while thus standing, a shell struck the ground in a few feet of him; but he coolly remarked to himself, "you cannot do that again!" During this time the battle was raging with great fury all along the line.

Most of General Johnston's staff having been sent off on duty except myself and Colonel ——, and the air seeming to be alive with whizzing bullets and bursting shells, Colonel —— would move his head from side to side, as if trying to dodge them. General Johnston turned toward him and smiling said: "Colonel, there is no use of dodging; when you hear them they have passed." Just after saying this a shell exploded immediately in his front, striking the General from his horse, severely wounded and unconscious. I immediately sprang forward, catching him up in my arms, carried him out of the enemy's fire. Others coming to my assistance we moved him back about a quarter of a mile, and laying him down, hastily sent for a stretcher.

He then regained consciousness, and finding that he had lost his sword and pistols said: "The sword was the one worn by my father in the old Revolutionary war and I would not lose it for ten thousand dollars; will not some one please go back and get it and the pistols for me?" And several others and myself volunteered. On returning to the battle-field we found our line had been considerably pressed back and the spot where General Johnston fell to be midway between the line of battle, which was blazing in all its fury, with men falling all around like leaves. I dashed through our line to the spot where the General had fallen, snatched up the sword and pistols, jumped upon my horse and was making back to our lines, when I hadn't got more than twenty yards when one of the pistols fell out of my hand. I quickly sprang to the ground, picked it up, when just as I did so a discharge of grape from a battery of artillery planted within a hundred and fifty yards from where I was, tore up the earth all around me; but I leaped upon my horse and reached our lines in safety, where I met one of the men who had volunteered to go back for the sword and pistols. He demanded me to turn them over to him. I said: "No; I will take them to the General myself." He replied, "I am your superior officer, and have the right to order you." I said, "Superior officer or not, you will not get this sword and these pistols unless you are a better man than I am, and I don't think you are."

Grievously wounded in the chest and shoulder, General Joseph E. Johnston (right) was thought by most observers to be dying when he was carried from the battlefield at Fair Oaks. Yet six months later he was able to return to active duty, assuming command of Confederate forces in Mississippi and Tennessee.

Although critically hurt, Johnston refused to be taken from the field until his sword (below) was saved from capture. The blade had been passed down to him by his father, Peter, a dashing young cavalry officer who had worn it while serving in the patriot forces of General Nathanael Greene in the Revolutionary War.

CAPTAIN BERNARD J. REID
63D PENNSYLVANIA INFANTRY, JAMESON'S BRIGADE

The 63d and the 105th Pennsylvania spearheaded Kearny's attack on the Rebel right. Fighting their way through Rodes' and Kemper's brigades, by nightfall the Pennsylvanians recaptured the southern portion of Casey's camp. But when Rebels closed in on their rear, General Jameson ordered his scattered units to retreat eastward—a dangerous undertaking that Reid described in a postbattle letter. Reid resigned his commission the following July after learning that his law practice was being mismanaged by an unscrupulous partner.

It was sundown and General Jameson had given the order for our whole brigade to fall back to an entrenched position, on the turnpike about a mile and a half to the rear, having the advantages of wide, open fields in front on both sides of the road, where our batteries would have a good range to guard against a night attack. Somehow or other, I believe from the cowardice or other default of our courier charged with the delivery of the order, it never reached us, and after the other regiments of the brigade had gone safely back, and the enemy had followed them a considerable distance along the turnpike behind us, we still held our position on the left of the road in the very front of where the hottest of the battle had been.

I knew well, from the direction of the firing on our right, that the enemy had succeeded in flanking us on that side, and there was still light enough to see fresh regiments beyond the houses moving toward our left. Our men had shot away all their ammunition, except perhaps one or two cartridges apiece, and had emptied besides, the cartridge boxes of our dead and wounded. Captain Kirkwood, of Company B, succeeding to the command as senior captain, asked my advice as to what he should do. I told him we had done all we could for that day; that under the circumstances to remain there longer was to expose what was left of the regiment to be sacrificed or captured as in a few minutes the only avenue of escape left us would be cut off. We had sent back all our wounded that we could find; the dead we could not possibly take with us through the slash and swamps we would have to cross.

Accordingly the captain gave the order to fall back slowly, just as it was growing dark. After I had seen that we had left none of our men behind and could get no further answer to my calls than the whiz of bullets that still came flying from the rifle-pits behind the houses, we turned our men into a by-path that diverged considerably from the main road, which was held by the enemy in force, and from which they

greeted us with random and harmless volleys. A little further on I was struck by a spent fragment of a shell, causing a slight smart for a few minutes, but without breaking the skin. That was the only time I was even touched that day by any of the enemy's missiles.

PRIVATE LEVI FRITZ
53D PENNSYLVANIA INFANTRY, FRENCH'S BRIGADE

At 2:30 p.m. McClellan ordered Sumner to cross the Chickahominy and march to the battlefield. The river was in flood and the troops faced an ordeal as they laboriously made their way across the rickety log bridges. Three brigades of Sedgwick's division arrived in time to blunt the Rebel advance at Fair Oaks, but Richardson's division did not reach the field until after dark. Fritz, a Pottstown, Pennsylvania, resident, wrote about the march to a newspaper back home.

Heavy rains had been falling and the Chickahominy was rising rapidly. The rude corduroy bridge was being fast washed away. The river must be crossed immediately, and so over we went our brigade in front of the division, and the 53d in front of the brigade. We held our cartridge boxes up, and we dashed on, and wading through mud and water for five hundred yards we made the other side. Gens. Richardson, Howard and Meagher, and most of their respective staffs, dismounted and waded through in front of their respective commands. Many amusing incidents occurred in the crossing of the stream but we have not space to dwell upon them. By five o'clock the whole division had got over, and, in quick time the forward line of march was taken up. About twilight a general halt took place. But orders came for us to forward on, so we did. Night had fairly set in and the cannonading had just ceased as we reached the battle ground. The night was dark and gloomy and threatened rain. Keeping our files closely dressed, we slowly forwarded on over the battle field. Treading carefully to avoid tramping on the dead and wounded, on we went. There was nothing to relieve the mysterious monotony of this slow and silent night march, but here and there the bright light from the lantern of some surgeon who was attending to the wounded. At midnight we were halted and forming line of battle, stacked our arms, and throwing ourselves upon the earth endeavored to get such repose as we could. It must be recollected that we had nothing with us but our accouterments, haversack and canteens.

Alfred Waud sketched soldiers of Sumner's II Corps crossing the so-called Grapevine Bridge over the Chickahominy shortly before sunset on May 31 (left). When Richardson's brigade arrived at the span, most of the structure was underwater. Colonel J. C. Pinckney of the 66th New York reported that "for at least half a mile the men waded in the water and marsh up to their waists."

With Johnston out of action, command of the Confederate forces fell to Major General Gustavus W. Smith (right). A native of Kentucky, Smith was a West Point-educated engineer who became New York City's street commissioner. He had such an impressive résumé that he was offered a commission as general by both the Federal and Confederate governments. But Smith proved unequal to the stressful challenge of command; what he described as "paralysis" was likely a mental breakdown.

PRIVATE J. RUFUS HOLLIS
4TH ALABAMA INFANTRY, WHITING'S BRIGADE

With Whiting acting as division commander, his former brigade was led into the fight by Colonel Evander M. Law, who by nightfall had pushed down the Nine Mile road to a point just south of Fair Oaks. Law's troops were not heavily engaged on May 31, and some of his men spent the night rummaging through the abandoned Yankee camps. Hollis, a 19-year-old farmer who had seen action at First Manassas, recalled his midnight adventure three decades after the fight at Fair Oaks.

O! how we did shiver after our blood cooled down. My commanding officer said to me: "If you wish you can get some volunteers and go into the Yankee camps and get some of their fine blankets they left in the retreat." Our boys were slow to volunteer, they didn't know but what some old Yank would be in his tent in the dark and souse a bayonet in them and they didn't care to go. However, I got three or four volunteers to go with me. I told them to be very quiet; we took our guns at a trail arms and went straight in their camps and about the first tent that we entered "shore nuf" an old Yank was ready for us. I told him to keep quiet or we would souse a bayonet thru him and he "shore did" as we had 4 to 1 this time and he had better keep quiet. We were not after Yanks but were after blankets and to see what they had in their camps stored away in their nap sacks. About the first one that we opened I found something rolled up nicely, and what do you reckon it was? A nice slice of ham and crackers they had put up for hard times, and how I did eat, as I was very hungry, and Oh! how many love letters we got, I can't now say, from the girls of the North to their sweethearts dressed in blue; they told them to "kill out all the boys dressed in gray and come home ending the cruel war at once."

We went back to the line of battle with all the blankets that we could conveniently carry. Left the old Yank in his tent for he did "shore" keep quiet. O! how the boys did beg for a blanket.

CORPORAL VALERIUS C. GILES
4TH TEXAS INFANTRY, HOOD'S BRIGADE

Giles writes of the paradox of a soldier's fearing ghosts more than live enemy troops. Arriving late in the fight at Fair Oaks, the four regiments of Hood's Texas Brigade remained in reserve until after dark on May 31, when they were shifted south across the tracks of the Richmond & York River Railroad. Halting in thick woods and swamp, the Texans deployed a picket line and waited uneasily for dawn.

I was frightened when I marched down into that dismal old swamp and when I was left alone in the matted jungle, enveloped in darkness so dense you could feel it; I was scared good and plenty! I knew there were dead men down there, for there had been considerable fighting in that part of the swamp late that afternoon. It may appear a little queer that a soldier would be frightened at dead men, who are powerless to harm him, and not care a snap for the live ones hidden in the brush ready and anxious to shoot him. Nearly every boy raised in the country, as I had been, has seen ghosts.

I had heard the weird yarns and ghostly stories of old Uncle 'Lisha and old Aunt Sarah when the chuck-will's-widows were calling down in the deep forest by the river and the lobo wolves were howling back on the hills. After listening to those fascinating horrors until we were thoroughly wrought up, we boys would form a line in front of Uncle 'Lisha's cabin door and make a dash for the big house a hundred yards away, and we always saw "something white" down by the barn or across the lane by the old gin.

As I stood in the gloomy solitude of the Chickahominy swamp that night I spied the biggest ghost I had ever seen before. I saw it rise up slowly out of the sluggish marsh not larger than a two-months-old calf at first, but the thing gradually grew broader, taller and whiter, until it looked to me as big as a box-car and high as a telegraph pole.

It lit up the dismal surroundings by a soft, pale light. It grew brighter for a few seconds, then rose slowly from the ground and disappeared in the thick foliage of the trees. It was a very decent sort of ghost. It never said a word, just flared up, wavered a little, and then vanished.

It was not long before I saw more of these "hants" floating around in the woods, and I felt relieved when the idea dawned upon me that it was only a phosphoric light rising from the noxious effluvia of the slimy old swamp. For a while there was a profound stillness, a distressing silence, and with those fantastic shadows waltzing all around me, I stood perfectly still until I got so tired that I began to grapple around in the dark feeling for a log or a stump to sit on. I was making some noise wading about in the dark when I heard the voice of my next post comrade call out and say: "You Company B fellow down there! Why the devil don't you climb a tree? No orders against that!"

Before the war 30-year-old Colonel Edward E. Cross (right) of the 5th New Hampshire Infantry had pursued an adventurous career on the western frontier as a journalist, scout, and soldier of fortune in the Mexican army. On the night of May 31 General Richardson detailed Cross' unit as the division advance guard, instructing the colonel, "Hold your position until you are whipped or relieved." During the fight on June 1 Cross was wounded in the left thigh.

SURGEON WILLIAM CHILD
5TH NEW HAMPSHIRE INFANTRY, HOWARD'S BRIGADE

Hunkered down in the wooded swamp south of the railroad and several hundred yards in front of Sumner's II Corps, the pickets of the 5th New Hampshire were only a stone's throw from their enemy counterparts in the Texas Brigade. One New Hampshire officer draped a blanket over his uniform coat and joined a group of Texans around their campfire, while Colonel Cross made a personal reconnaissance of the Rebel positions, detailed by Childs in his 1893 unit history.

About 1 o'clock in the morning the colonel saw lights in the woods on the right flank. He had been informed that they belonged to the Federals, but not being sure, he determined to investigate, sending Major Cook with Company B to reconnoiter. Cook soon reported that the lights were those of the enemy in the woods, according to the best of his belief. Then Cross went forward himself, alone, picking his way among the stumps, over the killed and wounded. He crossed a road running toward the depot when he was halted by the click of a rifle-lock, and a sharp voice said, "Who goes there?" Cross answered, "Wounded man of the Fifth Texas. Who are you?" "Picket of the Second Alabama," was the reply. "I wish to go to your fire," said Cross. "Pass around by the depot, and you will find the doctors," was the answer. Cross then drew off into the darkness and joined his regiment.

It thus having been learned that the enemy were upon our right flank a change of front became necessary. While doing this several prisoners were brought in who stated the pickets of the enemy were close upon us, but not aware that we were upon the field. One of these prisoners was captured by Lieutenant James E. Larkin, Company A. The man came out to pick up sticks for a fire, and stumbled upon our lines. The men being all quiet Larkin said, "What do you want?" supposing him one of our men. "I want some wood to make a fire." Said Larkin, rising up, "Who ordered a fire made?" "Why, Colonel Terry of the Fifth Texas." The words were no sooner out of his mouth than Larkin had him by the throat and a pistol at his ear.

LIEUTENANT WILLIAM N. WOOD
19TH VIRGINIA INFANTRY, PICKETT'S BRIGADE

At Longstreet's order, early on June 1 Brigadier General George E. Pickett brought his four Virginia regiments to Seven Pines, where he reported to D. H. Hill. Hill, not knowing the enemy's exact location, directed Pickett to join two of Huger's brigades in a movement toward the Richmond & York River Railroad. The Rebel units had lost sight of one another in the thick brush when, as Wood describes, the advance stumbled onto the waiting Yankees of Sumner's corps.

We stacked arms in the road and lounged about with indifference—many of the men picking up trinkets—old letters, packages of ground coffee, bundles of crackers, etc., which had been left by the enemy on the day before. A few tents had been left standing. We were getting to be interested—in fact, were having something of a picnic. I was standing near the head of the stacked arms looking Yankeewards, when suddenly puffs of smoke arose from the bushes about three hundred yards in front, followed by the report of musketry, whilst here and there the thud of bullets against stumps and the few standing trees brought the picnic to a sudden termination.

The command, "Fall in! fall in!" was given by the adjutant, and in a few minutes a body of well-drilled soldiers was marching toward the bushes from whence came the shots that put an end to the foraging.

General Pickett rode up, and the column was halted and the brigade formed in line of battle. "Forward, March!" "Steady, boys!" "Don't shoot until you see them!" and many similar expressions were used. We had to scramble through the chevaux-de-frise left in place by the enemy the day before and the various obstructions they had used to protect their rear when encamped on our picnic grounds. Marching forward through sharpened pine limbs, through patches of briars, the Nineteenth was stopped suddenly by an immense frog-pond and no enemy in sight. "By the left flank, march!" was the order and we went about two hundred yards to the left, halted, faced to the front and dressed upon the colors. Still no enemy in sight. We were in the edge of a forest—a road just in our rear separating the woods from an old field. "Lie down" was the next order which was cheerfully obeyed. I was standing near the centre of the regiment, far enough in the rear to see the road some distance to the left, and observed troops crossing the road going towards our rear. This I reported to the Colonel, who instructed me to display our flag "as they must be friends." Stepping back and looking again I saw the United States flag, and then knew they were not friends. Approaching the Colonel with this positive information, the tramp, tramp, is distinctly heard in front. The rustling of leaves comes nearer. Blue coats are seen through the bushes, more and more numerous, and coming directly towards us. The click of the minnie is heard as our boys prepare for action, and then the roar of musketry from the two lines of battle breaks upon the Sabbath day. Short, quick and decisive was the work done, the enemy leaving in less than eight minutes at a quick route step. Again inspecting the road, no sign of danger was seen, and to this day I have never learned what became of the troops that crossed the road on our left.

SERGEANT THOMAS L. LIVERMORE

5TH NEW HAMPSHIRE INFANTRY, HOWARD'S BRIGADE

When war began, Livermore—seen here after promotion to officer—was a 17-year-old student at Lombard University in Illinois. Following service in a 90-days outfit he joined the 5th New Hampshire and had his first taste of combat at Fair Oaks. Rushed forward to plug a gap between French's and Meagher's brigades, his unit lost 180 men—the most of any Federal regiment that day.

The light of the day of June 1, Sunday, had hardly crept around the shadows of the woods, when over the railroad, a little to the left of our front in the woods, a thundering roll of musketry broke forth, and increased in noise until it was almost deafening; and if there were shouts and loud commands they were drowned in that awful noise. Bullets commenced to whiz over our heads in piping tones; sometimes they sounded like a very small circular saw cutting through thin strips of wood, and sometimes like great blue flies; some flew high, and some low, but none hit any one that I observed. Presently old General Sum-

ner rode up to our colonel, and said in his deep voice, plain enough for us in the ranks to hear, "If they come out here, give 'em the bayonet; give 'em the bayonet, they can't stand that"; and rode away. The feelings of that first half-hour, while listening to our comrades in front, are indescribable. I can remember, though, that I waited with the most harrowing (if I may use the word) curiosity. The time was now come to shoot for country and liberty; we stood on our first field with the bullets whizzing around us. When *would* the time come? We did not see, that I recollect, any wounded men, and no horror abated the enthusiasm which the thunders of the fusillade excited; and yet we were all grave, and I for one was patient to rest or go, only the suspense was dreadful.

At length we moved forward in line of battle over the railroad. On the way some of the men in my company, poor fellows, marched into a pit full of water up to their chins, but they kept on. We lay down in the bushes at the edge of the woods and waited again. Up the railroad to our right the rebels we had driven out commenced to fire scattering shots at us, and I think our skirmishers replied. I do not know how near our troops connected on our right, but I believe that if the rebels could have known our exposed flank to be so near they could have made hot work for us. Some frightened, fleeing rebels came from the front right into our ranks, and were captured and told or shown how their lines must have been broken. In half an hour the musketry commenced subsiding, and suddenly our time came and we were commanded to rise up and march to the left on the railroad. The colonel was near our company on foot when he met General French on the railroad, his usual red face all afire and his eyes winking harder than ever; he was without a staff. The colonel asked him something about the fight, and he stammered out in the most excited way that his brigade (the 3d of our division) had met the enemy in the woods and were all cut to pieces. But the colonel, marching gallantly at our head, marched on, and when he had got just in rear of where the fight had been hottest, halted us. I think it was then that we saw two regiments of the Irish Brigade a little farther down the railroad, huddled into masses with their colors flying, trying to charge across the railroad, but as long as we saw them they only lost men and were unable to advance; they yelled, cheered, and swore, but somebody had got them into such an inextricable confusion they could do nothing.

Colonel Cross hurriedly strove to get orders from some one as to where to go in. General Howard had been wounded, and no one in command was near by, but time was not to be lost, so the gallant man ordered his line right forward.

PRIVATE DREWRY B. EASLEY
14TH VIRGINIA INFANTRY, ARMISTEAD'S BRIGADE

As they made their way through the woods in the center of the advancing Confederate line, Brigadier General Lewis A. Armistead's troops ambushed and scattered the 81st Pennsylvania Infantry, which had been deployed south of the railroad. The Rebels pushed on but were flanked and routed by a Federal counterattack. Easley, who was wounded in the encounter, returned to duty that fall and was captured in Pickett's charge at the Battle of Gettysburg.

> "I gave the driver my canteen and he got drunk on the first drink, and took me to Richmond, about seven miles, in a gallop, which came about as near killing me as the wound."

The Yankees fell back and Armistead advanced us into a worse thicket, halted us, and said: "Prepare to charge." I saw nothing to charge, and thought him looney. The Colonel said, "Fix bayonets!" and we did. The General said, "Lie down!" then "Ready!" and we cocked our rifles. Then he said, "Now men, if the Yankees step on you, don't a man shoot till I say fire," and I saw the point. There was a sapling down in front of me which made a good rest, so I knelt. I hap-

pened to look back and saw the brush shaking about fifty yards behind us. It turned out to be our other regiments coming in under a political colonel, without reporting to Armistead. On turning to the front, the brush was shaking there. Soon we saw their bayonets, then their heads. They must have been fresh troops, for their skirmishers were not more than fifteen or twenty feet in front of their line, and they were peeping back to where the brush was shaking behind us as if they were hunting turkeys. As they were about to step into us, Armistead yelled: "Fire!" The whole line disappeared, and I do not think many of them fired, as we lost only one or two killed and five or six wounded. The man in my rear put his gun just beside my face and fired, blacking my face, burning it slightly, and deafening me; and a ball struck me on the round bone which projects outside on the right knee and stopped about an inch above the ankle. It felt as if something heavy had fallen on it. I looked and saw a small hole in the only new uniform I got during the war. As it did not hurt, I started to reload, but got sick, and the captain told two men to take me off the field. They put me in a blanket, as we had no ambulance corps, took me back to the road, and put me in one of our regimental wagons. I gave the driver my canteen and he got drunk on the first drink, and took me to Richmond, about seven miles, in a gallop, which came about as near killing me as the wound.

Seeking a view of the battle at Fair Oaks, a Federal observer ascends in the basket of the balloon Intrepid (left). Aeronaut Thaddeus S. C. Lowe monitored the engagement from his base of operations near McClellan's headquarters, five miles north of the battlefield.

SERGEANT CHARLES A. FULLER
61ST NEW YORK INFANTRY, HOWARD'S BRIGADE

Fuller gave up his law studies in Ohio to return to his native New York and enlist. Led by a stern young Harvard graduate, Colonel Francis C. Barlow, the 61st moved forward with other units of Howard's Brigade and waged a point-blank duel with Mahone's Confederates. More than a quarter of Barlow's 432 men were cut down, but the Rebels were repulsed.

At this point the railroad ran through a piece of woods, and we, though facing occasional bullets from the enemy, could see but a short distance ahead of us. While in this place waiting further orders, Col. Barlow, himself, went forward into the woods to learn more of the situation.

From the stray bullets coming over some of our men were hit. It came to the mind of one, or a few ingenious men in the ranks, that a recumbent posture would conduce to safety, and he, or they, at once took it. This hint was taken up by others, and in a very short time every man was flat on his belly. Presently the Colonel appeared, and, perhaps, looked twice for his regiment he had left standing. He at once roared out, "Who ordered you to lie down? Get up at once." And every man was on his feet. Then the order came, "Forward, guide center. March!" and we entered the woods.

At this point the timber was quite heavy; there was considerable small growth, and under foot it was swampy. It was impossible to maintain a good line. In such an advance the naturally courageous will press forward, and the naturally timid will hang back, and the officers and file closers have their hands full to urge up the laggards.

In my place as orderly I was directly behind Lieut. Wm. H. McIntyre, commanding my company. Next to me, on the left, was Corporal Willey, an old friend from my town. As we were working our way to the front he spoke to me, and said, "Charley, am I hurt much?" I looked up and saw the blood running down the side of his face, and that a part of his ear had been shot away. I said, "No, nothing but a part of your ear is gone," and we pressed forward.

Soon we came upon the 52nd N.Y., I think of French's Brigade, lying on the ground in line of battle. I suppose they had exhausted their ammunition and were waiting for our appearance. We passed over them, and advanced a few rods, when the order was given to halt. Then strenuous efforts were made by our officers to get the men up in the ranks and to dress the line; while this was going on no firing was had on either side. I did not see a rebel, and did not think one was within musket shot. Lieut. McIntyre stood in the Captain's place, and I immediately behind him in the place of first sergeant. Suddenly a tremendous volley was fired by the enemy at short range, which was very destructive. McIntyre sank down with a deathly pallor on his countenance. He said, "I'm killed." I stooped down and said, "Lieutenant, do you think you are mortally wounded?" He replied, "Yes, tell them I'm killed." He never spoke again.

Colonel James Miller ordered the men of the 81st Pennsylvania to hold their fire while he identified the troops in their front. His inquiry was answered by the shout "Virginians!" and a volley that felled Miller and shattered his regiment.

Colonel Tennent Lomax (above), commanding officer of the 3d Alabama Infantry, was wearing this Confederate field officer's frock coat when he was killed in the fight at Fair Oaks on June 1. A 41-year-old lawyer from Montgomery, Lomax at the time of his death was awaiting confirmation of his promotion to brigadier general.

PRIVATE ERWIN LEDYARD
3D ALABAMA INFANTRY, MAHONE'S BRIGADE

With Armistead's troops and two of the three regiments in Mahone's brigade pinned down by enemy fire, the 3d Alabama continued to press on toward the Yankee line south of the railroad. The Alabamians held their own against two Federal units—the 52d New York and the 53d Pennsylvania—but the arrival of Barlow's 61st New York finally put the isolated Rebel regiment to flight. By the time Pickett's brigade came into action, Mahone and Armistead were in retreat.

Coming out of the bushes into a country road we found two Virginia regiments lying down, firing, they having reached the scene of action a little ahead of us. One of them belonged to our brigade and the other, I believe, to Armistead's Brigade. The fire of the enemy was from the dense undergrowth in front of us. There seemed to be no general present at the moment, although there may have been, and there was no definite plan of action. No skirmishers had been sent forward, as far as I could learn. Our regiment laid down in the road, a portion of it being partly behind one of the Virginia regiments. We were under command of General D. H. Hill, who I saw later in the day. General Hill was one of the bravest officers in the Confederate army, and a good division commander, but I think he was taken by surprise on this occasion. Our colonel was Tennant Lomax, of Montgomery, Ala., a gallant officer, who had served in the Mexican war and who had just received his commission as brigadier general. He none the less insisted on leading his boys in their first fight. His was not the spirit to act on the defensive. "I won't be dogged by these Yankees; charge them, boys!" he shouted. At the word the men rose to their feet with a yell, and plunged into the thick undergrowth in front of them. The Virginia regiments did not move forward. We broke one line of the troops opposing us, but we soon struck an overwhelming force. There we were, one regiment exposed to a heavy fire from all sides, for, in addition to the fire of the enemy one of the Virginia regiments of our brigade, thinking it was directing its fire against the Federals, poured several volleys into the backs and over the heads of our men. A member of my company, the Mobile Cadets, near me, was shot through the back and mortally wounded. The fire from the enemy was terrific. It seemed as if every tree in the wood was falling, and the undergrowth was so thick we could get no idea of the force opposed to us except by its fire.

From the edge of a wood east of Seven Pines, Alabamians of Wilcox's brigade fire into the oncoming ranks of the 71st New York Infantry (above). A unit of General Daniel E. Sickles' Excelsior brigade, the New Yorkers cleared the Rebel position at bayonet point, "the enemy," Sickles reported, "flying before them."

CAPTAIN WALTER A. DONALDSON
71ST NEW YORK INFANTRY, SICKLES' BRIGADE

On the morning of June 1 Sickles' regiments charged the Confederate line astride the Williamsburg road, east of Seven Pines. D. H. Hill ordered the hard-pressed brigades of Pryor and Wilcox to abandon their position and withdraw to the Yankee earthworks captured the previous day. Donaldson's skirmish line reoccupied the pillaged campground of Casey's division, but the Federals failed to follow up their success.

I was in command of the color company, and as we came into action, the men firing, a strange, hissing noise struck my ear; it came from a spot perhaps 20 feet to the rear of the men engaged. Calling to my Orderly, First Serg't Fox, I asked him the meaning of the strange sound. He replied: "Captain, we are in luck; the Johnnies are firing too high; their shot is going over our heads." I was really very glad to hear this, and sincerely hoped they would continue to shoot in the same direction.

Serg't Fox had served in the British army, was through the Crimea, consequently was posted on the little episode we were experiencing for the first time; he had been there before. The Confederates continued to unload their lead in our direction with rapidity and dispatch.

A few men had fallen. A rebel sharpshooter posted in a tree near a house on the right of the pike had been making some good shots, with Gen. Sickles and his staff as his target, being nearly in range with the colors. My attention was called to the lively and adventurous youth. Instantly the right of Co. F, including some 20 files, aimed for that tree, which unloaded its dead fruit as food for worms almost immediately.

By this time Col. Nelson Taylor had formed the 3d Excelsior on our left, but, strange as it may appear, his men were advancing with arms at a right-shoulder shift. Col. Brewster, with the 4th Excelsior, was moving forward on the right of the pike.

In this position of affairs some one on the right of the regiment yelled "Charge! Charge!" Supposing Lieut.-Col. Potter had given the order, I repeated it, running to the left, reiterating the direction to charge. It seemed to me to be the proper move to make, as Nelson Taylor's regiment was advancing. With a vigorous shout and cheer we broke with headlong speed toward the edge of the woods sheltering the enemy, whose volleys had been making things uncomfortable for the welfare and good health of Sickles's Brigade.

The onward movement was kept up until we reached the ditch separating us from the Confederate line, which rapidly disappeared. . . .

It was now about 10 a.m. of this memorable day, when I received orders to advance with the company of Capt. Owen Murphy, of the regiment, which now deployed as skirmishers to the right, and all hands moved forward toward the enemy, the right of Co. F resting on the Williamsburg pike. After proceeding a short distance my attention was drawn to an omnibus coming down the road with a citizen passenger seated inside, the driver on the box urging his horses toward us. I cautioned the men to keep out of sight, and allow the vehicle to get inside our lines, which was done, when I ran out of the woods, and covering him with my revolver, ordered him to halt. At the same time my men showed themselves, so preventing his retreat. At this moment the inside passenger jumped out, starting to run up the road toward Richmond. The skirmishers of the 4th Excelsior, who were in the woods on the other side of the road, in advance of Capt. Murphy, showed themselves and called to the fleeing citizen, ordered him to halt, but, continuing his flight, they shot the poor fellow.

PRIVATE ERWIN LEDYARD
3d Alabama Infantry, Mahone's Brigade

Having failed to pierce the Yankee line east of Fair Oaks, and with Mahone's and Armistead's brigades broken, D. H. Hill called off the attack and concentrated his forces at the earthworks west of Seven Pines. Longstreet directed Hill to retreat from the battlefield under cover of darkness, a movement recalled by Ledyard.

Some of the men drank water that was found in the furrows of a plowed field, which had more than a "suspicion" of blood in it. We had some "real" coffee in our haversacks, and some of my company got an iron pot from the barn and proceeded to build a fire. We soon had something to warm the inner man. All this time we were on the lookout for the enemy. Whenever an alarm was given we would man the entrenchments, standing on rails placed over the ditch. But no attack was made, and as the sun went down we had the most comfortable conviction that the day's fighting was over.

As night closed in the scene was a dreary one. We were directed to take such seats as we could place across the ditch referred to, which was in front of the entrenchments when held by the Federals, but was now in their rear as held by us. There we sat drying during the early hours of the night, in imminent peril of falling into the water beneath, filled with dead men and dead horses. A more uncomfortable position cannot well be imagined, for we were sitting on fence rails, and fence rails have their disagreeable features. The night was still. We knew that our troops were falling back and that we were covering the movement, but no neigh of horses or jingle of accoutrements was heard. The mysterious region of the Chickahominy had again lapsed into that slumber from which it had been awakened by the rude sounds of battle and the shrieks of human agony. At length about midnight the command was whispered for us to form line. Not a word was spoken aloud—the men had been charged against making the slightest noise—and like a regiment of spectres we moved into the Williamsburg road. We were the last regiment to leave the late scene of action. As we plunged knee deep in the mud of the Williamsburg road we saw a battery of artillery in position to open on the Federals if they should appear. The gunners stood silently by their pieces and the officers sat motionless on their horses. Not a word was spoken. We passed them silently and when about a quarter of a mile distant broke into a double-quick and in a couple of hours were safe within our lines.

Lee in the Wings

The clash that took place south of the Chick-ahominy was called the Battle of Fair Oaks by the Federals because it was at Fair Oaks that they did their best fighting. For the same reason, to Confederates it was the Battle of Seven Pines. By any name, it had been a major engagement, the biggest and bloodiest thus far waged in the East.

The battle was costly for both sides. The Confederates suffered 6,134 casualties, including 980 dead. The Federals lost 5,031 men, of whom 790 died. Not long after the fighting subsided, trains of ambulance wagons carrying the Confederate wounded descended on Richmond. Quickly the military hospitals and then the private hospitals were filled. The overflow of sufferers was placed in public buildings and in hotels, where they were tended by women of the town. And throughout the city, residents opened their homes to take in and care for wounded men when even these temporary hospitals became overcrowded.

Federal facilities were likewise overwhelmed. Military field hospitals, established throughout the Federal lines in abandoned farmhouses and barns, had already been filled with men sick from dysentery, malaria, and other diseases, and the battle casualties had to rely on nonmilitary aid. The wounded were taken by rail to White House landing on the York River, where a civilian agency, the U.S. Sanitary Commission, had moored a fleet of hospital ships in anticipation of a great bloodletting. "They arrived, dead and alive together, in the same close boxcar," reported noted landscape architect Frederick Law Olmsted, manager of the hospital fleet, "many with awful wounds festering and alive with maggots."

As the dead were buried and the wounded suffered on, both armies claimed victory. Yet neither side had profited from the battle. The Richmond newspapers touted the capture of 10 artillery pieces and a handful of prisoners, while Federal army communiqués claimed that the Confederacy was now on the ropes. In fact, however, the battle had ended in a stalemate: By dawn on June 2 the Confederates had withdrawn to prebattle lines, their backs against Richmond.

Artist Alfred Waud made this sketch of Federal soldiers recovering comrades' bodies and burning dead artillery horses in the yard of the twin houses that marked the center of General Casey's position during the Battle of Seven Pines.

And the Federals' strategic situation was little altered, except that Sumner's corps was now south of the Chickahominy instead of north of it.

The carnage seems to have shaken General McClellan, who on June 2 wrote his wife, "I feel sure of success, so good is the spirit of my men and so great their ardor. But I am tired of the battlefield, with its mangled corpses and poor wounded. Victory has no charms for me when purchased at such a cost."

For the benefit of his troops and no doubt the Northern public, McClellan proclaimed a glorious victory and predicted that the final and decisive battle was at hand. In a message to the troops on June 2, the Young Napoleon wrote, "You are now face to face with the rebels, who are at bay in front of their capital. . . . Let us meet and crush him here in the very center of the rebellion. Soldiers! I will be with you in this battle and share its dangers with you. . . . Let us strike a blow which is to restore peace and union to this distracted land."

Whatever the outcome of the fighting on the Chickahominy, McClellan himself had brought little influence to bear. He had spent much of the battle in bed, ailing with malaria, and had offered no leadership, except to prompt Sumner to send his troops across the river to rescue the threatened corps. Although the common soldiers still adored Little Mac, some of his subordinates were keenly aware of the inertness their general had displayed. One disgruntled officer wrote: "McClellan appeared on the field shortly after the fighting. He did nothing, which will be judged good or bad according as one may think as to the propriety of vigorous action at that time."

But neither did the Confederate leadership distinguish itself. Johnston and Longstreet had bungled their opportunity to crush the Federal left wing, then tried to make Benjamin Huger the scapegoat, blaming his inaction for their

own missteps. As for Johnston's immediate successor on the battlefield, Gustavus Smith, he had been frozen by indecision on June 1 and failed to support the Confederate attack. Smith clearly had crumpled under the burden of high command. Two days after the battle he left the army, his nerves shattered.

In view of these errors and of Johnston's having been rendered *hors de combat,* President Jefferson Davis made a move that would have a monumental effect on the course of the war. He named his military adviser, General Robert E. Lee, to be the new commander of the Confederate army in the East.

At the time Davis' selection was controversial, for Lee was widely seen as a soldier who had failed to live up to his potential. A highly regarded veteran of the Regular Army, with a reputation for personal bravery and competence gained during the Mexican War, Lee had accepted command of Virginia troops shortly after the war began and assumed the responsibility of preserving Union-leaning western Virginia for the Confederacy. He had developed a bold and complicated plan for evicting the Federals from that region, but it had miscarried, largely because his subordinates had served him poorly. In September 1861 Lee had suffered a defeat at Cheat Mountain and withdrawn his troops.

When Lee returned to Richmond from this frustrating venture, some Southern newspapers called him Evacuating Lee. His next assignment —what he called "another forlorn expedition"— was supervising the construction of fortifications along the coasts of Georgia and South Carolina.

Finally came his service as adviser to President Davis on military matters. Lee excelled in this job, masterfully launching Stonewall Jackson's successful campaign in the Shenandoah Valley and arranging for the defense of the Yorktown line on the Peninsula. But

these behind-the-scenes efforts went largely unrecognized by those outside the government, and Lee's reputation paled beside that of the man he was now replacing, Joseph Johnston, one of the heroes of Manassas.

When Lee's appointment was announced, the Richmond *Examiner* scathingly described the new commander as "a general who had never fought a battle, who had a pious horror of guerrillas, and whose extreme tenderness of blood inclined him to depend exclusively on the resources of strategy." The Richmond *Whig* was less severe but reported hearing much "disparagement, sarcasm and ridicule" of Lee. Indeed, some of Lee's new subordinates fretted that they were now being led by Johnston's inferior, a staff officer who had never shown that he possessed the determination and skill needed to successfully defend the Confederacy's capital. The greatest criticism of Lee among his fellow soldiers was his seeming preoccupation with fortifications. He tasked his infantrymen with the urgent construction of extensive defenses north and east of Richmond, work which most Confederate soldiers believed was better left to slaves conscripted from neighboring farms. Besides, they argued, Southern men were ill suited to static trench warfare and should boldly repel the Yankee invader in the open. Most were unaware that Lee viewed the earthworks as nothing more than a temporary expedient until he could reinforce his army.

There were some dissenters from the bleak view held of Lee. One of them was Colonel Joseph Ives, who had known him in South Carolina. Asked by a fellow officer if Lee was aggressive enough to withstand a numerically superior enemy force, Ives replied, "If there is one man in either army, Confederate or Federal, head and shoulders above any other in audacity, it is General Lee! His name might be

Audacity. He will take more desperate chances, and take them quicker, than any other general in this country, North or South." But as Richmond faced its severe test, most harbored doubts that Lee was the man for the job.

Ironically, the enemy commander concurred. McClellan, who had known both Johnston and Lee well during the Mexican War, expressed delight at the change of Confederate command. "I prefer Lee to Johnston," he wrote. "The former is too cautious and weak under grave responsibility—personally brave and energetic to a fault, he yet is wanting in moral firmness when pressed by heavy responsibility and is likely to be timid and irresolute in action."

Even so, the change in Confederate command did not induce McClellan to alter his own tactics. Still fretting over McDowell's absence and convinced that the Rebels outnumbered his forces, he grew even more cautious, digging in deep along his line, building elaborate defenses, bringing up more and more heavy guns for an intended siege of Richmond.

The Federal commander was confident that he had plenty of time to prepare meticulously for the siege. He was certain that the Confederates would remain on the defensive in their earthworks before the capital.

He was wrong. It was Robert E. Lee who would strike first. Lee's bolt out of the blue would fall at Mechanicsville, a few miles from the swampy battlegrounds of Seven Pines. The attack would bring on a series of sharp, bitter engagements known as the Battles of the Seven Days. And those battles would serve to introduce Lee as a bold new leader, a commander whose tactical brilliance, aggressiveness, and flair for risk and daring would become legendary, and whose influence on the course of the war would be greater, perhaps, than that of any other general on either side.

BATTLE OF WILLIAMSBURG CASUALTIES

CONFEDERATE

Killed	102
Wounded	1,368
Missing	133
Total	1,603

FEDERAL

Killed	456
Wounded	1,410
Missing	373
Total	2,239

BATTLE OF SEVEN PINES/FAIR OAKS CASUALTIES

CONFEDERATE

Killed	980
Wounded	4,749
Missing	405
Total	6,134

FEDERAL

Killed	790
Wounded	3,594
Missing	647
Total	5,031

SERGEANT ABRAHAM T. BREWER

61ST PENNSYLVANIA INFANTRY, ABERCROMBIE'S BRIGADE

Wounded on May 31, Brewer lay on the battlefield for two days before being re-moved to a makeshift field hospital. Four days later he was evacuated by rail to the hospital steamer Louisiana. The native of western Pennsylvania recovered in Philadelphia and returned to his regiment in August. Brewer fought at the Battles of Gettysburg and the Wilderness before receiving a discharge in September 1864.

About noon an enemy line of infantry formed twenty feet in rear of me, facing a Union line in the woods not far away. I was, therefore, between the lines so that after fighting began and the enemy lay down to fire, I would inevitably be killed. The Sergeant-Major of one the enemy's regiments stopped and talked to me in a very offensive manner, asking why I did not stay at home, etc. I replied that if his regiment began firing, I would be killed, and asked if he would be good enough to have me removed in rear of his line and laid behind a tree, where I would be in no danger from his fire and would be shielded from the Union fire. He declined, saying that they had enough to do to take care of their own wounded and then he departed.

Directly a fine looking officer came and spoke to me, saying that he was colonel of the 14th North Carolina Regiment and that his name was Anderson. He expressed regret the wounded had not been cared for on either side. Thanking him for his interest, I asked if he could have me placed in rear of his line. He said, "certainly," and called two of his men, directing them to move me in rear of the line and put me behind a big tree which he designated. This moving was a most painful process as the men had no stretcher and I weighed about a hundred sixty pounds. The regiment remaining in line, the colonel came to me again and talked for probably five minutes. Then he directed the two soldiers who had moved me to take me to the nearest Confederate field hospital. This the men started to do, but I could not endure the agony and begged them to lay me down, before going far, they complied with my request and placed me in a thicket of bushes with foliage well advanced. They then fastened several of the bushes together, making an arbor over my head to shield me from the hot sun and suspended a filled canteen so the water would run out by merely pushing it to one side. In this way they provided an arrangement, as nearly automatic as possible, for supplying water, the only thing I wanted and all that was then available. I saw nothing more of the 14th North Carolina, or its manly colonel, who, in time, became a distinguished general.

During the afternoon, some confederate soldiers stood around me and talked about the glorious victory they had won, driving the Union army back to, and at certain points, into the Chickahominy River. They said that the war would soon be over and the Confederacy would be a free and independent nation. After a good deal of such talk, to which I naturally made but scant reply, we heard great cheering toward the Union line followed by heavy musketry and artillery firing, many of the cannon shot crashing through the trees near us. My companions in-stantly started for their command, and I saw no more of the enemy on that field. The Union advance, starting with a brilliant charge of the New York Irish Brigade under General Meagher, came forward to with-in a hundred yards of where I lay, and then to my dismay, stopped, still leaving me between the two contending battle lines. Darkness came on again and the firing gradually ceased.

The second night on the field, Sunday, was uneventful except a gentle rain sifted for hours through the trees and dripped through my friendly arbor, furnishing sufficient moisture to prevent necrosis in the undressed wound. No troops, Union or Confederate, were in sight that next morning, and the dense woods seemed boundless. Nor was there any sound except an occasional discharge of small arms, which always happens when men are cleaning their guns and firing them at times to be sure they are in good order. If there was any water left in my hang-ing canteen, I had not strength to tip it to one side and drink. I could do nothing but wait, indulging whatever hope a wounded man had power to summon. About the middle of the forenoon, I heard voices which sometimes seemed to approach and then recede; whether they were friends or foes, I could not tell. Toward noon a drummer boy of our reg-iment, hunting for killed and wounded, came by and recognized me. This was natural as I was a sergeant in Company A; this company is always on the right of the regiment next to the band. The boy volun-teered to try to locate my brother, Thomas H. Brewer, also of Company A, and in a short time this brother and A. S. Work, a glorious man of our company, came with two other soldiers. They talked to me in low tones, saying that I was between the picket lines and that the rebel sharpshooters were not far away. With an improvised stretcher, they started to carry me off the field, but when they had proceeded a short distance, loud cheering was heard in the Confederate lines accompa-nied by the sound of moving horsemen, and someone said that a caval-ry charge was coming. Two of the men then dropped the stretcher and ran. My brother and Work, however, remained and in due time landed me at one of the field hospitals in rear of the Union lines.

Among the images taken by photographer George N. Barnard when he arrived at Seven Pines shortly after the battle was this view of a modest Virginia farmhouse used as a field hospital by soldiers of Brigadier General Joseph Hooker's division. In addition to the 129 wounded officers and men of their own command, Hooker's surgeons treated the wounded of Casey's division and enemy casualties left behind when the Confederates withdrew from the battlefield.

MAJOR HILARY A. HERBERT

8TH ALABAMA INFANTRY, PRYOR'S BRIGADE

At dusk on May 31, Herbert joined one of the details sent onto the battlefield to recover Confederate wounded. After the Peninsula campaign, Herbert rose to command the 8th Alabama before a severe wound, suffered at the Wilderness, forced him to retire. Later he served seven terms in the U.S. House of Representatives and was appointed secretary of the navy by Grover Cleveland in 1893.

After nightfall we were moved forward and occupied a portion of the field from which the enemy, Casey's Division, had been routed, and here the writer, now Major, was ordered with a detail of 300 men to look after and gather up the wounded on both sides. Casey had been attacked while his men were cooking and what we now saw in camp indicated clearly how complete at that point our victory had been. Men had dropped everything where it was. Pots were still swinging over fires still smouldering; bacon, crackers, sugar, coffee, clothing and other paraphernalia of camp were promiscuously scattered; still standing, here and there, were sutlers' tents filled with canned foods, liquors in great variety, and knick-knacks, such as Confederate soldiers had of late seen only in their dreams. We exulted of course in all these evidences of success, but it soon became painfully evident that our victory, that afternoon at this point, had not been won without great sacrifices. The Federal wounded were more numerous than ours, but though we relieved hundreds of wounded Federals, we came upon many a poor Confederate who also sadly needed our help. A brother-in-law of the writer, George Cook, of the 6th Alabama, lay dead on that field, but it was fortunately not for me to find his body. We were not examining the dead, only answering the

piteous cries of the wounded that came up to us from all sides.

At 3 o'clock in the morning we finished our task. The writer, taking shelter from the rain, crawled into a little tent. Inside was a man sprawled out, occupying nearly the whole space. Lying down by his side I shook him and said, "Get further!" He was dead and already stiff. Another tent was found close by.

CONSTANCE CARY HARRISON
RESIDENT OF RICHMOND

Constance Harrison traveled to Richmond in 1861 when her husband, Burton N. Harrison, accepted the post of secretary to Confederate president Jefferson Davis. Until the Battle of Seven Pines she spent her spare time sewing silk battle flags for the army with her sisters and cousins in one of the many Richmond "sewing circles." When the war came to her doorstep in the form of wounded soldiers from the battlefields of the Peninsula, she volunteered her services as a nurse.

When on the afternoon of the 31st it became known that the engagement had begun, the women of Richmond were still going about their daily vocations quietly, giving no sign of the inward anguish of apprehension. There was enough to do now in preparation for the wounded; yet, as events proved, all that was done was not enough by half. Night brought a lull in the cannonading. People lay down dressed upon beds, but not to sleep, while the weary soldiers slept upon their arms. Early next morning the whole town was on the street. Ambulances, litters, carts, every vehicle that the city could produce, went and came with a ghastly burden; those who could walk limped painfully home, in some cases so black with gunpowder they passed unrecognized. Women with pallid faces flitted bareheaded through the streets searching for their dead or wounded. The churches were thrown open, many people visiting them for a sad communion-

Stretcher bearers unload wounded Yankees alongside the Richmond & York River Railroad tracks in this drawing by Arthur Lumley at Fair Oaks Station on June 3. Lumley's notes point out the name of the locomotive—the Exeter—and the use of leafy branches to shade the wounded. Hundreds made the trip to Cumberland Landing on the Pamunkey River to be carried aboard hospital ships to Northern ports.

service or brief time of prayer; the lecture-rooms of various places of worship were crowded with ladies volunteering to sew, as fast as fingers could fly, the rough beds called for by the surgeons. Men too old or infirm to fight went on horseback or afoot to meet the returning ambulances, and in some cases served as escort to their own dying sons. By afternoon of the day following the battle, the streets were one vast hospital. To find shelter for the sufferers a number of unused buildings were thrown open. I remember, especially, the St. Charles Hotel, a gloomy place, where two young girls went to look for a member of their family, reported wounded. We had tramped in vain over pavements burning with the intensity of the sun, from one scene of horror to another, until our feet and brains alike seemed about to serve us no further. The cool of those vast dreary rooms of the St. Charles was refreshing; but such a spectacle! Men in every stage of mutilation lying on the bare boards, with perhaps a haversack or an army blanket beneath their heads,—some dying, all suffering keenly, while waiting their turn to be attended to. To be there empty-handed and impotent nearly broke our hearts. We passed from one to the other, making such slight additions to their comfort as were possible, while looking in every upturned face in dread to find the object of our search. This sorrow, I may add, was spared, the youth arriving at home later with a slight flesh-wound. The condition of things at this and other improvised hospitals was improved next day by the offerings from many churches of pew-cushions, which, sewn together, served as comfortable beds; and for the remainder of the war their owners thanked God upon bare benches for every "misery missed" that was "mercy gained." To supply food for the hospitals the contents of larders all over town were emptied into baskets; while cellars long sealed and cobwebbed, belonging to the old Virginia gentry who knew good Port and Madeira, were opened by the Ithuriel's spear of universal sympathy. There was not much going to bed that night, either; and I remember spending the greater part of it leaning from my window to seek the cool night air, while wondering as to the fate of those near to me. There was a summons to my mother about midnight. Two soldiers came to tell her of the wounding of one close of kin; but she was already on duty elsewhere, tireless and watchful as ever. Up to that time the younger girls had been regarded as superfluities in hospital service; but on Monday two of us found a couple of rooms where fifteen wounded men lay upon pallets around the floor, and, on offering our services to the surgeons in charge, were proud to have them accepted and to be installed as responsible nurses, under direction of an older and more experienced woman.

JOHN BEAUCHAMP JONES
CLERK, CONFEDERATE WAR DEPARTMENT

Born in Baltimore, Jones spent his childhood in the border states of Kentucky and Missouri. In 1840 he became editor of the Baltimore Saturday Visitor and had some success as a novelist. In April 1861 Jones resigned as editor of the Philadelphia-based Southern Monitor and traveled to Richmond to work for the new government. In his diary he recorded events in Richmond after Seven Pines, including claims by detectives in the city's provost marshal's department.

The battle was renewed to-day, but not seriously. The failure of Gen. Huger to lead his division into action at the time appointed, is alleged as the only reason why the left wing of the enemy was not completely destroyed. But large masses of the enemy did cross the river, on bridges constructed for the purpose, and they had 50,000 men engaged against a much less number on our part; and their batteries played upon us from the north bank of the Chickahominy. The flying foe kept under shelter of this fire—and these guns could not be taken, as the pontoon bridge was defended by heavy artillery.

All day the wounded were borne past our boarding-house in Third Street, to the general hospital; and hundreds, with shattered arms and slight flesh wounds, came on foot. I saw a boy, not more than fifteen years old (from South Carolina), with his hand in a sling. He showed me his wound. A ball had entered between the fingers of his left hand and lodged near the wrist, where the flesh was much swollen. He said, smiling, "I'm going to the hospital just to have the ball cut out, and will then return to the battle-field. I can fight with my right hand."

The detectives are jubilant to-day. They say one of their number, ——, did heroic feats of arms on the field, killing a Yankee colonel, and a private who came to the rescue. At all events, they brought in a colonel's sword, pistols and coat, as trophies. This story is to be in the papers to-morrow!

PRIVATE R. B. MCCULLY
81ST NEW YORK INFANTRY, PALMER'S BRIGADE

The 81st New York suffered heavy casualties—138 officers and men—early in the fighting at Seven Pines. McCully and his comrades returned to the battle-field on June 3 to recover their own dead and inter some of the hundreds of bodies, both Rebel and Yankee, that littered the field. Years later, in response to a letter from a fellow veteran, McCully wrote to describe the experience. The letter was printed in the National Tribune in 1888.

There had been advances and retreats for three days, so that the dead rebels and Yanks were lying together all over the field.

The weather was extremely hot, and the bodies were decomposed beyond recognition. There were also a great many horses killed, so that the stench was terrible. The bodies we buried were of those killed the first day, principally from Casey's Division. The greater part of our men's clothing, and in some cases (especially of officers) the entire clothing, had been removed. In searching for bodies we found under a Sibley tent (I think they were called by that name—they were a round tent with a center-pole) 12 dead rebels, that were wounded and had crawled under there and died.

The 81st N.Y. were camped on this same ground when the battle commenced, and this was one of their tents. Near this tent was a well about six feet deep, with an incline dug to it to walk down to the water. In this lay a dead rebel with his head under the water. He had been wounded, and had crawled down to get a drink and could not get back. On that portion of the field there were many more of the rebels than our men; on other portions more of ours than theirs. We found but one man who was yet alive. A young rebel about 20 years old, who was wounded in the breast, had crawled into some underbrush, and had been left by the rebels while carrying off their wounded. He was delirious and would call piteously the name of some girl, which we concluded was his sweetheart, as we found on his body an ambrotype of a beautiful girl. We gave him a better burial than the others, because we could handle the body. We also found his name, company and regiment, which I have forgotten. We dug his grave, laid him carefully in, put his coat over his face and covered him, got a piece of cracker-box for a head-board, and wrote his name, company and regiment as best we could with a lead-pencil. This was a pathetic incident. It was in the early part of the war, and our hearts were still tender. The other bodies we buried in this manner: We would dig a hole close to the body about

18 inches deep, tip the remains with our shovels into the grave as quickly as possible and cover it. We used pieces of hardtack boxes for headboards; but the most of our men were buried in unknown graves, as it was impossible to get their names, as everything that would give any clew to their identity had been taken by the enemy. The most of the bodies were in such a state of decomposition that they were swollen to double their size.

LIEUTENANT CHARLES S. FLEMING
2D FLORIDA INFANTRY, GARLAND'S BRIGADE

Fleming was wounded in the hip while trying to recover the body of his colonel, George T. Ward, during the Battle of Williamsburg. Left in a field hospital, he was captured and wrote of being a prisoner of war after his exchange in August 1862.

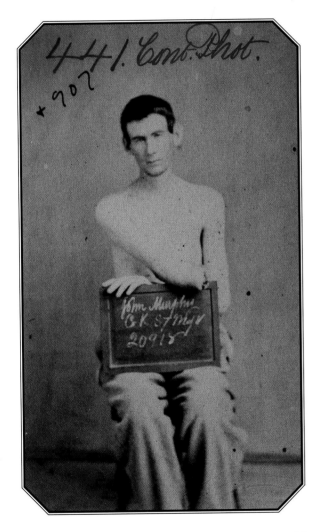

A gaunt Private John Murphy displays the stump of his amputated forearm in this photograph taken at the request of the Union army medical department as part of a project to study the effects of battlefield injuries. Murphy was one of 58 men of the 87th New York Infantry wounded during the fighting on May 31.

*I*n the first place I was wounded by a rifle or musket-ball which entered the center of my right side, about an inch above my hip-bone, and came out alongside of my back-bone. I suppose that Frank wrote you that he left me at a private house, where I was taken about three o'clock that night. The Yankees, who came in town next morning, did not have me removed to a hospital but let me remain at the same house; where I was, indeed, very lucky to get, for the lady who staid there was just as kind and attentive to me as though I were her own and only child. There was nothing that I wanted that was not gotten for me, if it could be had in town. I was confined to my bed for about seven weeks, during which time I suffered more from fever than the actual pain that my wound occasioned. . . .

As soon as I got well enough to be sent away from Williamsburg, I was sent to Fort Monroe, and from there to Fort Wool, commonly known as the Rip Raps, which is an artificial island at the mouth of Hampton Roads. . . . The island is about two hundred yards long and one hundred yards wide, with not a particle of vegetation upon it, and is used at present as a prison. There was strict guard kept over us; our fare was salt meat, bread and coffee; but the coffee was not fit to drink; and our beds consisted of one blanket each. It was no very pleasant thing to be a prisoner; but such is the result of war, and we must take our chances. I intend giving them another trial, and expect that I will have a good opportunity to do so, as the Second Florida is under orders to march to-morrow, and I hear its destination is Jackson's army. I want at least to pay one Yankee off for what they did to me.

Captain Horatio Gibson sits astride his horse in the midst of Battery C, 3d U.S. Light Artillery, in this photograph taken near Fair Oaks in early June. Gibson's battery, part of the Artillery Reserve, missed the battle at Seven Pines but joined the rest of the army to renew the advance on Richmond.

MAJOR GENERAL GEORGE B. MCCLELLAN

COMMANDER, ARMY OF THE POTOMAC

McClellan, shown here with his wife, Ellen, issued this confident general order following Seven Pines. With the failure of the Confederates to halt his advance, Richmond seemed ripe to fall to his army, and McClellan was certain that the entire rebellion could be ended in one grand battle.

Headquarters Army of the Potomac
Camp near New Bridge, Va., June 2, 1862
Soldiers of the Army of the Potomac:

I have fulfilled at least a part of my promise to you. You are now face to face with the rebels, who are at bay in front of their capital. The final and decisive battle is at hand. Unless you belie your past history the result cannot be for a moment doubtful. If the troops who labored so patiently and fought so gallantly at Yorktown, and who so bravely won the hard fights at Williamsburg, West Point, Hanover Court-House, and Fair Oaks now prove worthy of their antecedents, the victory is surely ours. The events of every day prove your superiority; wherever you have met the enemy you have beaten him; wherever you have used the bayonet he has given way in panic and disorder. I ask of you now one last crowning effort. The enemy has staked his all on the issue of the coming battle. Let us meet and crush him here in the very center of the rebellion.

Soldiers, I will be with you in this battle, and share its dangers with you. Our confidence with each other is now founded upon the past. Let us strike the blow which is to restore peace and union to this distracted land. Upon your valor, discipline, and mutual confidence that result depends.

Geo. B. McClellan
Major-General, Commanding.

GENERAL ROBERT E. LEE

COMMANDER, ARMY OF NORTHERN VIRGINIA

Lee's order, published and read to all commands, announces his appointment to command the army and pays tribute to its former leader, the wounded Joseph Johnston. More ominously, the second part of the directive warns the army to prepare for action.

Special Orders No. 22.
Headquarters, Richmond, Va., June 1, 1862
I. In pursuance of the orders of the President, General Robert E. Lee assumes command of the armies of Eastern Virginia and North Carolina.

The unfortunate casualty that has deprived the army in front of Richmond of the valuable services of its able general is not more deeply deplored by any member of his command than by its present commander. He hopes his absence will be but temporary, and while he will endeavor to the best of his ability to perform his duties, he feels he will be totally inadequate to the task unless he shall receive the cordial support of every officer and man.

The presence of the enemy in front of the capital, the great interests involved, and the existence of all that is dear to us appeal in terms too strong to be unheard, and he feels assured that every man has resolved to maintain the ancient fame of the Army of Northern Virginia and the reputation of its general and to conquer or die in the approaching contest.

II. Commanders of divisions and brigades will take every precaution and use every means in their power to have their commands in readiness at all times for immediate action. They will be careful to preserve their men as much as possible, that they may be fresh when called upon for active service. All surplus baggage, broken-down wagons, horses, and mules, and everything that may embarrass the prompt and speedy movement of the army will be turned into depot. Only sufficient transportation will be retained for carrying the necessary cooking utensils and such tents or tent-flies as are indispensable to the comfort and protection of the troops.

GLOSSARY

abatis—A defensive barrier of fallen trees with branches pointed toward the enemy.

ambrotype—A photograph produced with a wet, glass-plate process.

bastion—A projecting portion of a fort's rampart into which artillery is placed, or any fortified place.

Berdan's Sharpshooters—The 1st U.S. Sharpshooters Regiment, named after its founder, Hiram Berdan, a well-known marksman.

breastwork—A temporary fortification, usually of earth and about chest high, over which a soldier could fire.

brevet—An honorary rank given for exceptional bravery or merit in time of war. It granted none of the authority or pay of the official rank.

butternut—The color, variously described as yellowish brown, tan, or brownish gray, of the common homespun Confederate uniform for those who could not afford to acquire cloth of the official gray. It became a general Northern term for a Confederate soldier.

caisson—A cart with large chests for carrying artillery ammunition; connected to a horse-drawn limber when moved.

chevaux de frise—A movable defensive barrier made of logs with sharpened spikes.

color company—The center company of a regiment in line of battle, which included the color guard and carried the regimental flags or colors.

Columbiad—A large cast-metal, smoothbore cannon adopted for all U.S. seacoast defenses in 1860. The largest, a 15-inch Columbiad, threw a 320-pound shell more than a mile. The tube alone weighed almost 25 tons.

contraband—A slave who sought the protection of Union forces.

corduroy road—A road with a surface of logs laid together transversely.

Dahlgren gun—A standard U.S. Navy smoothbore developed by John A. Dahlgren. These guns were distinctively bottle shaped and massive—the barrel alone of a 15-inch Dahlgren weighed more than 10 tons.

double-shotted artillery—Artillery charged with two projectiles rather than the normal one.

echelon—A staggered or stairsteplike formation of parallel units of troops.

embrasure—An opening in a fort wall through which a cannon was fired.

file closer—A soldier marching in the rear of a line of battle to make sure that the formation stayed in order.

forlorn hope—A last-ditch, desperately difficult or dangerous assignment, or the body of soldiers given such a task.

friction primer—A tube containing combustible material that ignited when a wire coated with a friction-sensitive igniter was withdrawn by pulling the lanyard. The device was inserted into the vent of a cannon to discharge the piece.

gabion—An open-ended cylindrical basket of brush or metal strips woven on stakes and usually filled with dirt or cotton. Used to create or reinforce earthworks.

glacis—The outer rim of the defensive ditch protecting a fort's rampart. It usually sloped down toward the enemy.

grapeshot—Iron balls (usually nine) bound together and fired from large-caliber coastal or siege cannon. Resembling a cluster of grapes, the balls broke apart and scattered on impact. The terms "grape" and "grapeshot" are commonly misapplied to the much smaller canister and case shot used in field artillery.

in battery—A cannon placed in a position to fire; a piece of artillery, particularly one mounted on a swiveling carriage, returned to its firing position after loading or recoil.

Irish spoon—A shovel or spade.

limber—A two-wheeled, horse-drawn vehicle to which a gun carriage or a caisson was attached.

lunette—A crescent-shaped fortification, usually for artillery.

masked battery—Any concealed or camouflaged battery of artillery.

Napoleon—A smoothbore, muzzleloading artillery piece developed under the direction of Napoleon III. It fired a 12-pound projectile (and therefore was sometimes called a 12-pounder). Napoleons were originally cast in bronze; when that material became scarce in the South, iron was used.

oblique—At an angle.

order arms—The position for holding a shoulder arm in which the weapon, with its butt resting on the ground, is held vertically along the soldier's right side.

parallel—A trenchwork for artillery dug parallel to the face of an enemy fortification in order to cover an advancing siege party.

parapet—A defensive elevation raised above a fort's main wall, or rampart.

Parrott guns—Muzzleloading, rifled artillery pieces of various calibers made of cast iron, with a unique wrought-iron reinforcing band around the breech. Patented in 1861 by Union officer Robert Parker Parrott, these guns were more accurate at longer range than their smoothbore predecessors.

Pioneers—Construction engineers.

rampart—The main wall of a fort, usually a mound of earth with a flattened top.

redoubt—An enclosed, defensive stronghold.

rifle pits—Holes or shallow trenches dug in the ground from which soldiers could fire weapons and avoid enemy fire. Foxholes.

right shoulder shift—A position for holding a musket in which the butt of the gun was held in the right hand at just below chest height, the breech area rested on the right shoulder, and the muzzle pointed skyward. The rough equivalent of the modern *shoulder arms*.

secesh—A slang term for secessionist.

section of artillery—Part of an artillery battery consisting of two guns, the soldiers who manned them, and their supporting horses and equipment.

Sibley tent—Tent resembling the tepee of the Plains Indians; named for its inventor, Confederate general Henry Hopkins Sibley. Conical, erected on a tripod, with a smoke hole at the top, the tent could easily accommodate 12 men and their equipment.

spike—To render a piece of artillery unserviceable by driving a metal spike into the vent.

trail arms—To grasp a musket at about midpoint and carry it at one's side, roughly parallel to the ground.

vedette—A sentry on horseback (often spelled *vidette*).

vent—A small hole in the breech of a weapon through which a spark travels to ignite the powder charge and fire the piece.

ACKNOWLEDGMENTS

The editors wish to thank the following for their valuable assistance in the preparation of this volume: Eva-Maria Ahladas, Museum of the Confederacy, Richmond; Dale Biever, Civil War Library and Museum, Philadelphia; Elizabeth Bilderbach, University of South Carolina, Columbia; Edith Butler, Union County Historical Foundation, Union, S.C.; Paul A. Carnahan, Vermont Historical Society, Montpelier; Chris Carter, U.S. Naval Academy Museum, Annapolis, Md.; Chrysler Museum of Art, Norfolk, Va.; Steven Cox, Tennessee State Museum, Nashville; Edwin Finney, Washington Navy Yard, Washington, D.C.; Claudia Jew, Mariners' Museum, Newport News, Va.; Michael Lynn, Stonewall Jackson House, Lexington, Va.; Bob McDonald, Glassboro, N.J.; Sue Miller, *Civil War Times Illustrated,* Harrisburg, Pa.; Teresa Roane, Valentine Museum, Richmond; Janice Smith, Washington Navy Yard, Washington, D.C.; William Styple, Kearny, N.J.; Steve Wright, Civil War Library and Museum, Philadelphia.

PICTURE CREDITS

The sources for the illustrations are listed below. Credits from left to right are separated by semicolons, from top to bottom by dashes.

Dust jacket: front, Library of Congress, Neg. No. LC-B8171-377; rear, Massachusetts Commandery of the Military Order of the Loyal Legion and the U.S. Army Military History Institute (MASS-MOLLUS/USAMHI), copied by A. Pierce Bounds.

All calligraphy by Mary Lou O'Brian/Inkwell, Inc.

6, 7: Art by Paul Salmon. 8: Minnesota Historical Society, St. Paul. 15: Map by Peter McGinn. 16: MASS-MOLLUS/USAMHI, photographed by Robert Walch. 17: Library of Congress, Neg. No. LC-B8184-4448. 18: MASS-MOLLUS/USAMHI, copied by A. Pierce Bounds. 19: National Archives, Neg. No. LC-111-B-3804; Massachusetts Historical Society, Boston. 20: Cook Collection, Valentine Museum, Richmond. 21: From *The Papers of Randolph Abbott Shotwell*, Vol. 1, edited by J. G. de Roulhac Hamilton, North Carolina Historical Commission, Raleigh, 1929, copied by Philip Brandt George—Museum of the Confederacy, Richmond, photographed by Larry Sherer. 22: Courtesy Mississippi Department of Archives and History, Jackson. 23: Frank & Marie-Thérèse Wood Print Collections, Alexandria, Va. 24: Collection of Michael J. McAfee; U.S. Army Military History Institute (USAMHI), copied by A. Pierce Bounds. 26: Massachusetts Historical Society, Boston; MASS-MOLLUS/USAMHI, copied by A. Pierce Bounds. 27: Courtesy Bureau of State Office Buildings, Commonwealth of Massachusetts, photographed by Douglas Christian; MASS-MOLLUS/USAMHI, copied by A. Pierce Bounds. 29: Frank & Marie-Thérèse Wood Print Collections, Alexandria, Va. 30, 31: Library of Congress, Waud #375. 32: Courtesy Friends of Fort Ward, from *A Confederate Soldier's Memoirs*, by Edgar Warfield, Masonic Home Press, Richmond, 1936. 33: Print Collection, Miriam and Ira D. Wallach Division of Art, Prints and Photographs, New York Public Library, Astor, Lenox and Tilden Foundations. 34: MASS-MOLLUS/USAMHI, copied by A. Pierce Bounds. 35: Library of Congress, Neg. No. LC-B8171-648. 37: From *Yankee in Gray: The Civil War Memoirs of Henry E. Handerson*, Press of Western Reserve University, 1962, courtesy Cleveland Health Sciences Library, copied by Philip Brandt George. 38: Courtesy Vermont Historical Society, Montpelier. 43: Map by Walter W. Roberts. 44: Chrysler Museum of Art, Norfolk, Va., gift of Anson T. and Philip T. McCook, 54.5.2. 45: Courtesy collection of William A. Turner, copied by Larry Sherer; Museum of the Confederacy, Richmond, photographed by Katherine Wetzel. 47: Milwaukee Public Museum, photographed by Leo Johnson. 48, 49: Library of Congress—Frank & Marie-Thérèse Wood Print Collections, Alexandria, Va. 50: U.S. Naval Historical Center photograph. 51: Alabama Department of Archives and History, Montgomery. 54: MASS-MOLLUS/USAMHI, copied by A. Pierce Bounds. 55: Courtesy U.S. Naval Academy Museum, Annapolis, Md.; Museum of the Confederacy, Richmond, photographed by Larry Sherer. 56: Frank & Marie-Thérèse Wood Print Collections, Alexandria, Va.; Smithsonian Institution, Washington, D.C. 57: Courtesy Mariners' Museum, Newport News, Va. 58: Library of Congress, Neg. No. LC-B8171-4866. 59: From *Civil War Times Illustrated*, April 1974. 61: Library of Congress, Waud #696. 62: Ed Boots Collection at the USAMHI, copied by A. Pierce Bounds—Library of Congress, Waud #1104. 63: Collection of Michael J. McAfee. 64, 65: Copyright, Virginia Historical Society, 1996, all rights reserved. 66: Edward A. Dowling III Collection at the USAMHI, copied by A. Pierce Bounds. 67: From *Confederate Veteran*, Vol. 22, August 1914, copied by Richard Baumgartner—C. Pat Cates Collection at the USAMHI, copied by A. Pierce Bounds. 68: Courtesy Brendan Synnamon, photographed by Henry Mintz; New Jersey State Archives, Trenton, courtesy the USAMHI, copied by A. Pierce Bounds. 69: MASS-MOLLUS/USAMHI, copied by A. Pierce Bounds. 70: Sarah B. Jones Collection at the USAMHI, copied by A. Pierce Bounds. 71: Courtesy Vermont Historical Society, Montpelier. 73: M & M Karolik Collection, courtesy Museum of Fine Arts, Boston. 74, 75: West Point Museum Collections, photographed by Henry Groskinsky—Old Courthouse Museum, Vicksburg, Miss., copied by Henry Mintz. 76: MASS-MOLLUS/USAMHI, copied by A. Pierce Bounds. 77: Library of Congress, Neg. No. LC-B8171-656. 78: Copyright, Virginia Historical Society, 1996, all rights reserved. 79: MASS-MOLLUS/USAMHI, photographed by Robert Walch. 81: Courtesy Vermont Historical Society, Montpelier—MASS/MOLLUS-USAMHI, copied by A. Pierce Bounds. 82: Collection of Michael J. McAfee. 83: Courtesy Vermont Historical Society, Montpelier. 84: Collection of Michael J. McAfee. 85: Frank & Marie-Thérèse Wood Print Collections, Alexandria, Va. 86: From *Yankee Rebel: The Civil War Journal of Edmund DeWitt Patterson*, edited by John G. Barrett, University of North Carolina Press, Chapel Hill, 1966. 89: Old Courthouse Museum,

Vicksburg, Miss., copied by Henry Mintz. 90: Gil Barrett Collection at the USAMHI, copied by A. Pierce Bounds—collection of C. Paul Loane, photographed by Robert J. Laramie (2). 91: Courtesy Bureau of State Office Buildings, Commonwealth of Massachusetts, photographed by Douglas Christian; collection of Michael J. McAfee. 92: Pete Hakel Collection at the USAMHI, copied by A. Pierce Bounds—courtesy collection of William A. Turner. 93: Copyright, Virginia Historical Society, 1996, all rights reserved. 95: Courtesy William Styple; Avoca Museum and Historical Society. 96, 97: Copyright, Virginia Historical Society, 1996, all rights reserved. 98: Library of Congress, Waud #501A. 99: Courtesy William Styple; Division of Military and Naval Affairs, New York State Adjutant General Office, Albany, N.Y., copied by A. Pierce Bounds. 100, 101: Virginia Historical Society, Richmond—courtesy Brian Pohanka; Library of Congress, Waud # 760D. 102: Wisconsin Veterans Museum, Madison. 103: Roger D. Hunt Collection at the USAMHI, copied by A. Pierce Bounds. 104: Courtesy Bryan Craddock, copied by Henry Mintz. 106: Bentley Historical Library, Ann Arbor, Mich. 107: Copyright, Virginia Historical Society, 1996, all rights reserved. 108: M. & M. Karolik Collection, courtesy Museum of Fine Arts, Boston. 109: MASS-MOLLUS/USAMHI, copied by A. Pierce Bounds. 111: State Historical Society of Wisconsin, Madison, WHi (x3)51072; MASS-MOLLUS/USAMHI, copied by A. Pierce Bounds. 112: Library of Congress, Neg. No. LC-B8171-1214. 115: Maps by Walter W. Roberts. 118: Courtesy Brian Pohanka—Civil War Library and Museum, Philadelphia. 119: MASS-MOLLUS/USAMHI, copied by A. Pierce Bounds. 121: Library of Congress, Waud #180. 122: Special Collections Library, Duke University; Library of Congress, Neg. No. LC-B8171-2353. 123: Library of Congress, Neg. No. LC-B8171-428. 124: Civil War Library and Museum, Military Order of the Loyal Legion of the U.S., Philadelphia, copied by

A. Pierce Bounds—Pennsylvania Capitol Preservation Committee, Harrisburg. 125: MASS-MOLLUS/USAMHI, copied by A. Pierce Bounds. 126: Courtesy Rusty Hicks, copied by Henry Mintz. 127: MASS-MOLLUS/USAMHI, copied by A. Pierce Bounds. 128: Collection of Michael J. McAfee. 129: Pennsylvania Capitol Preservation Committee, Harrisburg. 130: MASS-MOLLUS/USAMHI, copied by A. Pierce Bounds—courtesy Joe Woolard Collection, photographed by Henry Mintz. 131: North Carolina Department of Cultural Resources, Division of Archives and History, Raleigh, photographed by Larry Sherer. 133: South Carolina Confederate Relic Room and Museum, photographed by Larry Sherer—courtesy Union County Historical Foundation, Union, S.C. 134: MASS-MOLLUS/USAMHI, copied by A. Pierce Bounds. 135: Tennessee State Museum, Tennessee Historical Society Collection, Nashville. 136: MASS-MOLLUS/USAMHI, copied by A. Pierce Bounds. 137: Valentine Museum, Richmond—Museum of the Confederacy, Richmond, photographed by Larry Sherer. 139: Library of Congress, Waud #42A—Library of Congress, Neg. No. LC-USZ62-77934. 140: MASS-MOLLUS/USAMHI, copied by A. Pierce Bounds. 142: USAMHI, copied by A. Pierce Bounds. 143: Library of Congress, Neg. No. LC-5562-11838. 144: New York State Division of Military and Naval Affairs, Military History Collection, copied by Randall Perry; MASS-MOLLUS/USAMHI, copied by A. Pierce Bounds. 145: Alabama Department of Archives and History, Montgomery, photographed by Robert Fouts. 146, 148: Library of Congress. 153: MASS-MOLLUS/USAMHI, copied by A. Pierce Bounds. 154: Library of Congress, Waud #190. 157: Collection of Michael J. McAfee; Museum of the Confederacy, Richmond, copied by Katherine Wetzel. 158: Library of Congress, Neg. No. LC-B8171-431. 159: Courtesy Brian Pohanka; courtesy Mark Katz, Americana Image Gallery.

BIBLIOGRAPHY

BOOKS

Abbott, Henry Livermore. *Fallen Leaves: The Civil War Letters of Major Henry Livermore Abbott.* Ed. by Robert Garth Scott. Kent, Ohio: Kent State University Press, 1991.

Andrews, W. H. *Footprints of a Regiment: A Recollection of the 1st Georgia Regulars, 1861-1865.* Atlanta: Longstreet

Press, 1992.

Armistead, Drury L. "The Battle in Which General Johnston Was Wounded." In *Southern Historical Society Papers,* Vol. 18. Wilmington, N.C.: Broadfoot, 1990.

Averell, William Woods. *Ten Years in the Saddle: The Memoir of William Woods Averell.* Ed. by Edward K.

Eckert and Nicholas J. Amato. San Rafael, Calif.: Presidio Press, 1978.

Battles and Leaders of the Civil War: North to Antietam, Vol. 2. Ed. by Robert Underwood Johnson and Clarence Clough Buel. New York: Castle Books, 1956.

Blackford, Susan Leigh, comp. *Letters from Lee's Army: Or Memoirs of Life in and out of the Army in Virginia during the War between the States.* Ed. by Charles Minor Blackford III. New York: Charles Scribner's Sons, 1947.

Boatner, Mark Mayo, III. *The Civil War Dictionary.* New York: David McKay, 1959.

Bratton, John. "The Battle of Williamsburg." In *Southern Historical Society Papers,* Vol. 7. Wilmington, N.C.: Broadfoot, 1990.

Brewster, Charles Harvey. *When This Cruel War Is Over.* Ed. by David W. Blight. Amherst: University of Massachusetts Press, 1992.

"Carleton." *Stories of Our Soldiers.* Boston: Journal Newspaper Co., 1893.

Child, William. *A History of the Fifth Regiment New Hampshire Volunteers in the American Civil War, 1861-1865.* Bristol, N.H.: R. W. Musgrove, 1893.

Coker, James Lide. *History of Company G, Ninth S.C. Regiment, Infantry, S.C. Army, and of Company E, Sixth S.C. Regiment, Infantry, S.C. Army.* Greenwood, S.C.: Attic Press, 1979.

Cooling, Benjamin Franklin. *Symbol, Sword, and Shield: Defending Washington during the Civil War.* Hamden, Conn.: Archon Books, 1975.

Cullen, Joseph P. *The Peninsula Campaign 1862: McClellan & Lee Struggle for Richmond.* New York: Bonanza Books, 1973.

Davis, Nicholas A. *The Campaign from Texas to Maryland with the Battle of Fredericksburg.* Richmond: Presbyterian Committee of Publication of the Confederate States, 1863.

Davis, William C., ed. *The Confederate General.* Harrisburg, Pa.: National Historical Society, 1991.

De Leon, T. C. *Belles Beaux and Brains of the 60's.* New York: G. W. Dillingham, 1974 (reprint of 1907 edition).

De Trobriand, Regis. *Four Years with the Army of the Potomac.* Trans. by George K. Dauchy. Boston: Ticknor, 1889.

Dickert, D. Augustus. *History of Kershaw's Brigade.* Dayton: Press of Morningside Bookshop, 1973.

Dowdey, Clifford. *The Seven Days: The Emergence of Robert E. Lee.* New York: Fairfax Press, 1978.

Dutcher, Salem. "A Graphic Story of the Battle of May 5, 1862." In *Southern Historical Society Papers,* Vol. 17. Wilmington, N.C.: Broadfoot, 1990.

Esposito, Vincent J., ed. *The West Point Atlas of American Wars: 1689-1900,* Vol. 1. New York: Frederick A. Praeger, 1959.

Fisk, Wilbur. *Anti-Rebel: The Civil War Letters of Wilbur Fisk.* New York: Emil Rosenblatt, 1983.

Fleming, Francis P. *Memoir of Capt. C. Seton Fleming, of the Florida Infantry, C. S. A.* Jacksonville, Fla.: Times-Union Publishing House, 1881.

Freeman, Douglas Southall. *Lee's Lieutenants: A Study in Command,* Vol. 1. New York: Charles Scribner's Sons, 1970.

Fuller, Charles A. *Personal Recollections of the War of 1861.* Sherburne, N.Y.: News Job Printing House, 1906.

Giles, Valerius Cincinnatus. *Rags and Hope: The Recollections of Val C. Giles, Four Years with Hood's Brigade, Fourth Texas Infantry, 1861-1865.* Comp. and ed. by Mary Lasswell. New York: Coward-McCann, 1961.

The Guns of '62. Vol. 2 of *The Image of War: 1861-1865.* Garden City, N.Y.: Doubleday & Co., 1982.

Handerson, Henry E. *Yankee in Gray: The Civil War Memoirs of Henry E. Handerson.* Cleveland: Press of Western Reserve University, 1962.

Haydon, Charles B. *For Country, Cause & Leader: The Civil War Journal of Charles B. Haydon.* Ed. by Stephen W. Sears. New York: Ticknor & Fields, 1993.

Hays, Gilbert Adams, comp. *Under the Red Patch: Story of the Sixty Third Regiment Pennsylvania Volunteers, 1861-1864.* Pittsburgh: Sixty-Third Pennsylvania Volunteers Regimental Association, 1908.

Holbrook, Arthur. "With the Fifth Wisconsin at Williamsburg." In *War Papers Being Read before the Commandery of the State of Wisconsin Military Order of the Loyal Legion of the United States,* Vol. 3. Wilmington, N.C.: Broadfoot, 1993.

Holien, Kim Bernard. *Battle at Ball's Bluff.* Orange, Va.: Moss Publications, 1985.

Hudgins, Robert S., II. *Recollections of an Old Dominion Dragoon: The Civil War Experiences of Sgt. Robert S. Hudgins II, Company B, 3rd Virginia Cavalry.* Ed. by Garland C. Hudgins and Richard B. Kleese. Orange, Va.: Publisher's Press, 1993.

Hunter, Alexander. *Johnny Reb and Billy Yank.* New York: Neale, 1905.

Hyde, Thomas W. *Following the Greek Cross: Or, Memories of the Sixth Army Corps.* Boston: Houghton, Mifflin, 1894.

Jones, J. B. *A Rebel War Clerk's Diary at the Confederate States Capital,* Vol. 1. Philadelphia: J. B. Lippincott, 1866.

Keeler, William Frederick. *Aboard the USS Monitor: 1862* (Naval Letters series). Ed. by Robert W. Daly. Annapolis, Md.: U.S. Naval Institute, 1964.

Krick, Robert K. *Lee's Colonels: A Biographical Register of the Field Officers of the Army of Northern Virginia.* Dayton: Press of Morningside Bookshop, 1979.

Livermore, Thomas L. *Days and Events, 1860-1866.*

Boston: Houghton Mifflin, 1920.

Loehr, Charles T. "The First Virginia Infantry in the Peninsula Campaign." In *Southern Historical Society Papers,* Vol. 21. Wilmington, N.C.: Broadfoot, 1990.

McDaniel, J. J. *Diary of Battles, Marches and Incidents of the Seventh S.C. Regiment.* N.p., n.d.

McRae, D. K. "The Battle of Williamsburg—Reply to Colonel Bratton." In *Southern Historical Society Papers,* Vol. 7. Wilmington, N.C.: Broadfoot, 1990.

Maury, Richard L.:
"The Battle of Williamsburg and the Charge of the Twenty-fourth Virginia of Early's Brigade." In *Southern Historical Society Papers,* Vol. 8. Wilmington, N.C.: Broadfoot, 1990.
"The Battle of Williamsburg, Va." In *Southern Historical Society Papers,* Vol. 22. Wilmington, N.C.: Broadfoot, 1990.

Maxfield, Albert, and Robert Brady Jr. *Roster and Statistical Record of Company D, of the Eleventh Regiment Maine Infantry Volunteers.* New York: Press of Thos. Humphrey, 1890.

Meyers, Augustus. *Ten Years in the Ranks, U.S. Army.* New York: Arno Press, 1979.

Miller, Edward M. *U.S.S. Monitor: The Ship That Launched a Modern Navy.* Annapolis, Md.: Leeward Publications, 1978.

Mills, George Henry. *History of the 16th North Carolina Regiment (Originally 6th N.C. Regiment) in the Civil War.* Hamilton, N.Y.: Edmonston Publishing, 1992.

Morgan, William H. *Personal Reminiscences of the War of 1861-5.* Lynchburg, Va.: J. P. Bell, 1911.

Naglee, Henry M. *Report of Brig. Gen. Henry M. Naglee: Commanding First Brigade, Casey's Division, Army of the Potomac.* Philadelphia: Collins, 1862.

Norton, Oliver Willcox. *Army Letters: 1861-1865.* Dayton: Press of Morningside, 1990.

Osborne, William H. *The History of the Twenty-ninth Regiment of Massachusetts Volunteer Infantry, in the Late War of the Rebellion.* Boston: Albert J. Wright, 1877.

Parker, William Harwar. *Recollections of a Naval Officer: 1841-1865.* New York: Charles Scribners' Sons, 1883.

Patterson, Edmund DeWitt. *Yankee Rebel: The Civil War Journal of Edmund DeWitt Patterson.* Ed. by John G. Barrett. Chapel Hill: University of North Carolina Press, 1966.

The Rebellion Record: A Diary of American Events, Vol. 3. Ed. by Frank Moore. New York: D. Van Nostrand, 1866.

Riley, Franklin Lafayette. *Grandfather's Journal.* Dayton: Morningside, 1988.

Ripley, Warren. *Ammunition of the Civil War*. New York: Promontory Press, 1970.

Sauers, Richard A. *Advance the Colors!: Pennsylvania Civil War Battle Flags,* Vol. 1. Harrisburg, Pa: Capitol Preservation Committee, 1987.

Sears, Stephen W. *To the Gates of Richmond: The Peninsula Campaign*. New York: Ticknor & Fields, 1992.

Shotwell, Randolph Abbott. *The Papers of Randolph Abbott Shotwell,* Vol. 1. Ed. by J. G. de Rouihac Hamilton. Raleigh: North Carolina Historical Commission, 1929.

Stevens, George T. *Three Years in the Sixth Corps*. Albany, N.Y.: S. R. Gray, 1866.

Stuyvesant, Moses S. "How the 'Cumberland' Went Down." In *War Papers and Personal Reminiscences: 1861-1865,* Vol. 1. Wilmington, N.C.: Broadfoot, 1992.

United States War Department:

The War of the Rebellion: A Compilation of the Official Records of the Union and Confederate Armies, Series 1, Vol. 5. Washington, D.C.: Government Printing Office, 1881.

The War of the Rebellion: A Compilation of the Official Records of the Union and Confederate Armies, Series 1, Vol. 9. Washington, D.C.: Government Printing Office, 1883.

The War of the Rebellion: A Compilation of the Official Records of the Union and Confederate Armies, Series 1, Vol. 11, Part 1. Washington, D.C.: Government Printing Office, 1884.

The War of the Rebellion: A Compilation of the Official Records of the Union and Confederate Armies, Series 1, Vol. 11, Part 3. Washington, D.C.: Government Printing Office, 1884.

Wainwright, Charles S. *A Diary of Battle: The Personal Journals of Colonel Charles S. Wainwright, 1861-1865*. Ed. by Allan Nevins. New York: Harcourt, Brace & World, 1962.

Warfield, Edgar. *A Confederate Soldier's Memoirs*. Richmond: Masonic Home Press, 1936.

Warner, Ezra J.:

Generals in Blue: Lives of the Union Commanders. Baton Rouge: Louisiana State University Press, 1964.

Generals in Gray: Lives of the Confederate Commanders. Baton Rouge: Louisiana State University Press, 1959.

Wistar, Isaac Jones. *Autobiography of Isaac Jones Wistar: 1827-1905*. Philadelphia: Wistar Institute of Anatomy and Biology, 1937.

Wood, William Nathaniel. *Reminiscences of Big I*. Ed. by Bell Irvin Wiley. Jackson, Tenn.: McCowat Mercer Press, 1956.

PERIODICALS

Acton, Edward A. " 'Dear Mollie': Letters of Captain Edward A. Acton to His Wife, 1862." Ed. by Mary Acton Hammond. *Pennsylvania Magazine of History and Biography,* 1965, Vol. 89.

Boots, E. N. "Civil War Letters of E. N. Boots, Virginia 1862." Ed. by Wilfred W. Black. *Virginia Magazine of History and Biography,* 1961, Vol. 69.

Cary, Harriette. "Diary of Harriette Cary, Civilian, of Williamsburg." *Tyler's Quarterly Historical and Genealogical Magazine,* 1928, Vol. 9.

Childs, H. T. "The Battle of Seven Pines." *Confederate Veteran,* n.d., Vol. 25.

Coxe, John. "With the Hampton Legion in the Peninsular Campaign." *Confederate Veteran,* 1916, Vol. 24.

Craven, Milton. "Fair Oaks." *National Tribune* (Washington, D.C.), November 8, 1883.

Dennis, Frederick E. "The 8th New Jersey: How It Faced the Music at the Battle of Williamsburg." *National Tribune,* September 16, 1886.

Donaldson, W. A. "Fighting before Richmond." *National Tribune,* March 8, 1894.

Drake, W. F. "Eye-Witness Story of Battle of Ironclads." *Raleigh News & Observer,* n.d.

Easley, Drewry B. "Experiences at Seven Pines." *Confederate Veteran,* 1929, Vol. 37.

Fritz, Levi. "Letter from the Army." *Montgomery Ledger* (Pa.), June 3, 1862.

Geer, John. "Fighting at Fair Oaks." *National Tribune,* June 4, 1914.

Gibbs, George Alphonso. "A Mississippi Private at 1st Bull Run and Ball's Bluff." *Civil War Times Illustrated,* April 1965.

Grimsley, Mark, ed. "We Prepare to Receive the Enemy Where We Stand." Trans. by Bernatello Glod. *Civil War Times Illustrated,* May 1985.

Herbert, Hilary A. "History of the Eighth Alabama Volunteer Regiment, C.S.A." Ed. by Maurice S. Fortin. *Alabama Historical Quarterly,* 1977, Vol. 39.

Hunter, Alexander. "Battle of Seven Pines." Philadelphia *Weekly Times,* February 17, 1883.

Lawrence, John. "The Congress and the Merrimack." *National Tribune,* April 7, 1904.

Ledyard, Erwin. "Smoke at Seven Pines." Philadelphia *Weekly Times,* October 22, 1887.

Littlepage, Hardin Beverly. "A Midshipman Aboard the Virginia," part 1. *Civil War Times Illustrated,* April 1974.

McCully, R. B. "Burial Details." *National Tribune,* November 29, 1888.

Miller, Robert H. "Letters of Lieutenant Robert H. Miller to His Family, 1861-1862." Ed. by Forrest P. Connor. *Virginia Magazine of History and Biography,* 1961, Vol. 70.

Minnich, J. W. "Incidents of the Peninsular Campaign." *Confederate Veteran,* 1922, Vol. 30.

Nielson, Jon M., ed. "Debacle at Ball's Bluff." *Civil War Times Illustrated,* January 1976.

Page, Selden. "Hooker's Boys." *National Tribune,* June 19, 1884.

Reblen, William. "A Glorious Action: The Battle between the Cumberland, Congress and Merrimac." *National Tribune,* June 5, 1890.

Sharpe, Alexander B. "The Battle of Drainsville." *Wellsboro Agitator* (Pa.), March 2, 1886.

Walker, Albert R. "The Second New Hampshire at Williamsburg." *National Tribune,* n.d.

Webster, William E. "The Battle of Williamsburg." *National Tribune,* October 22, 1914.

Whetten, Harriet Douglas. "A Volunteer Nurse in the Civil War: The Letters of Harriet Douglas Whetten." Ed. by Paul H. Hass. *Wisconsin Magazine of History,* 1964-1965, Vol. 48.

OTHER SOURCES

Brower, A. T. "The Woolen Shawl." Unpublished manuscript, n.d., *Civil War Times Illustrated* Collection. Carlisle Barracks, Pa.: U.S. Army Military History Institute.

Fite, John A. Memoirs, n.d., Civil War Collection: Confederate and Federal, 1861-1865. Nashville: Tennessee State Archives.

Fowler, Frederick K. Letters, n.d., Civil War Miscellaneous Collection. Carlisle Barracks, Pa.: U.S. Army Military History Institute.

Gleason, John F. Papers, n.d. Worcester, Mass.: American Antiquarian Society.

Hollis, J. Rufus. Memoirs, n.d., Civil War Collection: Confederate and Federal, 1861-1865. Nashville: Tennessee State Archives.

Jenkins, Robert Alexander. "From Harper's Ferry to the Surrender." Unpublished manuscript, n.d., Gertrude Jenkins Papers. Durham, N.C.: Duke University, Special Collections Library.

Kilmer, George L. "The Lottery of War." Unpublished manuscript, n.d. Montgomery: Alabama Department of Archives and History.

Ward, George H. Letter, October 21, 1861. Worcester, Mass.: Worcester Historical Museum.

INDEX

Numerals in italics indicate an illustration of the subject mentioned.

TIME LIFE BOOKS ® Time-Life Books is a division of Time Life Inc.

TIME LIFE INC.
PRESIDENT and CEO: George Artandi

TIME-LIFE BOOKS
PRESIDENT: Stephen R. Frary
PUBLISHER/MANAGING EDITOR: Neil Kagan

VOICES OF THE CIVIL WAR

DIRECTOR OF MARKETING: Pamela R. Farrell

THE PENINSULA

EDITOR: Paul Mathless
Deputy Editors: Harris J. Andrews (principal), Kirk Denkler, Philip Brandt George
Art Director: Ellen L. Pattisall
Associate Editor/Research and Writing: Annette Scarpitta
Senior Copyeditors: Judith Klein (principal), Anne Farr, Mary Beth Oelkers-Keegan
Picture Coordinator: Lisa Groseclose
Editorial Assistant: Christine Higgins

Initial Series Design: Studio A

Special Contributors: James Michael Lynch, John Newton, Brian C. Pohanka, Dana B. Shoaf, David S. Thomson, Henry Woodhead (text); Paul Birkhead, Charles F. Cooney, Steve Hill, Robert Lee Hodge, Susan V. Kelly, Beth Levin, Henry Mintz, Dana B. Shoaf (research); Roy Nanovic (index).

Correspondent: Christina Lieberman (New York).

Director of Finance: Christopher Hearing
Directors of Book Production: Marjann Caldwell, Patricia Pascale
Director of Publishing Technology: Betsi McGrath
Director of Photography and Research: John Conrad Weiser
Director of Editorial Administration: Barbara Levitt
Production Manager: Marlene Zack
Quality Assurance Manager: James King
Chief Librarian: Louise D. Forstall

Consultants
Brian C. Pohanka, a Civil War historian and author, spent six years as a researcher and writer for Time-Life Books' Civil War series and Echoes of Glory. He is the author of *Distant Thunder: A Photographic Essay on the American Civil War* and has written and edited numerous works on American military history. He has acted as historical consultant for projects including the feature film *Glory* and television's *Civil War Journal*. Pohanka participates in Civil War reenactments and living-history demonstrations with the 5th New York Volunteers and he is active in Civil War battlefield preservation.

Dr. Richard A. Sauers is director of the Soldiers and Sailors Memorial Hall in Pittsburgh, Pa. As chief historian for the Pennsylvania Capitol Preservation Committee he directed the research and documentation of more than 400 Civil War battle flags and wrote *Advance the Colors!* the two-volume study of Pennsylvania's Civil War flags. He is active in Civil War and local historical societies and is involved in battlefield preservation. He is assistant editor of *Gettysburg* magazine. His published works include *A Caspian Sea of Ink: The Meade-Sickles Controversy* and *"The Bloody 85th": A Supplement to the History of the 85th Pennsylvania.* He has also compiled a critical bibliography of the Gettysburg campaign.

First printing. Printed in U.S.A.
School and library distribution by Time-Life Education, P.O. Box 85026, Richmond, Virginia 23285-5026.

TIME-LIFE is a trademark of Time Warner Inc. U.S.A.

Library of Congress Cataloging-in-Publication Data
The Peninsula / by the editors of Time-Life Books.
    p. cm.—(Voices of the Civil War)
    Includes bibliographical references and index.
    ISBN 0-7835-4715-3
    1. Peninsular Campaign, 1862.
    I. Time-Life Books. II. Series.
E473.6.P46 1997
973.7'31—dc21   97-34623
                                   CIP

OTHER PUBLICATIONS:

HISTORY
What Life Was Like
The Civil War
The American Indians
Lost Civilizations
The American Story
Mysteries of the Unknown
Time Frame
Cultural Atlas

SCIENCE/NATURE
Voyage Through the Universe

DO IT YOURSELF
The Time-Life Complete Gardener
Home Repair and Improvement
The Art of Woodworking
Fix It Yourself

TIME-LIFE KIDS
Library of First Questions and Answers
A Child's First Library of Learning
I Love Math
Nature Company Discoveries
Understanding Science & Nature

COOKING
Weight Watchers® Smart Choice Recipe Collection
Great Taste~Low Fat
Williams~Sonoma Kitchen Library

For information on and a full description of any of the Time-Life Books series listed above, please call 1-800-621-7026 or write:

Reader Information
Time-Life Customer Service
P.O. Box C-32068
Richmond, Virginia 23261-2068